BETRAYALS

Politics of Colonial Policy
Guerillas and Grenadiers
Atlantic Merchant-apothecary
The English Atlantic 1675–1740

BETRAYALS

*Fort William Henry
and the "Massacre"*

IAN K. STEELE

New York   Oxford
OXFORD UNIVERSITY PRESS
1990

Oxford University Press

Oxford   New York   Toronto
Delhi   Bombay   Calcutta   Madras   Karachi
Petaling Jaya   Singapore   Hong Kong   Tokyo
Nairobi   Dar es Salaam   Cape Town
Melbourne   Auckland

and associated companies in
Berlin   Ibadan

Copyright © 1990 by Ian K. Steele

Published by Oxford University Press, Inc.,
200 Madison Avenue, New York, New York 10016

Library of Congress Cataloging-in-Publication Data
Steele, Ian Kenneth.
Betrayals : Fort William Henry and the "massacre" / Ian K. Steele.
p.   cm.   Includes bibliographical refrences.
ISBN 0-19-505893-3
1. Fort William Henry (N.Y.)—Capture, 1757.
2. Massacres—New York (State)—Fort William Henry—History—18th century.
I. Title.
E199.S82   1990   973.2′6—dc20   89-16266

68267

1 3 5 7 9 8 6 4 2

Printed in the United States of America
on acid-free paper

To the Memory of

GERALD S. GRAHAM
JOSEPH J. MALONE
GEORGE METCALF

PREFACE

The compelling events of the brief existence of Fort William Henry, explored while studying the treatment of prisoners of war, have simply demanded a careful retelling. The well-documented realities were much more subtle and revealing than James Fenimore Cooper's mythical classic *The Last of the Mohicans* (1826). The mixture of Indian, colonial, and European values produced cooperation, conflict, and confusion within the armies that fought for the Albany–Montreal corridor. The Battle of Lake George demonstrates the confusion accompanying the unprecedented commitment of European military resources to the persistent colonial rivalries on this frontier. The fort itself was an assertion of the European military presence on builders, garrisons, and enemies in this wilderness. The seige of 1757 displayed the uneasy, but effective, combination of Indian, colonial, and European warfare. The climactic "massacre at Fort William Henry" was a foreseeable collision of attitudes about prisoners of war, rather than the drunken or "homicidal" rage that has been depressingly popular as an explanation among historians.

The remembering of Fort William Henry has served a variety of purposes over the centuries. The conflict between European and colonial values and methods has been a favorite theme of historians seeking the roots of American and Canadian identity. The "massacre," which left more killed and missing than those at Deerfield or Lachine, became powerful in American folk memory, confirming attitudes toward American Indians that justified "removals" and wars. From this distance, the short and tragic story seems to have been part of the nineteenth century's "usable past." The twentieth century has, perhaps with humane intention, tended to forget Fort William Henry, or leave it to the "literature" of James Fenimore Cooper, Francis Parkman, or H.-R. Casgrain. What follows is a retelling based on new as well as familiar sources, an analysis of casualties and consequences, and an essay on the witnesses and the historians. This reopening of a sensitive subject is offered with the hope that readers will agree that understanding is preferable to forgetting.

Naming the people and places, like the rest of this faceted story, is not simple or value free. I have labeled the opposing armies "English" and "French," as their opponents did in recognition of their kings or the dominant languages in each. While the English empire was becoming more British at this time, the term "British" here refers to natives of Britain. "Americans" was in use for English colonists, though in the military the term "provincials" was more common. The Chippewa are here called the "Ojibwa," and the Iroquois in Canada are usually named the "Caughnawaga," after their major settlement, to distinguish them from their kin farther south. The struggle on the frontier between New York and Montreal was also a war of place names. Albany (L'Orange), Fort Edward (Lydius), Fort William Henry (Fort Georges), Fort Carillon (Ticonderoga), and Fort St. Frédéric (Crown Point) are given the names assigned by their possessors during this story. The disputed Lac St. Sacrement might well have borne that name here, but the serenity of the "holy lake" was gone after the autumn of 1755, when William Johnson pretentiously claimed it, renamed it, and fought a battle that has been called the Battle of Lake George ever since.

Special thanks are due to a number of people who assisted with aspects of this book. The University of Western Ontario helped with research time and resources. Archivists who helped beyond legitimate expectations include Galen Wilson of the William L. Clements Library; Martha Briggs of the Huntington Library; State Archivist Frank C. Mevers of New Hampshire; Voorhees Dunn of the State of New Jersey Division of Archives and Records Management; Pat Robinson and Michel Wyczynski of the National Archives of Canada; and Jane M. Lape of Fort Ticonderoga. My colleagues Professors F. A. Dreyer, R. L. Emerson, and G. N. Emery have offered valuable criticism of parts of this study. Herta Steele, who has given the author's life much of its meaning, has given even more than her customary interest and effort to the research and thorough copy editing of the entire manuscript. Surviving errors remain the exclusive property of the author.

London, Ontario   I.K.S.
June 1989

CONTENTS

ILLUSTRATIONS

TABLES

BETRAYALS

1

APPROACHES

Midsummer day 1749 was ideal for Pehr Kalm, a Swedish professor of economic natural history, to begin exploring the wilderness between British and French America in search of plants that might profitably be introduced into Sweden. This perceptive, multilingual neutral used the long days to collect flowers and seeds, to note evidence of the war that had ended, and to gather impressions of people who did not know that a new war was already brewing. He did not know that he was touring battle routes when he traveled the wild 225 miles between Albany and Montreal, and back again, in the summer and fall of 1749. The Peace of Aix-la-Chapelle had been proclaimed in the British colonies and was being honored by Canadian authorities months before Pehr Kalm saw the peace formally proclaimed in Montreal.[1] A peace that called for a return to normal in America could be expected to function well on this particular frontier, where Iroquois neutrality and Albany complicity had made so little of the last war.[2] In choosing the route, the guides, and William Printup as interpreter, Kalm had the advice of William Johnson, who, in the eleven years since he arrived from Ireland, had become a prominent fur trader and landowner, an adopted Mohawk chief, and New York's most influential intermediary with the Iroquois.[3]

Kalm had not gone far along a good road north of Albany before he saw signs that the frontier had not been in tranquil neutrality. Within ten miles of Albany, all the farm buildings had been burned, and farmers were just beginning to reoccupy lands they had fled. At Saratoga, Kalm learned about a ruse organized by St. Luc de la Corne that had netted forty prisoners for his Canadian raiding party in 1747, after which the English decided to burn their own palisaded fort. (Kalm may not have been told that this settlement and fort had also been destroyed in an earlier raid, which had opened King George's War on this frontier in November 1745.) Beyond the abandoned fields and meadows of Saratoga, Kalm's party found few signs of habitation except burned saw mills. The humans were faring poorly here compared with the sassafras trees, the purslane, and the muskrats. Above the falls of the Hudson, the travelers forded the river, abandoned their heavy canoe, and followed an overgrown trail through the forest along the east side of the Hudson to the shrub-covered remains of Fort Nicholson[4] (Figure 1).

One hard day's travel north from the remnants of Fort Nicholson took Kalm across the watershed into French-claimed territory. Whether he went northwesterly to the head of Lac St. Sacrement or northeasterly to the headwaters of Wood Creek, Kalm entered the watershed of the St. Lawrence River. Both the lake and the creek fed Lake Champlain, which drained down the Richelieu river to the St. Lawrence, carving canoe routes that completely breached the mountainous wilderness that otherwise kept New France and its English neighbors relatively insulated from each other. People heading northward that summer, whether to ransom captives, to smuggle, or to gather seeds, followed those waterways funneling to Montreal. In wartime this geography made the English colonies easy to surprise and Montreal easy to defend. Pehr Kalm's advisers chose the more arduous Wood Creek route, perhaps because boatmen would have been visible and vulnerable on the open waters of Lac St. Sacrement in the uncertain twilight of a war. At night, the naturalist was studied by the gnats, wood lice, and mosquitoes that he studied during the day, and "our fear of snakes and especially of the Indians made the night's rest very uncertain and insecure."[5] As they reached Wood Creek, Kalm found the burned site of Fort Anne effectively occupied by mice; the nearby apple and plum trees were the most enduring legacies of English occupation nearly forty years earlier. As he viewed the charred remains of old Fort Anne, Kalm wondered aloud why the English had burned yet another of their own forts. A cynical companion claimed

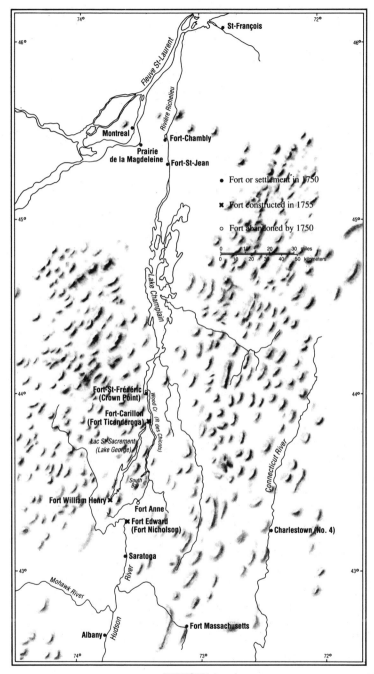

FIGURE 1
The Albany–Montreal corridor, 1749–1757. (© Ian K. Steele)

that it was the profiteers who built and burned them, wanting both to hide their poor workmanship and to make money building again. In these borderlands, forts and roads were ambivalent defenses that became menacing if they fell into the hands of an enemy.[6] Kalm's journey down Wood Creek was obstructed in various ways. Two days were spent at the Fort Anne site while one guide built a bark canoe and another recovered from illness. Beaver dams distracted the naturalist and blocked his passage, as did the occasional dead tree. When they came upon a still-burning campfire, around which several people had slept, Kalm and his companions were initially unconcerned. Later in the day, when they met six French soldiers escorting three English travelers south to Saratoga, Kalm learned that the campfire had belonged to six Indians from Canada seeking to avenge the death of one of their own, before formal peace came to Canada. Farther north, Kalm found Wood Creek entirely clogged for six miles with trees the French had felled three years earlier to obstruct a threatened English invasion. Kalm's group exchanged their canoe at the south end of the blockade for one in the French escort's cache at the north end. Kalm and his guides then lost their way in the reeds of what was variously known as the "Drowned land," "12-mile swamp," "*grand marais*," or "*rivière de chicôts.*" The unarmed travelers spent a night without fire or sleep and a day without provisions before reaching Fort St. Frédéric. Kalm's twelve-day journey was eventful enough and suggests the more grueling treks of runaway captives or wounded scouts who could not look to Fort St. Frédéric as a haven in this wilderness.[7]

Physically and psychologically, Fort St. Frédéric (Figure 2) easily dominated these borderlands from its site at the narrows of Lake Champlain, known to the English as Crown Point. The thick black limestone walls, the bomb-proof four-story inner tower, and the forty mounted cannon were in stark contrast to the burned remnants of wooden palisades that had been the English frontier presence at Fort Saratoga, Fort Nicholson,[8] and Fort Anne. The differences were not lost on English traders and travelers, or on Kalm. He reported:

> The Englishmen insist that this fort is built in their territory and that the boundary between the French and English colonies in this locality lies between Fort St. Jean and the Prairie de la Madeleine; on the other hand, the French maintain that the boundary runs through the woods, between Lake St. Sacrement and Fort Nicholson.[9]

Fort St. Frédéric was an assertion of the French watershed theory of the boundary and had grown from a wooden palisade to a major fortification in less than twenty years.[10] The English had continued to

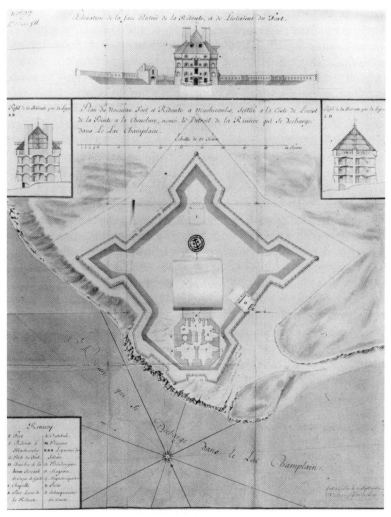

FIGURE 2
Plan of Fort St. Frédéric, 1737.
(Courtesy of Centre des Archives d'Outre-Mer, Aix-en-Provence, France)

complain that the fort was built on Mohawk land deeded to New Yorkers, but that hardly mattered in 1749. Kalm saw a "pretty little church" outside the fort, stone houses of officers and men of the garrison, kitchen gardens, and houses and farms of retired soldiers.[11] They, like the New York frontier farmers, had returned that summer after having withdrawn to safer places during the war that had just ended. During that war, Fort St. Frédéric had been the scourge of the English. It was from here that Paul Marin's raiders annihilated Saratoga in November 1745, taking 103 prisoners and ending two generations of tacit neutrality on the New York frontier. It was also from Fort St. Frédéric that Pierre Rigaud led seven hundred men in the successful siege of Fort Massachusetts two years later, returning with twenty-nine prisoners.[12] Dozens of other raiding parties had terrorized the frontiers of New Hampshire, Massachusetts, Connecticut, and New York from the safety of this well-located fortress. It was also clear that any effective challenge to Fort St. Frédéric would require siege cannon that would have to be pulled as far as Pehr Kalm had traveled.

The more offensive function of Fort St. Frédéric became apparent to Kalm within a few days of his arrival. While dining with the civilized and urbane commandant, Paul-Louis Dazemard de Lusignan,[13] he heard several "bloodcurdling" cries from the south. The same six Ottawa, Nipissing, and Abenaki warriors whom Kalm's party had missed a week earlier on Wood Creek were returning in triumph from an attack on Charlestown, New Hampshire, in the Connecticut River Valley. To avenge a comrade who was killed in an unsuccessful attack on that fort three years earlier, they had killed and scalped a sergeant who was harrowing a field near the fort, and had taken a nine-year-old boy captive. Although the raid had been forbidden by the governor of Montreal, and discouraged by Lusignan, "the latter could not at present deny them provisions and whatever else they wanted for their journey, because he did not think it advisable to exasperate them."[14] Lusignan, holder of a nearby seigneury and an experienced Canadian post commander who later bought a black captive from Abenaki raiders,[15] was conducting border diplomacy. He had sent six men south to protect three English travelers from this war party. He had sent a warning about the Indians to the English officials at Albany, but he tolerated the warriors rejoicing while dressed in bits of the dead man's clothing, and Lusignan left the retrieval of the captive boy to be handled, promptly, by the governor of Montreal.[16] At this checkpoint, as elsewhere along this route of illegal traders, warriors, captives, and naturalists, there was a complex and incongruous mixture of attitudes to war and to peace.

Kalm sailed north on Lake Champlain aboard the regular packet boat that maintained summer communications between Fort St. Frédéric and its supply base, Fort St. Jean. After a night anchored near the uninterrupted forest that surrounded Lake Champlain, the boat proceeded to its destination. Fort St. Jean, situated above the rapids of the Richelieu River, had been rebuilt the previous year. With a new wagon road from there to Montreal, it was claimed that Fort St. Frédéric could be reinforced within forty-eight hours. The strength of Fort St. Jean, palisaded and boasting two four-story bastions facing the lake, was the only evidence that English land claims reached the rapids of the Richelieu.

Fort St. Jean had been rebuilt on the orders of Roland-Michel Barrin de La Galissonière, the man who impressed Pehr Kalm the most during his four-month stay in Canada. Kalm was amazed by the range and depth of knowledge displayed by the acting governor of New France, as well as by the man's initiative and hospitality. La Galissonière had synthesized the views of his predecessors and subordinates to produce a plan for asserting the watershed version of the Anglo-French boundary in North America. He sent an expedition to the Ohio Valley to stake claims, influence Indians, and gather information preliminary to the initiatives that later provoked war. He eyed the English Fort Oswego on Lake Ontario as a blatant invasion of the St. Lawrence watershed that had been tolerated for too long. He rebuilt Fort St. Jean to reinforce Fort St. Frédéric more effectively and support the farming communities he sought to encourage there. Although La Galissonière left for France while Kalm was still in Canada, the marquis became a commissioner for negotiating the boundaries betwen English and French in North America, and his assertiveness was continued by his successors.[17]

Pehr Kalm returned through the lands between Fort St. Frédéric and the Hudson later that year, noting that "not a human being lives in these waste regions and no Indian villages are found here."[18] The trip that had been twelve days' travel northward by way of Wood Creek took ten less-strenuous days southward via mountain-fringed Lac St. Sacrement. In a total of twenty-two days in this no-man's-land, Kalm recorded seeing three small escorted groups concerned with returning prisoners and smuggling, one Indian raiding party, and several Indian deer hunters. On the longer autumn nights of this return trip, he was chilled by the fireside bragging of Canadians who had been in earlier scalping parties using this route.[19] Although this area had been familiar to the French and English for nearly a century, Kalm's guides northward had become lost in the reeds of Wood Creek, and his Canadian escort southward had trouble finding the portage at the south end of Lac St. Sacrement. Dense pine forest covered a path that led sixteen miles to the Hudson, offering no premonitions that within eight years this end of that log-strewn trail would be the site of a bloody day-long battle, a substantial fort that would be subjected to a full-scale artillery siege, and a "massacre."

Pehr Kalm had not intended to survey the strength of the contenders during a recess in the Anglo-French battle for North America, which only enhances his value as a witness. Although he described them as "an unimportant body" vastly outnumbered by the English Americans, the Canadians appeared strong despite odds of more than thirty to one. The people of the colony of New York alone outnumbered all of New France by three to two.[20] Kalm had visited solid, well-garrisoned French forts, after camping amid an army of mice at Fort Anne's razed site. He had heard of ferocious Canadian raids on Saratoga and Fort Massachusetts which had been answered only with an abortive invasion scheme that caused recriminations among the factious English colonists, the Iroquois, and the British government. While New England had taken Louisbourg and been forced to give it back, the Albany–Montreal corridor looked as though new France had won King George's War. It is not surprising that, having described the English counterclaims to the whole area, Kalm described the whole country between Fort St. Frédéric and the Hudson as "a part of Canada."[21]

II

Like the New York settlers whom Kalm saw reoccupying clearings north of Albany and the *habitants* he saw returning to the Lake Champlain frontier, Susannah Johnson and her husband James responded to news of peace in 1749 by migrating with their baby from Winchester, New Hampshire, to the frontier village of Charlestown, previously known simply as No. 4. This fort was the most northerly English settlement on the Connecticut River. Two years previously, a small garrison under Captain Phineas Stevens had withstood a five-day siege by some five hundred Canadians and Indians. The Johnsons were there only a few days when a small Indian raiding party avenged their losses in that earlier fight by killing a man and capturing young Enos Stevens, who, they may not have known, was a son of the same Captain Stevens. Pehr Kalm saw Enos and his captors as they passed through Fort St. Frédéric. Although Enos was returned promptly from Montreal by way of Albany, confidence in the peace came slowly to Charlestown and the settlers lived in the fort itself for three more years. The Johnsons moved to their own nearby farmstead in the summer of 1753, and peaceful trading with the Indians was a major part of their livelihood. Rumors of renewed war caused the Johnsons to consider returning to the fort with their three young children, but the move was not made. Before dawn on August 30, 1754, Abenaki raiders captured the five Johnsons, Susannah's fourteen-year-old sister, Miriam Willard, as well as Ebenezer Farnsworth and Peter Labarree, both of whom happened to be in the house after a night of neighborly merrymaking.[22]

Amid her initial screams, Susannah forgot that she was as naked as the three children the Indians flushed from their bed. The Abenaki claimed captives individually by grabbing them, then cooperated to tie up the men and plunder the house. Susannah was given several gowns from the plunder and managed to find her shoes before being hurried away from the house. While ten warriors repacked their loot for the journey, the eleventh ran back to the house, but returned even faster "with marks of fear in his countenance." They had missed one man in the house, who had hurried off to sound the alarm at the fort. Susannah later learned that the garrison intended to give chase, but Susannah's father convinced his superior officer that the raiders would kill their slowest captives if chased and Susannah was nine months pregnant. The captives were hurried through thorny thickets even faster once the alarm guns of the fort began firing. Susannah lost a shoe in the scramble and was winded within a mile and half. When she sat down, a warrior pulled his scalping knife, but used it only to cut the waistband of her gown before pushing her onward. The group hurried on for another three miles before the Abenaki felt confident enough to stop and eat.[23]

Susannah later recalled a complete change in the mood of her captors from this point in her journey. As she sat looking at her bleeding legs and feet, the Abenaki brought her bread, raisins, and apples taken from her own house. A stray horse, which the Johnsons knew by name, was caught with the help of James, who had earlier been unbound to help hurry his children along. The procession now included one young and ten middle-aged Abenaki warriors, none of whom spoke English, shepherding Susannah on Scoggin with blankets and loot, as well as the three captive men, Miriam Willard, Sylvanus (six years old), Susannah (four), and Polly (two), none of whom spoke Abenaki or French. On the rainy second day of their captivity, Mrs. Johnson's labor pains prompted the group to stop, build a shelter, and allow her husband and sister to help Susannah with the birth of her third daughter, rather whimsically named Captive. The Abenaki remained at a distance throughout the birthing, with the other prisoners and Susannah's crying children. Her new master, whom she regarded as clever and compassionate, was pleased, announcing "two monies for me." He helped clothe the infant, and the rest of the day was spent building another shelter for the mother and babe and preparing a litter for the next day's journey. The litter to carry Susannah and her baby was useful only as long as the captive men could carry it; they were exhausted after only two miles, prompting the Indians to consider leaving Susannah. She accepted the nearly as terrifying prospect of riding a horse in her condition. Probably because the raiding party had been more successful than they had expected, and had been slowed by Susannah, their food proved insufficient. Game was not to be found and, on the fifth day of the trip, Scoggin was butchered. Susannah now had to walk, but she remembered the prisoners being offered the choice pieces of meat.[24]

Susannah had not walked more than half a mile on the sixth day before she collapsed and fainted. In a third contentious discussion among the warriors, Susannah's master again defended the life of his bothersome captive. Saved again, Susannah stumbled on, amazed that the Abenaki built shelters for her to sleep in, stopped to dry her clothes after a river crossing, and shared food more than fairly with their captives. A cache of bear meat, flour, and tobacco, stored by the warriors on their way south to Charlestown, now saved the finicky English from the freshly smoked horse meat. The only irritants Susannah recalled came from the youngest of the Abenaki, who "delighted himself by tormenting my sister, pulling her hair, treading on her gown, and numerous other boyish pranks." Near the middle of the ninth day the caravan reached East Bay of Lake Champlain, ending the foot-destroying hundred-mile walk of the poorly shod captives.[25]

After a night in canoes, the Abenaki held a victory dance near the fringe of the French settlement at Fort St. Frédéric, presumably for the benefit of the commandant. Each prisoner was given an individual song to sing and was forced to dance, "and the best dancer was the most violent in motion" as they circled the fire. Susannah did not know whether this was diversion or a religious ceremony, but found it painful and offensive. Then they were all taken into the fort, where Commandant Lusignan treated them to brandy, a good dinner, and a change of clothing. After four days of kindness and civility along lines she better understood, a refreshed Susannah was returned to her

Abenaki captors. Before the whole party boarded the packet boat for St. Jean, the Johnsons were able to send a letter home by way of Albany. Susannah recalled further gestures of kindness from the commander at Chambly, where she slept in a bed for the first time since captivity, drank brandy, and "lived in high style." At another village the parish priest was hospitable but, like the other Canadians, was not willing to interfere in an accepted traffic that saw the prisoners off once again with their Abenaki masters.[26] As the Abenaki approached their home village of St. François, another halt was made. The captives were again forced to dance and sing around a fire, and this time they were each painted with stripes of vermilion and bear grease for the triumphal entry into the village. As the canoes landed, there was tremendous yelling and the village emptied to form a gauntlet to the water's edge. Susannah expected a severe beating, but the prisoners were given only a ceremonial pat by each villager as they were led to their masters' wigwams. At a village council the next day, Susannah's compassionate master traded her and Captive for Sylvanus, who was to be taught the skills of a hunter. Susannah and Captive now belonged to a principal chief of the Abenaki, Magouaouidombaouit or Joseph-Louis Gill. He was the son of two New England captives himself, but had been born in St. François, married the daughter of the chief sachem, and lived as the most prosperous farmer and trader in the settlement.[27] This white chief of the Abenaki formally adopted Susannah, as she understood from the interpreter.

Susannah, her baby, and her son, Sylvanus, were the only members of the captive group to be adopted into the tribe. Susannah and her accompanying infant were not taken in for their skills. Susannah milked cows but was still weak, was a novice at canoe making, and saw some truth in her adoptive sister's occasional complaints that Susannah was a "no good squaw." Sylvanus was adopted to become a hunter, a considerable investment in a six year old unless he was also being adopted to replace a lost son. Peter Labarree was apparently tested as a hunter by his master and found unsatisfactory. He and the other captives, including Susannah's husband and two older daughters, were promptly sold in Montreal.[28] The adoption process might be expected to bypass the adult males, but it also ignored three girls aged fourteen, four, and two. The choice of Susannah may have been compassionate, may even have involved some clever calculation of a mother's ransom, but seemed to her simply a matter of chance.

Susannah lived in a village of some thirty wigwams inhabited by people who were devout and deferential to their aged Jesuit missionary, Père Joseph Aubery.[29] They "lived in perfect harmony, holding most of their property in common," Susannah learned, but she did not mention whether the individual claim of prisoners was for prestige or whether the sale of a prisoner was a personal reward. It is not surprising that the Puritan mother found the Abenaki rather indolent "and not remarkable for neatness," but interesting that she felt "they were extremely modest, and apparently averse to airs of courtship." Susannah spent much of her time visiting her adoptive relations, becoming particularly fond of her new brother, Sabbatis, who was about the age of her own son, who was away hunting.[30] Susannah's general appraisal of the community within which she lived for two months was very favorable, for none of her family suffered wanton cruelty and she was confident that no "civilized conquerors" would have been as solicitous of her health or adopted her as a sister.[31]

The peacetime traffic in captives had economic and social significance that deserves notice. The Johnson party received generous treatment from Canadians they had met, but the observant mother of four young children saw no French or Canadian inclined to purchase or rescue them from their Abenaki captors. As Governor Ange de Menneville, Marquis de Duquesne, had explained a year earlier, the captives taken in peacetime were regarded as slaves of their Indian captors. Assuming that New Englanders knew about slaves, he added that these became "slaves fairly sold" when bought by Canadians. The government of New France could not legally force masters to give them up, as could be done with prisoners of war.[32] Another New Hampshire captive, in Montreal when the Johnsons arrived, claimed that the Indians

> cannot make Money half so fast any other Way, as by taking Englishmen, and selling them for Slaves; and the French are very ready to buy them; for when they buy a Man, or Woman for 3 or 400 Livres, they pay in Paper Money or Goods, and they will ask double in Silver; and they make 'em live and work like Negro's, till they pay just what they ask.[33]

This acidic description by a victim suggests the variety of experiences that might await those sold to the Canadians by the Abenaki.

James Johnson and his two younger daughters were taken to Montreal for sale, as were Farnsworth, and Labarree. These two men were sold to prosperous Montreal gentlemen, while little Polly Johnson was bought by the mayor of Montreal, whose wife seemed determined to raise her as her own. Susannah, aged four, was sold to three elderly and prosperous sisters, who apparently doted on her. Miriam Willard was bought by Governor Duquesne, whose personal help concerning the plight of the Johnsons made it clear that he was no more buying a worker than were the purchasers of the two little girls. James Johnson was probably sold, too, but was soon treated as the militia officer that he was. His wife and infant daughter were brought to Montreal after being with the Abenaki for two months, and Susannah learned that the governor had paid a surprising 700 livres for them. Such a valuation compared favorably with the prices of slaves in New France at the time.[34] James was given two months' parole to return to New Hampshire, and gather cash to redeem his family. On November 12, 1754, James set out for Albany with two Indian guides who were to remain there until his return. The Canadian governor wanted spies in Albany, but that did not lessen the humanity of his efforts.[35]

From Albany, James returned to Boston, where ambitious plans for the next year's campaign had already begun. James applied to Governor William Shirley and the General Court of Massachusetts for redemption money for his and other families of New England captives. The General Court gave him £10 toward his expenses, but negotiations for additional help did not succeed. The Massachusetts authorities wished for a broader mandate for Captain Stevens to redeem captives and did not want to use the proposed Albany merchants as intermediaries.[36] His own New Hampshire government granted £150 sterling for redemption of Johnson's party, as well as eight others captured on the Merrimack River that summer. Johnson set out for Albany overland. Instead of carrying cash, he was bearing letters for two prominent merchants, Cornelius Cuyler and Robert Sanders, who were involved in the illegal trade between Albany and Montreal and therefore in a position to transfer payments to Canadians.[37] Johnson reached no farther than Worcester, Massachusetts, when he was intercepted by order from Governor Shirley. Johnson's parole from Canada had already expired, but he was forbidden to proceed for fear that information about Massachusetts' preparations for expeditions against Acadia and Fort St. Frédéric could be forced from the frantic husband and father.[38]

The best days of Susannah's captivity had been those spent in Governor Duquesne's house that winter. She recalled numerous "general tokens of generosity which flow from a humane people." Although she needed an interpreter in Montreal, as in St. François, Susannah found special kindness in the family of Louis Charly Saint-Ange, where another Englishwoman captured in Maine was a purchased slave treated like the merchant's daughter.[39] Susannah and Miriam enjoyed the company and carriage rides of the young Saint-Ange ladies. Susannah also met Captains Robert Stobo and Jacob Van Braam of the Virginia militia, who were hostages for unfulfilled terms of George Washington's surrender at Fort Necessity. As hostages taken in peacetime by a formal government force, these men were given considerable freedom, including the freedom to trade. They were affluent enough to give Susannah a substantial gift of cash.[40] Susannah also succeeded in recovering her daughter Polly from the mayor's reluctant wife. The child not only was returned without compensation, but also was accompanied by a considerable wardrobe. Susannah's adaptability showed when infant Captive was seriously ill. Not only did she yield to exhortations to have her baptized a Catholic, but the governor stood as godfather and the child was named Louise after Madame Duquesne.[41]

Life changed abruptly for Susannah and her sister when the Indian guides returned to Montreal from Albany without James. Governor Duquesne's own sense of honor, which was well developed, could not tolerate this breach of parole. The sisters were banished from the governor's house and from polite society. After their funds were exhausted, they worked as seamstresses. Finally, in May 1755, James gained Governor Shirley's permission to go to Albany and William Johnson's permission to return to Montreal.[42]

James Johnson arrived in a very different Montreal at the end of June. Governor-General Pierre-François de Rigaud, Marquis de Vaudreuil, had just arrived and was taking New France into war. Even before Braddock's papers revealed that Stobo had smuggled a plan of Fort Duquesne to his superiors, Vaudreuil was furious that the hostage Virginians had been given the freedom of the city and neighboring Indian villages.[43] Not only was James Johnson a prisoner who had broken parole, he was also carrying bills of exchange that implicated prominent Candians like St. Luc de la Corne[44] in the illegal trade to Albany. War not only made this offense more serious, but also made Lieutenant Johnson a potential source of damaging military intelligence about the defenses of New France. He might also be usable in subsequent exchanges of prisoners of war. James Johnson was jailed in Montreal, while his wife provided sympathy for former acquaintances who began arriving as newly taken prisoners of war.[45] Her own party, taken as slave captives of the Abenaki and redeemed first by the Canadians as preliminary to a repayment in cash or labor that would set them free, was also now seen as a group of prisoners of war.

Although Miriam, Farnsworth, and Labarree had managed to pay their ransom, they were not allowed to go home.[46] Within a few weeks, Susannah, James, and their two younger daughters were sent off to Quebec, where they were incarcerated in the criminal prison. All four contracted smallpox, and Susannah was sent to the hospital once with a fever, but they survived five months of close confinement in desperate circumstances. They managed to communicate with fellow prisoners Stobo and Van Braam, whose treason charges were pending. Relief did not come for the Johnsons until December, when Intendant François Bigot intervened with Vaudreuil's permission. The Johnsons were moved to the civilian prison and were given beds, fuel, candles, and a lieutenant's pay. Their confinement within the prison yard was a major improvement from the cell they had occupied in the criminal prison, but more confining than the liberty of many prisoners of war. Susannah was allowed a weekly outing to buy provisions.[47]

On one of her days of freedom, Susannah visited two recent captives of the Indians who had been bought by Governor Vaudreuil and sent to the Ursuline convent for education. In addition to meeting the two girls and being impressed with how well they were treated, Susannah talked to the assistant superior, Sister Esther-Marie-Joseph de l'Enfant-Jésus. Sister Esther asked to be remembered to her brother in Boston, whom she had not seen in the fifty-two years since she had been taken captive in an Abenaki raid on the Maine frontier.[48]

Confusion about the status of the Johnsons continued. It was May 1757 before they were given freedom within the town of Quebec, which included the company of officers of the former garrison at Fort Oswego, led by Peter Schuyler, the wealthy and generous colonel of the New Jersey Blues. A cartel ship arrived, promising release to the prisoners by the indirect route home through England. Vaudreuil refused to set James free, but gave permission for Susannah, Miriam, Polly, and Captive to go. Susannah agonized about leaving her beloved husband in Quebec, her eldest daughter in Montreal, and her son among the Abenaki. A coffeehouse conference chaired by Colonel Schuyler convinced her to go to England, and then back to America.[49]

Like many English captives and commentators, Susannah Johnson saw the treatment of captives in Canada not only as barbaric, but also as hypocritical. France under Louis XV set the standards for humane treatment of prisoners of war, yet civilian captives were enslaved in peacetime by Indian captors, often sold to Canadians, and then required to redeem themselves in cash. The Johnson case indicates that

Governor Vaudreuil did not distinguish clearly among captives, hostages taken in peacetime (Captains Stobo and Van Braam), and prisoners of war. The coming of war prompted Vaudreuil to consider James Johnson as a captured militia officer and a criminal who had broken parole. The treatment of Susannah reinforced the impression that captives were subject to rather capricious political authority. The Abenaki quest for captives, and their sale in Canada, was not visibly affected by the coming of war. The trade had made them more anxious to take prisoners, rather than scalps, and to bring their captives back in reasonable health. The traditional village triumph was moderated, but preserved, and captives could fulfill other traditional roles if adopted, or be exchanged for trade goods by warrior-hunters of an area that no longer supported trappers. What the English regarded as the hypocrisy of the French, the arbitrariness of the Canadians, and the cruelty of the Abenaki, was actually the result of a value system in transition. The Abenaki and other domiciled Indians in Canada were integrated into the money economy. They were less integrated into the French value system than were the Canadians, and much less than some of their missionaries hoped. These differences were not always serious, and could be symbiotic, but they still had the potential to produce explosive misunderstandings.

III

Unlike the Abenaki, the sachems of the Six Nations of the Iroquois were ostensibly as neutral as Pehr Kalm in the Anglo-French contest, though better informed about it and more affected by it. Neutrality had salvaged the strength of their league at the opening of the century and had been beneficial since in trade and diplomacy. When the English and French had returned to war in 1744, the wisdom of Iroquois neutrality was again evident, reinforced by concern for their relatives the Caughnawaga, descendants of the Mohawk who had migrated to Canada generations earlier. The Caughnawaga still visited their Mohawk kin and were involved in the clandestine trade between Montreal and Albany, a trade which had powerful supporters in New York politics.[50]

Iroquois neutrality was, however, something of a mirage. The Mohawk, Oneida, Tuscarora, Onondaga, Cayuga, and Seneca member tribes each acted with considerable independence of their formal confederacy council at Onondaga. Individual family clans, with marriage links across the member tribes, could also mount "mourning wars" against nonmembers of the league, revenge-seeking expeditions that could produce more deaths and even larger retaliatory expeditions. A few years earlier it had been estimated that about one-eighth of the fifteen hundred Iroquois warriors were inclined toward the French.[51] This interest was strongest with the most westerly Seneca, who honored and protected a trader and diplomat from Montreal, Nitachion, who was feared by the New Yorkers under his family name, Joncaire.[52] While the Seneca keepers of the league's western door were predominantly pro-French, many Mohawk keepers of the eastern door were clearly pro-English. By 1745 the Mohawk had adopted Warraghiyagey, "Chief Much Business," that brash and flamboyant Irish newcomer and leading trader at Oswego, hated by the French as William Johnson.[53] Many wise heads and genuinely friendly advisers saw Iroquois neutrality as the preferable course, but the tensions of the fifteen years after 1744 demanded more flexibility.

Those Iroquois who eventually ignored their league's official neutrality in order to join the New Yorkers refrained from doing so in the first years of King George's War. Prominent among the Mohawk sachems were the venerable Theyanoguin (Figure 3), orator, warrior, and Protestant who had visited England twice and was known to them as Chief Hendrick or Hendrick Peters;[54] Karaghtadie, fellow sachem of the Wolf clan of the Mohawk, known to the English as Nicks or Nicholas;[55] and the valiant Gingego, "the chief warrior of all the Nations."[56] At a 1745 conference between the Iroquois and representatives of Pennsylvania, Connecticut, Massachusetts, and New York, Theyanoguin aired complaints about land sales and the price of trade goods. He admitted that the Mohawk had joined other Iroquois in visiting Canada that summer, and he warded off all efforts to involve the Iroquois in the war that had already brought Canadian Indian raids to the Massachusetts frontier.[57] Governor George Clinton of New York tried to organize a campaign against Fort St. Frédéric to protect the New York frontier and aid the New Englanders.[58] Theyanoguin may have hoped that the pattern he remembered from Queen Anne's War would repeat itself, with war between New England and Canada and neutrality along the New York frontier. Destruction of Saratoga did not change the Mohawk position, though some English worried that the Indians on both sides were keeping a tacit neutrality among themselves while using the opportunity to destroy non-Indians.[59] Even the seemingly successful conference at Albany in August 1746, where some seven hundred representatives of all six Iroquois

FIGURE 3
Theyanoguin, or Chief Hendrick, in the early 1750s.
(Courtesy of The New-York Historical Society, New York City)

nations and the Mississauga exchanged belts with the English, had failed to recruit many warriors for the intended invasion of Canada.[60] While this conference was in progress, the Iroquois neutrality saved the New York frontier once more. Several Mohawk scouts captured by the French near Fort St. Frédéric were well treated, given presents, and sent home to encourage Iroquois neutrality.[61] Canadian and Indian reinforcements, sent to protect Fort St. Frédéric from this rumored attack, were soon able to go on the offensive as the invasion aborted. Rigaud led a seven hundred-man force southward, intending to raid Schenectady. Caughnawaga objections to attacking their kin who might be there led to a new target, and the capture of Fort Massachusetts.[62]

The Mohawk who entered the war were not simply lured by William Johnson, though "Chief Much Business," now Colonel of the Six Nations, was generous with the inducements that Governor Clinton had offered.[63] The Mohawk had their own concerns. Their position within the Iroquois League was in decline, and they were under more pressure from land speculators than were the other tribes. The Mohawk relationship with Johnson would prove advantageous in the longer term with regard to Iroquois politics, the diplomacy of gifts, and the protection of tribal lands.[64] The Mohawk also shared Johnson's self-interested objections to the fur trade carried on so profitably by the Caughnawaga to Albany. English military initiatives along the Lake Champlain route would enhance Johnson's Oswego trade and strengthen Mohawk land claims. It was also believed that the Caughnawaga would return to their homeland if their fur porterage declined.[65] War would also bring stricter enforcement of French trade restrictions, especially through Fort St. Frédéric.

The first of Johnson's raiders who went north in the autumn of 1746 divided into two parties, a war party that raided successfully north of Montreal and a diplomatic mission to the Caughnawaga. Theyanoguin led the latter group, which reassured the Caughnawaga, gave them a wampum belt "to stop their mouths," and went on to a meeting with Governor Charles de la Boische de Beauharnois of New France in Montreal, where they were given many presents. This trip marked Theyanoguin's own entry into the war; on their way home they attacked a small crew of French carpenters who were building on Ile La Motte, at the north end of Lake Champlain, then known as Iroquois Lake to some of the English and Iroquois, and "the Gate of Canada" to the Caughnawaga.[66]

Despite initial successes and eventual advantages, their support for the New Yorkers in the next two years brought the Mohawk repeated disaster. The great army that was supposed to take Fort St. Frédéric on the way to Canada in 1746 did not proceed because the promised British contingent did not arrive. Small Mohawk war parties, which would not even need approval by the tribal elders, collected a few scalps and prisoners during the subsequent winter. These raids provoked New France to declare war on them, though not on the rest of the Iroquois Confederacy.[67] In the spring Johnson's parties, including Mohawk, Oneida, Seneca, as well as English and Dutch, brought in fourteen scalps and twenty-five prisoners, at the cost of several of their own prominent warriors.[68] Theyanoguin, now sixty-six, led a major war party of Iroquois and English into a disastrous ambush above

Montreal, at the Cascades of the St. Lawrence, that June. Although Theyanoguin escaped, a number of leaders were killed and those captured included Karaghtadie.[69] Condolence wars by the Iroquois escalated the involvement, as did bounties, wampum belts, and the diplomacy of Johnson. In August 1747, some 318 Iroquois of all six tribes joined Johnson for yet another planned attack on Fort St. Frédéric. Again the attack did not materialize because of a change of priorities in England. Johnson himself led these warriors and an equal number of New York militiamen on an excursion north as far as Lac St. Sacrement.[70] The final blow for the Mohawk came in March 1748, when Gingego was shot and scalped, and his body was mutilated by a party of Caughnawaga.[71]

When the Iroquois gathered at Albany to meet with Governors Clinton and Shirley in July 1748, the complaints, like Pehr Kalm's observations, made it clear that the French had won King George's War on the Lake Champlain frontier. The English were rightly accused of leading the Iroquois to make sacrifices while the English remained safely on the defensive. This charge should have had a special sting for James De Lancey, political leader of the effective opposition to Clinton's war effort.

The blunt accusations of the Iroquois were used by the royal governors in an attempt to rouse administrators in Britain. In reporting on the conference to the Lords of Trade and Plantations in London, the governors emphasized that Iroquois contempt for the English was reaching unprecedented levels, while French influence was growing. The governors sent a number of their French prisoners to Canada in exchange for five imprisoned Iroquois chiefs, including Karaghtadie. This gesture was prompted by fear that the Mohawk would come under more French influence or appear more independent than the English wished, if these Indians accepted the Canadian invitation to negotiate the release of their own warriors. The troubled governors also wanted the peace to be used to reorganize the funding of British colonial defense. This involved the generations-old claim that New York, Massachusetts, and New Hampshire bore the burdens of war, while other governments, except that of Connecticut, balked at assisting in what was actually their own defense.[72]

Fort St. Frédéric had a special place in the complaints of the Mohawk raiders to Governors Shirley and Clinton, and in these governors' laments to the Lords Commissioners for Trade and Plantations in London. The governors argued that from this fort the French

were enabled to send out parties of Indians & French to harrass the
Frontiers of New York & New England and it served their parties as a
secure retreat in case of their being pursued by a superior force; it being
only three days travelling from the English Frontiers & about half way
between Albany & Montreal in Canada; Whereas the parties sent from
New York into Canada were under great difficulties by their being
obliged either to pass near that Fortress or to go a great way round thro'
a vast Mountainous Dessert, & had no place of retreat for their security,
or for recruiting either with Provision or Ammunition.

Even in the Indian-style guerrilla war of mobile raiding parties, this
conventional European fortress affected the military geography of this
no-man's-land. After wishing that the fort could be demolished by
negotiation, which was attempted, the governors offered the more
realistic suggestion that one or more forts be built on the major routes
to Canada and as near to Crown Point (as the English invariably
called Fort St. Frédéric) as practicable. This was a project for which
the governors wanted the British Crown to require intercolonial cooperation.[73]

The Mohawk lost their war and suffered with their fellow Iroquois
in the belligerent peace that followed. Mohawk prestige was low in
1748 and gained nothing from their acceptance of English negotiation
for the release of those Mohawk held prisoner in New France. Negotiating for release of prisoners was not in the Iroquois martial tradition, and the French could mock the implied dependence of a proud
people. Despite generous intentions, particularly those of Governors
Clinton and Shirley, the negotiations went on into 1750.[74] Although
these negotiations were opportunities for spying and smuggling, the
delay became another Mohawk grievance and further evidence of the
weakness of their patrons, William Johnson and Governor Clinton. In
1751, Johnson resigned as New York's agent with the Iroquois, disgusted with the government's unwillingness to pay his accounts, to
continue presents for the Indians, or to seize initiatives in disputed
areas during the peace.[75] By the summer of 1751, there was mounting
evidence that the Mohawk had supported the losing side.

Canadian influence was also growing during the five years after
1749, both within the Iroquois League and with their Ohio Valley
clients and allies. When Joncaire had taken eighty Iroquois sachems to
Montreal for a conference the previous year, the Mohawk were the
only tribe absent.[76] In 1749, the French encouraged the Ottawa to
attack and scatter the Mississauga, who were recent allies of the

English. The Mississauga received no help whatever from English America;[77] the Mohawk noticed. That same year, Abbé François Picquet established his strategically placed mission for the Iroquois at La Présentation (Oswegatchie, New York). Despite being razed by Mohawk one year later, this rebuilt settlement housed nearly four hundred Iroquois of various tribes by the summer of 1753.[78] The rebuilding of Niagara and the construction of Fort Rouillé (Toronto) in 1750 were two other Canadian initiatives enhancing the French presence among the western Iroquois. That summer a senior English Indian agent, Conrad Weiser, complained that the new chief sachem of the Iroquois was a Roman Catholic Onondaga and that his tribe, as well as the Cayuga and Seneca, had "turned Frenchmen."[79]

Rivalries in the upper Ohio Valley proved central in the rekindling of international violence, and Iroquois influence there was decreasing. As this region filled with Indians fleeing European encroachment farther east, the Iroquois tried to reassert authority over their former hunting lands. They were urged on by the English, who had found Iroquois claims useful in acquiring lands from some of their client tribes, but the English gave no direct support. Increasingly, even Iroquois migrants to the Ohio Valley were conducting independent diplomacy.[80] The Iroquois of the homelands heard that the British colonies of Virginia and Pennsylvania conducted talks directly with the Ohio Iroquois and tribes that the Onondaga claimed as clients.

The Canadians were also moving into the upper Ohio Valley in force. After Céleron de Blainville's rather cavalier expedition of 1749, which combined diplomacy and the burying of lead plates claiming sovereignty, the French became more assertive. The Ottawa destroyed the Miami town of Pickawillany, and the ceremonial cannibalism that followed was a gruesome symbol of the risks of being allied with the English. Then, in April 1753, some apprehensive Iroquois sighted what proved to be a force of about two thousand men under Sieur de Marin heading for the upper Ohio Valley. This army built two forts that year, establishing a secured route from Lake Erie to the Alleghany River that was extended to the forks of the Ohio the following year. Ominously, that army's five hundred Indians included a number of Seneca who, the English were assured, went along solely as hunters.[81]

Theyanoguin and sixteen companions from his Canajoharie settlement in the Mohawk Valley undertook a desperate mission two months later. Theyanoguin led his party into New York City for a formal conference with Governor Clinton, members of his council, and other notables. William Printup, Pehr Kalm's interpreter four years earlier, served similarly on this memorable occasion, with William Johnson also attending. Theyanoguin began by doubting English attachment to the sacred "covenant chain" that had bound them to the Iroquois and by insisting that the Mohawk had remained faithful to it when other tribes of the confederacy had not. New York's neglect of the frontier was castigated, and the new French threat on the Ohio made the Mohawk feel that the French "now dayly stand with a knife over our heads to destroy us."[82] Theyanoguin called for a redress of grievances, threatening that otherwise all links between New York and the Six Nations would be broken. After Mohawk land grievances were discussed and investigated by the governor and council, the Indian conference resumed. Governor Clinton, politically blocked by the De Lancey faction, could urge only self-help. On the land frauds, Clinton offered nothing but reference to the Albany commissioners, whom Theyanoguin dubbed "no people but Devils." Angry and disappointed, he said that "as soon as we come home we will send a Belt of Wampum to our Brothers the 5 Nations to acquaint them the Covenant Chain is broken between you and us," and he and his delegation stalked out.[83] With its closest Iroquois allies angry, the government of New York was alarmed and "allmost every Body was afeared of an Indian Warr."[84]

Theyanoguin's outburst had an impact that may well have exceeded that wily diplomat's calculations. Predictably, Clinton sent Johnson back to his estate in the Mohawk Valley to placate the angry delegates and to confirm that the supreme Onondaga Council of the Iroquois had neither planned nor sanctioned Theyanoguin's position.[85] When reported to the British government, Theyanoguin's threat prompted action that Governors Clinton and Shirley had pleaded for in vain after the upsetting conference with the Iroquois five years earlier. London authorities now urged Clinton's successor to call a major conference with the Iroquois, with all British colonies between Virginia and New Hampshire represented, for which royal presents for the Iroquois would be provided. The Albany Congress of 1754, remembered primarily for its abortive plans for inter-colonial union, was called to consider cooperative measures of defense, to placate disgruntled Mohawk, and to renew the covenant chain with the Iroquois.[86]

For the Mohawk, and particularly for those from Canajoharie led by Theyanoguin, the Albany Congress was a diplomatic success. The commissioners from seven colonies, assembled by New York's Lieutenant Governor James De Lancey, whose unexpected accession to power made him responsible for defense of New York's frontier, waited more than a week for Theyanoguin's party to make its entrance. The sachem's reply to De Lancey's committee-written opening speech had a power that survived translation. To De Lancey's only complaint, that the Iroquois were dispersing, Theyanoguin insisted that Abbé Picquet's new mission succeeded because the English neglected the Iroquois, while the French exerted themselves to win the Six Nations. He noted, "The Govr of Virginia and the Govr of Canada are both quarrelling about lands which belong to us." This argument was emphasized by formal presentation of another wampum belt, which paragraphed Iroquois diplomacy. Theyanoguin then denounced the Albany commissioners again, insisting that they had only smoked pipes with Canadian Indians in the last three years, that their warehouses were full of beaver from Canada, and that money, guns, shot, and powder had gone from Albany to Canada to help with French schemes against the Iroquois in the Ohio Valley. The British colonies were condemned for failed expeditions against Canada and for burning their own forts. He finished with a remark showing his understanding of the English audience: "Look at the French, they are Men, they are fortifying everywhere—but, we are ashamed to say it, you are like women, bare and open without any fortification."[87]

Most of the replies to Theyanoguin were lame, though Conrad Weiser performed well when called on to recount the recent history of the Ohio Valley.[88] The congress had effectively turned aside serious consideration of defense measures by insisting that a plan of intercolonial union be developed before defense contributions could be discussed. The commissioners had cause for serious worry; only 150 Iroquois had attended this major meeting. As was customary, those Iroquois who did not sympathize with Theyanoguin stayed away. As his supporters left the conference, with thirty wagons of presents, they could still feel content with their own performance.[89]

The small pro-English element among the Iroquois had used harsh words to convey justified exasperation with a weak ally. There was more evidence of English weakness while the congress was in session; George Washington's Virginia garrison surrendered the aptly named Fort Necessity on terms that sent Captains Stobo and Van Braam to Canada as hostages. Canadian Indians raided the backwoods settlements of Massachusetts and New Hampshire that summer, including the attack that captured the Johnsons at Charlestown, New Hampshire. Abenaki mission Indians from Becancourt destroyed New York farms within fifteen miles of Albany and captured all the Scachtacook Indians, a small Hudson River tribe who had been at the Albany Congress. These raids from the north, all using Fort St. Frédéric as a base, were warnings for the Mohawk.[90] The wagons of presents hauled away from the Albany Congress seemed to represent a prepaid price on the lives of those Iroquois who followed Theyanoguin.

2

TO BATTLE FOR
LAKE GEORGE

"All North America will be lost if these practices are tolerated, and no war can be worse to this country, than the suffering [of] such insults as these," stormed the Duke of Newcastle on hearing that the French had forced George Washington to surrender Fort Necessity.[1] The duke's government made no diplomatic protest; all negotiations on Anglo-French boundaries in North America were to wait until the British had recovered some military initiative. It soon became clear that Britain could not face war with France without a major ally, yet Britain's alliance with Austria was lame, and that with Russia was even more dubious. War would also ruin Newcastle's own plans for revenue reform in England. He and his closest allies in cabinet wanted retaliation limited to sending some regular army officers to America to train colonials for their own defense and to providing some financial assistance. Although this course of action fitted well with King George II's own resistance to sending any of his prized regular troops to America, the scheme was outflanked by those who wanted more initiative.[2]

When consulted about army officers to go to America, William Augustus, Duke of Cumberland, went directly to his father, King George, and successfully argued for two regular regiments to lead the response to French "encroachments." Cumberland, Captain General of the British Army and a tough soldier with command experience in

Europe and Scotland, promptly sketched an operational plan to counter French advances. The forks of the Ohio, Fort St. Frédéric, and the isthmus linking Nova Scotia to the continent were the central areas of attention. These three targets were to be attacked *seriatum*, with diplomatic negotiations between victories.[3] The cabinet decisions of September 1754, to send regiments to America under Major General Edward Braddock of Cumberland's own Coldstream Guards, were made on the assumption that no full-scale war with France would ensue. Secretary of State Sir Thomas Robinson wrote colonial governors about preliminary plans to send two regiments of five hundred men each, to be augmented in America to seven hundred men each. He also authorized the revival of two regular regiments of Americans, each brought to full strength of one thousand men, led by Governor Shirley of Massachusetts and Sir William Pepperrell.[4]

In the preparation of Braddock's secret instructions, the British cabinet heard a different perspective from the ambitious and industrious President of the Lords Commissioners for Trade and Plantations, the Earl of Halifax. Arguing that the Ohio campaign involved needless risks deep in the wilderness, Halifax urged attacks on Fort Niagara and Fort St. Frédéric. This strategy, he argued, was a more convenient way to challenge the French, affording better communications and stronger Indian support from the Iroquois than the southern colonies had been able to muster to help Washington. With Niagara taken, the French presence in the Ohio would be so precarious that southern English colonies could complete the conquest themselves. A simultaneous attack on Fort St. Frédéric would divide the forces in Canada, and could be undertaken by New York, New Hampshire, and Massachusetts, colonies with vital reasons to wish that fort taken.[5] The resulting instructions, dated November 25 but not known to colonial planners until the following April, called for attacks on Fort Niagara and Fort St. Frédéric in addition to the Ohio and Acadian campaigns.[6]

Lieutenant Governor James De Lancey of New York had received Robinson's letter by the time Braddock sailed for America at the end of the year. De Lancey's reply, which foretold much about the next three years, offered his views of what was needed on the northern frontier. He began with the plea that, because there were "not above twenty two miles land carriage between Crown Point and through this Province to the Ocean, I apprehend we are in great danger." The colony had no forts beyond Albany, and an attack from Canada was expected as the French tried to distract English forces from the Ohio

Valley. De Lancey wanted a regiment of regulars and a money quota from neighboring colonies to build forts, and he specified forts at Wood Creek and at the south end of Lac St. Sacrement. He said that these forts would protect New York and its neighbors from attacks launched out of Fort St. Frédéric, facilitate future action against that fort should a war be declared, and assert British land claims against French "watershed" pretensions.[7] When the more ambitious scheme for 1755 had failed, these were to become the New York arguments for building Fort William Henry.

De Lancey's response confirmed his reputation as an "anti-imperialist," especially when compared with the initiatives taken by Governor Shirley on the basis of the same Robinson letter. Shirley, who had been active in plans to attack Fort St. Frédéric in 1746, 1747, and 1748, and who had tried to have the fort declared on English territory while he served on the Anglo-French boundary commission during the next few years, was now planning again. Although he was already preparing an expedition against Acadia with Governor Charles Lawrence, Shirley's own regiment was being recruited by early January on the understanding that it was bound against Fort St. Frédéric.[8] The following month he convinced the Massachusetts General Court to provide twelve hundred men for such an expedition, and he began negotiating with neighboring governments for more. He sent the well-connected Thomas Pownall to convince their mutual friend, James De Lancey, to use the opportunity provided by impending initiatives on the Ohio and in Acadia to build a fort to neutralize Fort St. Frédéric. The expedition, Shirley suggested, should be led by William Johnson, and a fort should be built to withstand anything the French might send against them. Shirley, like De Lancey, stayed within the limits of a peacetime effort to counter French initiatives. He did not suggest taking the French border fort, though he was impatient with that restraint.[9]

William Johnson was understandably reluctant to take command of such an intercolonial expedition. He had previously sent scouting and scalping parties to Fort St. Frédéric and had taken a small expedition of Iroquois and New York militia to Lac St. Sacrement in 1747, but he had no conventional military experience whatever. Rather than lead colonial troops in building a road and then a fort, while subject to endless raids and ambushes, Johnson proposed destroying the French fort with Iroquois. Johnson also mentioned attacking Fort Niagara, apparently without knowing that Lord Halifax had earlier suggested the same. Shirley, who insisted on Johnson for command against Fort

St. Frédéric, came to think much more highly of Johnson's Niagara suggestion.[10]

The shape of the 1755 campaign was affected by Shirley's strenuous efforts, but became clear at the April meeting of colonial governors with General Braddock. Braddock had been in Virginia for two months and had moved his camp to the frontier town of Alexandria by the time he met with Admiral Augustus Keppel and the governors of Virginia, Maryland, Pennsylvania, New York and Massachusetts. The surprising progress made by the northern colonies in raising troops made Braddock's secret instructions read differently. Instead of a series of measures by a single army, with the possibility of spasmodic negotiations with the French between phases, armies were ready to attempt four nearly simultaneous strikes. This was a much more aggressive strategy, even if all the targets were what the English regarded as "encroachments." Braddock was already beginning his campaign against Fort Duquesne, and the New England expedition against the Acadian Fort Beauséjour was able to sail within six weeks of the Alexandria meeting.

William Johnson was now definitely to lead an intercolonial expedition to take Fort St. Frédéric, as well as becoming superintendent of Indian affairs on the northern borders. The major change that would directly affect Johnson's expedition was the launch of a separate attack on Fort Niagara, under Governor Shirley. It was ironic that Shirley, who had spearheaded efforts against Fort St. Frédéric for nearly a decade, was now to lead a force through New York and Iroquois country to attack Fort Niagara. Johnson, who had first interested Shirley in an attack on Fort Niagara and had been a leading trader on that frontier, was to attack Fort St. Frédéric, with a commission from Major General Shirley rather than from Braddock.[11]

William Johnson, "Chief Much Business" and former colonel of the Six Nations, was no more prepared for his assignment than were his troops. His limited military experience was as paymaster of Indian warriors who lived off the land, struck suddenly at vulnerable and unsuspecting targets, and then melted into the woods, defending nothing. Johnson and his Iroquois allies were now to join forty-four hundred recruits from the farms and villages of six English colonies on an assignment that involved cutting a road, building forts, hauling cannon and supplies, and then besieging a fort. The objective was derived from conventional European warfare; the means had to be conventional, and the men must try to be like regulars. Johnson studied Braddock's own camp for an introduction to efficient organization, and he accepted advice readily. A month later, however, he confessed to Braddock: "I am truly sensible of my own Inability to be at the head of this undertaking & I am afraid I shall have but few with me to assist & strengthen my Incapacity. None that can be called an Engineer. . . ."[12] Many of his problems were already being solved, since Braddock was sending him Captain William Eyre. A military engineer with the British army in the Netherlands and in Scotland, Eyre impressed Johnson's colleagues as "a gentleman of smart powers, understands his business well";[13] he was soon acting as quartermaster general as well as engineer for the expedition.

Amid the growing complexities and frustrations of mounting an intercolonial expedition, William Johnson spent considerable time in the more familiar world of Iroquois diplomacy. He commissioned several colonials with frontier experience to recruit Iroquois, but warned one of them that "they are not to go a Scalping as in the last War, only to march with me wherever I go."[14] With his captains, Johnson visited the Mohawk, urging them to war and to attend his major conference.[15] During the last two weeks of June and the first few days of July, nearly one thousand Iroquois men, women, and children gathered at Johnson's estate (Figure 4). Predictably, the Mohawk were the largest group (408), and the large Oneida presence (200) reflected their pro-English inclinations. The Onondaga legation (100) mattered more to Johnson, as it was the most neutral and distinguished tribe. The Cayuga (103) made their reticence known and were carefully courted. The Seneca were underrepresented (67), and some were suspected of spying for the French. The Tuscarora contingent (64) was not a surprise, but the arrival of 130 Delaware and their allies represented the broader reach of the Iroquois connection, as did the late arrival of a Mississauga chief, and a letter from Scarouday, half-king of the Iroquois interest in the upper Ohio Valley.[16] Johnson was aided by his secretary, Peter Wraxall; by four interpreters, including William Printup; and by Johnson's newly commissioned captains.

The speeches at the conference bore the marks of careful orchestration by Johnson and by the Mohawk, and the politeness, the feasting, and the dancing could suggest that everything went well. Yet when Johnson tried to obtain firm commitments and conclude the conference, the reticence of the Iroquois became evident. Concern for the Caughnawaga was a predictable one, reinforcing practical reasons why the Iroquois preferred to wait and measure the relative strength and resolve of the two European contestants.[17] Two weeks after the conference ended, Johnson wrote a frank appraisal of it:

FIGURE 4
E. L. Henry, *Johnson Hall.*
(Courtesy of the Collection of the Knox Family)

> I found all the Nations except the Mohawks extreamly averse to taking
> any part with us in the present Active Measures against the French.
> [T]his Arose from two Principal Sources; the Most prevalent was their
> Fear of the French, owing to our long passiveness & their Activity, & the
> shameful hand we have always made of our former Expeditions. The
> other was, from a real attachment in many of their most leading Men to
> the French Interest.[18]

Johnson observed that everything rested on a vigorous and spirited
conduct of the current season's campaign.

A week after the conference, interpreter Daniel Claus wrote from
Theyanoguin's village of Canajoharie that "the Indians here observed
it was true enough that the English had fallen asleep in their under-
takings and Expeditions."[19] The Mohawk had already seen some signs
of the confusion and delay that made them ignore Johnson's immediate pleas for warriors. The competition between Governor Shirley
and William Johnson for Iroquois support was confusing in view of
Johnson's supposed new powers in all Indian affairs. Shirley's methods of Iroquois recruitment included offering them pay by the day,

organizing them into companies like militia, and insisting that Shirley was Johnson's commander. Johnson fumed at these expensive and alien recruiting methods, which made the Mohawk reluctant to join either expedition.[20] Johnson also objected to Shirley's authority, legitimately in the sphere of Indian diplomacy and less plausibly on other issues. Shirley had commissioned and instructed Johnson, and the instructions included receiving additional commands from Shirley. Johnson attempted to counter this jurisdiction with an identical set of instructions from New York Lieutenant Governor De Lancey. These latter had one significant variation: Johnson was not subject to further instruction, but was to use his own judgment aided by his officers acting as a council of war.[21] The dispute between Shirley and Johnson cost both of them Iroquois support, but Johnson lost more in the contest to launch two campaigns out of Albany. Shirley diverted one thousand men from Johnson's force to his own; half of them were Massachusetts volunteers, and the others served under a popular New Jersey colonel, Peter Schuyler. The competition for cannon, wagons, and whaleboats was overt, but the shortages of other equipment and supplies were also due to the two contending enterprises.[22]

Delays for supplies and boats were particularly crippling, and the Iroquois were able to observe their own doubts being confirmed. Delay meant that the expected French reinforcements from Europe arrived, further strengthening Fort St. Frédéric. Delays also affected the morale of the army that gathered at Albany. Colonel Ephraim Williams, heading one of the Massachusetts regiments of volunteers, had waited a full month before marching to Albany because of lack of equipment, including guns for men who had not brought their own.[23] The surgeon's mate of that regiment, Perry Marsh, reported early in July, "I see no prospects of our marching this month: no Governor; no stores; no medicines; no battoes, at least there is not one ready."[24] His colonel worried about sickness if the men did not march soon, a legitimate concern in regiments of newly raised rural recruits whose sanitary habits were notorious.[25] This concern, as well as the vulnerability to epidemic diseases for those used to living in relative isolation, was aggravated by the shortage of kettles, causing many of the men "to eat their victuals almost as salt as brine."[26] The Connecticut regiment, under Major General Phineas Lyman, had arrived before the end of June and was impatient for action. Although better supplied than the Massachusetts troops, they had brought some boats with them that proved too small to be useful.[27]

Early in July, when both Governor Shirley and William Johnson arrived personally in Albany, the town became the site of more frantic preparations by the two armies, competing for men, materials, and supplies. By the middle of the month, there were signs of order in Johnson's command. Men were still arriving, particularly from New York and New Hampshire, but Johnson had muster sheets indicating nearly twenty-seven hundred effectives. Regimental quarter guards were reporting some attempted desertion and insubordination, but the new levies were being conditioned to the routine of guard duty.[28] Together with the urgent work of building boats and gathering supplies, teams, and other materials, guard duty seemed to consume the energy of the camp, with little time for training exercises to bring effective cooperation among the gathered volunteers. At mid-month Seth Pomeroy, lieutenant colonel of a Massachusetts regiment, could report that "Mr. Johnson's army are generally well & in heigh spiritts for marching, but are unhapaly detained for want of our stores."[29]

Two days later, the first contingent of fourteen hundred Massachusetts and Connecticut troops, under Major General Lyman, were ordered to cut a wagon road up the Hudson to the Great Carrying Place. The road was to be thirty-feet wide and well cleared. Although this was a long-traveled route, Lyman's force found the going slow. A week later Lyman wrote from Stillwater, reflecting the complaints of his men by asking whether it was not excessive

> to Cut down all ye Trees & Small bushes which if we do we must make Such a Pile or heap of Timber in the Thickest Places in ye woods that will be a Com pleat fort for ye Indians to Ly behind & fire on the army & by Cutting ye Small Low bushes which grow but abt 3 feet high the Troops will be more Exposed by the Stubs than by Leaving them Standing.[30]

Like Pehr Kalm, Lyman's army crossed the Hudson near Saratoga, but their ford was waist deep, meaning that men, horses, guns, and provisions hauled by wagon became very wet.[31] This contingent was also wrestling large whaleboats over the numerous falls of the upper Hudson.[32] At the Great Carrying Place, near the ruins of Fort Nicholson and on the site where Fort Edward would be built that autumn, Lyman was to oversee construction of bark-covered log magazines for the whole army's ammunition and supplies. Johnson ordered friendly Indians to wear a red headband and call out his Mohawk name, Warraghiyagey, to distinguish them from hostile Indians, who had been seen around the

Albany camp. Many of the troops had difficulty repeating or recognizing this password, and the French soon learned of it.[33]

This first display of English momentum had not even begun when the depressing news arrived from the Ohio Valley. Reports of Braddock's defeat, which reached Johnson and the senior officers with whom he shared the secret on July 21,[34] added to the persistent pessimism fed by the unending difficulties about the entire absence of supplies for the New Hampshire troops, jurisdictional disputes in the commissaries, and contests between Shirley and Johnson that did not improve even after Braddock's defeat made the two New York expeditions more crucial to each other. Johnson was now being advised to keep his force together, to consider joining with Shirley to try to recapture Braddock's artillery train, and to retaliate by giving no quarter to the French but to "destroy and scalp as they do."[35] Suspicious that European reinforcements had reached Canada, Shirley ordered Johnson to go on the defensive at any sign of superior French strength, and to retreat to Albany and protect the New York frontier.[36] With mounting evidence that the Iroquois were becoming even more cautious about helping the luckless English, Johnson wrote a despondent letter to Lieutenant Governor De Lancey suggesting withdrawal to Albany after strengthening Lyman's post at the Great Carrying Place with more artillery. De Lancey replied supportively that Braddock's defeat was "entirely owing to the European Troops being unaccustomed to and unacquainted with Wood Fighting."[37] This exaggeration may have helped the colonial army that assembled under Johnson at the Great Carrying Place in mid-August, but by then the prospect of taking Fort St. Frédéric was fading.

As August began, Johnson ordered a second contingent of eleven hundred men to take the field artillery to Major General Lyman at the Great Carrying Place. Braddock's defeat, and the risk of losing sixteen cannon and three mortars, made Johnson's cautions to Colonel Moses Titcomb more elaborate than those for Lyman when he had set out to prepare the wagon road. Formal guard arrangements were specified, with stops every half hour to ensure that the column stayed together. Strict discipline was to be enforced "as the Troops who are to march under Your Command have not been used to a regular Military . . . and to establish & preserve that relative Subordination without wch every Military Undertaking will be Shameful & very probably fatal."[38] These were strange words for a general of the Iroquois, but Johnson was following the military manuals and protecting himself from his own superior, the increasingly unsympathetic William Shirley. Johnson was still extremely nervous about the impact of Braddock's defeat on the Iroquois, who still had not arrived. Johnson warned that any irresponsible firing at Indians would be disastrous if a friendly warrior were killed or wounded. After reviewing the red band code, he advised that small parties of Indians, like those coming to join him, were not hostile so long as units stayed together, "& a single Indian is not to be dreaded & indeed but as a Friend will not show himself."[39] Neither Johnson's objectives nor his methods on this campaign permitted any irregular warfare. His second contingent was nine days reaching Lyman's camp, and the men were weary and wet from wrestling three-ton cannon around the falls of the upper Hudson.[40] Like Pehr Kalm, Johnson's army followed the west bank of the Hudson to Saratoga, and then crossed to the east side for the trip to the proposed site of Fort Edward.

There was a definite New England character to Johnson's army, some of which he did not appreciate. Raw levies electing their own officers was one peculiarity Johnson disliked, since it encouraged widespread failure to enforce orders and courts-martial that failed to do their duty.[41] Incidents of insubordination, mutiny, and desertion were handled very leniently.[42] There was little drill or training done amid the building, digging, and guard duty, though there had been some practice in coordinating three ranks to fire and reload while giving ground.[43] A New England militiaman on the same frontier three years later wrote that it "greatly surprised me, to think that I must stand still to be shot at."[44] Johnson's American troops were being trained for a conventional battlefield rather than woodland warfare.

The New Englanders were anti-professional, idealizing the militia. Equipped with a variety of muskets, and hatchets rather than bayonets, the New Englanders were a military hybrid that could sometimes perform well in what was a hybrid war. There was also a special ferocity to their warfare compared with that of eighteenth-century European armies. Born of an earlier Europe that fought an ostensibly religious total war, New Englanders were inclined to seek final extirpation and destruction of their enemies. This approach had been reinforced by their vulnerability to Indian raids, the uselessness of forts, the limits of treaties, and their racist views of Indians. The three wars fought against Canada, in which neither side had European regulars, had reinforced the New England preference for complete destruction and total war. The limited objective of the newer European wars between related landowners, and the code of honor of the European professional officer dealing with his enemy counterpart, were as unfamiliar to New Englanders as was the contrasting brutality of the internal discipline within eighteenth-century European armies.[45] Another uncommon feature of the New England troops was their religious concerns. In the spring Johnson was advised that "Prayers have often a good effect, especially among New England men, a well gifted New England Parson might therefore be a usefull implement."[46] The diaries confirm that the New England parsons, and Reverend John Ogilvie of New York, were much appreciated.[47] Reverend Stephen Williams, who had been taken captive to Canada as a boy half a century earlier, was particularly inspiring.[48] Colonel Ephraim Williams of Massachusetts was piously disgusted with some of the army that was assembling:

> We are a wicked profane army, more especially New York troops & Road Island, nothing to be heard among a great part of them but the language of Hell. I assure you Sir if ever the place is taken it will not be for our sakes, but for those good people left behind.[49]

New England regiments did not take any women with them, and difficulties arose since the New York and Rhode Island units had laundresses, nurses, wives, and prostitutes in their camps. Johnson, whose own womanizing was notorious, responded to complaints from his second-in-command, Colonel Lyman, late in July: "As to bad Women following or being harboured in our Camp I shall discountenance it to the utmost of my Power. As to Men's Wives while they behave Decently they are suffered in all Camps & thought necessary to Wash & mend." Johnson went on, without increasing his credibility: "Immorality of all kinds I will use my utmost power to suppress & chastise. I hope we shall not soil the Justice of our Cause with a Conduct rebellious against that Al(mighty) Power upon whose Favour depends the Success of all human Enterprises."[50] Nearly a month later, after Johnson had come to Fort Edward, Lyman succeeded in having a council of war send all women back to Albany with orders not to allow any to return.[51] The most severe punishment imposed by a court martial on this expedition was for "Profane Swaring & a Sodomittical atempt" for which a soldier received one hundred lashes, was drummed out of the army, and was imprisoned until the end of the campaign.[52]

When Johnson left Albany with the third and final contingent, including only fifty Indians and no New Hampshiremen, the second contingent was still on the road to Fort Edward. Lyman had some three hundred men cutting a thirty-foot wagon road from Fort Edward to Wood Creek, along the same northward route Pehr Kalm had traveled six years earlier. The troops had cut eight miles of road when the work was suddenly stopped.[53] The Wood Creek route had been used in earlier expeditions and might well be favored by a Connecticut man like Lyman. Fortification on this route would protect Connecticut and western Massachusetts more than would a fort on the Lac St. Sacrement route. Yet there were objections that the low water levels made Wood Creek impractical; the route could be commanded by a single well-placed French battery; and the route was clogged with the logs Kalm had encountered, to which more could readily be added. Scouting parties reconnoitered both routes and reported to the council of war that Johnson held at the Fort Edward camp on August 22.[54] The choice of the Lac St. Sacrement route was favored by those thinking seriously about moving cannon to Fort St. Frédéric.

As Johnson was aware, the French became more powerful with every passing day.[55] By mid-August, Thomas Pownall told Johnson that the taking of Fort St. Frédéric was increasingly unlikely that year, and he supported the building of a fort "in some Place that might for ye present cover ye Country & from whence we might in future when we are better & stronger appointed, annoy ye Enimy, & so at length carry ye [Crown] Point."[56] The Mohawk, returning from an unsuccessful attempt to keep the Caughnawaga neutral, conveyed fears that as many as six thousand French regulars had landed at Quebec and were being moved to Fort St. Frédéric, and confirmed that supplies from Montreal were being rushed through Fort St. Jean to Fort St. Frédéric in great quantities. Johnson's council of war at the Great Carrying Place on August 22 resolved to call for reinforcements for their 2932 effectives and to proceed by the Lac St. Sacrement route. Johnson was undermanned (Colonel Williams' hint that eight to nine thousand additional troops were needed was not an exaggeration for the expected task) and had fewer than sixty Iroquois with him.[57] As now became evident, the advance was to build a road with a fort at the end of it near the lake, similar to the fortified-road technique used by General George Wade in the Scottish highlands. If provincial reinforcements arrived in time, they could proceed from that new base. If reinforcements did not come, the fort would help deter Canadian raiders and traders, including the Caughnawaga whose trade with Albany irritated the Mohawk and Johnson. What no one argued, because it was desperately obvious, was that the fort was also to prevent French access to the new road itself, a seventy-mile wagon and cannon road that led to Albany and had made northern New York more vulnerable to regular troops from Canada than ever before.[58]

Johnson himself took command when fifteen hundred militiamen and forty Indians set off on four days of road cutting that expanded the log-strewn, overgrown walking path (which Kalm had followed south to the Hudson in 1749) into a road for their supplies, boats, and artillery. When they reached Lac St. Sacrement, named a century earlier by the intrepid Jesuit Isaac Jogues, Johnson immediately, and prematurely, asserted English claims by renaming it Lake George after his king. Johnson found "not a foot of land cleared" in the dense pine forest that went to the water's edge. The army set about clearing a stony rise of land that proved ideal for a defensible camp and began building temporary shacks for provisions and stores. The Iroquois now arrived. Although fewer than had accompanied Johnson there in 1747, they numbered more than two hundred well-equipped warriors led by Theyanoguin himself. On September 3, most of the remaining force from Fort Edward came up to the lake, convoying two hundred wagons and the rest of the artillery. The army had completed a vulnerable trek with only two men lost to the enemy; men herding cattle near Fort Edward had been attacked by Indians, leaving one dead and one taken prisoner.[59]

Boats were still needed to launch the attack down Lake George, and the army improved their camp in the meantime. With Captain Eyre's arrival, the site of Fort William Henry was chosen and clearing began. Johnson had left Fort Edward lightly manned, with a rear guard of about five hundred, half of them workmen finishing the fort that Captain Eyre had planned.[60] The advance of most of Johnson's troops to Lake George was less cautious than he had been earlier. Perhaps the arrival of the Indians put spirit into Warraghiyagey. His army could not retreat to a strong point in case of danger, but there had been little sign of the enemy.

On September 3, scouts discovered the tracks of 150–200 Indian allies of the French who had gone by South Bay, apparently headed for Schenectady. Johnson's pursuit party proved unsuccessful, and the security around the Lake George camp was strengthened.[61] The relative security of the camp was further shattered on September 7, when Theyanoguin told a council of war that Indians returning from scouting at Crown Point found three large roads made by many men who had marched from South Bay toward Fort Edward the day before. Guards were doubled, the men were ordered "to lay on their Arms all Night," more scouting parties were organized, and a Jacob Adams volunteered to ride Johnson's horse with a warning for Colonel Joseph Blanchard, whose four hundred New Hampshiremen had supplemented the small garrison at Fort Edward.[62]

II

The sixteen men-of-war that sailed from Brest on May 3, 1755, were the French response to British initiatives for North America. Although the squadron was rated at nearly one thousand guns, with the seventy-four-gun *L'Esperance* as Admiral Du Bois de La Motte's flagship, a nine-vessel armed escort saw them out of European waters because only three of La Motte's ships had all their guns mounted. The men, kit, and supplies of 6 of France's 395 battalions of regular infantry were crammed into ships that were too crowded to mount guns.[63] These three thousand *troupes de terre* were to be commanded by Maréchal de camp Jean-Armand, Baron de Dieskau, who had been a protégé of the legendary Maréchal de Saxe and a cavalry colonel at the Battle of Fontenoy, and more recently served as military governor of the port from which the fleet sailed.[64] These regulars, like Braddock's, were proof that the imperial powers had come to fight for North America and to change the inconclusive pattern of two-thirds of a century of Anglo-French intercolonial warfare. Dieskau's instructions made it very clear that he was under the military orders of his fellow passenger on *L'Esperance* and now Governor-General of New France, Pierre-François de Rigaud de Vaudreuil de Cavagnal, Marquis de Vaudreuil. This fifty-eight-year-old Canadian soldier had established his reputation as tough, ruthless, and effective as governor of Louisiana.[65] The fleet, which had a crossing of less than four weeks to Newfoundland waters, represented French determination to defend its version of the boundaries between empires in North America.

Like the British, the French government had a generous view of its own possessions in North America and shared a belief that its aggressive opponent would not risk war. Early in October 1754, the French ambassador to Britain, Duc de Mirepoix, had reported the British decision to send Braddock and two regiments to Virginia. The British ambassador in Paris was the Earl of Albemarle, who happened to be colonel of Braddock's regiment, father of the commodore of the fleet that took Braddock to Virginia, titular governor for seventeen years of a Virginia he had never visited, a member of the inconclusive boundary commission that had failed to delineate the Ohio or Nova Scotia boundaries, and the diplomat assigned to seeking release of several English traders taken prisoner in the Ohio Valley and shipped to France. Under questioning by Louis XV, Albemarle insisted that the measures were entirely defensive and conventional, though no one regarded the sending of regulars to North America as customary.[66] A month later, Minister of Marine Jean Baptiste de Machault d'Arnou-ville ordered Governor Duquesne of Canada to remain on the defensive, use only Indians to retaliate, and not expect a complete rupture with the British.[67] Although Machault's ministry developed a comprehensive plan for victory short of war, involving French control of the St. Lawrence and Mississippi drainage basins, the cautious orders to Duquesne were repeated in a letter which announced that Vaudreuil and six battalions of regulars were bound for New France in the spring. The only action ordered, to be portrayed as defensive and without royal support, was the conquest of a small post that Shirley had built in 1754 on the upper Kennebeck River.[68] Vaudreuil carried private instructions that also insisted on a defensive posture and the use of Indian allies to stall or retaliate for minor aggressions. Yet there were hints that war was now considered possible.[69]

After its smooth passage to the Grand Banks, de La Motte's fleet met different weather in more than one sense. Gales, fogs, and icebergs dispersed and threatened his ships. On June 6 the passengers on the flagship, then accompanied by only three other vessels of the squadron, saw ten sail in the distance. Their failure to respond to signals made it clear that these were British men-of-war, not part of the scattered French squadron. Fog intervened to protect de La Motte's four ships from Admiral Edward Boscawen's force, which carried orders to attack, take, or sink this fleet for Canada, even if doing so provoked war. Boscawen's fleet did not learn of de La Motte's presence until the next day, first from an English fishing vessel and then by spotting three French vessels off Cape Race. Boscawen, now with eleven ships, gave chase on the clear morning of June 8, and the *Dunkirk* overhauled the fleeing *l'Alcide*. *L'Alcide's* captain was assured by the *Dunkirk's* captain, only seconds before a close-range broadside disabled his ship, that the two nations were still at peace. The capture of *l'Alcide* and the *Lys* completed the Anglo-French side into war.[70] When news of the event reached London, in mid-July, Ambassador Mirepoix departed immediately without taking official leave.[71] By the time the news reached Quebec a week later, telling Vaudreuil that his younger brother François-Pierre de Rigaud and 330 of the French regulars were taken to England as prisoners of war, the war had already begun for Vaudreuil.

Although Vaudreuil's arrival at Quebec on June 23 was accompanied by appropriate festivities, nothing could mask the dire threats to New France. Within days he learned that forts Beauséjour and Gaspereau had fallen ignominiously to the New England volunteers led by

Colonel Robert Monckton, severing links to the Acadians as well as land links to Louisbourg. Scouting reports indicated that three thousand men under Braddock had advanced to Fort Necessity, preparing for a final push against Fort Duquesne. More immediately, there were two enemy armies assembling at Albany, reportedly nine thousand men, some bound for Fort Oswego to threaten Fort Niagara and Fort Frontenac, and the rest (overestimated as five thousand men) mustering under William Johnson to attack Fort St. Frédéric. It was too late to attempt to help Fort Duquesne, named for the retiring governor whom Vaudreuil later accused of negligence. Vaudreuil deserved no credit for the surprise victory over Braddock at Fort Duquesne, though he did attempt to claim responsibility. Vaudreuil could not initiate his preferred policy (one that later became clear to a disgusted John Campbell, Earl of Loudoun, when he read Vaudreuil's papers captured aboard *l'Alcide*) of guerrilla warfare to distract and disrupt the enemy.[72] To meet the English, Vaudreuil had two thousand regulars, perhaps an equal number of *troupes de la marine* (recruits from France officered and trained by Canadians), about eight thousand militia, and Indian allies who were unnumbered but unimpressed with the European conventions of battle that suddenly were coming to dominate this contest.[73]

Initially, Vaudreuil put priority on protecting French interests on Lake Ontario by mounting a force to attack Oswego, and to defend Fort Frontenac and Niagara in the process. The speed with which this campaign was launched, compared with Johnson's difficulties at Albany, was testimony to the value of unified command in Canada, regular army organization, and advanced planning from France. The force was composed of about forty-three hundred men: two thousand regulars, eighteen hundred Canadians, and five hundred Indians from the mission villages of Canada.[74] While New France had interior lines of defense that were made more effective by good water transport on the St. Lawrence, this gamble was predicated on the assumption that Johnson's army would not be an immediate threat. On August 12, Vaudreuil received an exaggerated report claiming that Johnson's force, said to include one thousand regulars, were within two days' march of Fort St. Frédéric.[75] Vaudreuil's attack on Fort Oswego was postponed, and Dieskau was diverted with three thousand men to stop the threat to Fort St. Frédéric. Within three days, Vaudreuil received other reports that Johnson's second contingent, hauling artillery, had just begun moving north of Albany.[76] Hearing that Fort St. Frédéric, which so frightened British American colonists, "is threatening to fall on all sides, in consequence of the walls being too weak to support the terraces,"[77] Vaudreuil had good reasons to employ his preferred strategy of a spoiling raid.

Dieskau's force set out in contingents from Montreal between August 10 and 20, buoyed by the news of the great victory over Braddock.[78] Seven hundred French regulars of La Reine and Languedoc regiments joined some sixteen hundred Canadians, mostly militia but including some three hundred colonial regulars, and over six hundred Indians, half of whom were Caughnawaga from the missions of Sault St. Louis and Lac de Deux Montagnes. Vaudreuil had made a special appeal to the Indians and was anxious about their role in the venture. Anticipating that Johnson's Mohawk would attempt to stall the raid by sending legates, Vaudreuil provided a belt that was to carry a friendly but negative reply to the relatives of the French Mohawk.[79] The Caughnawaga were given one interpreter, while two were sent with the Abenaki, including Joseph Boucher de Niverville, who had led them on successful raids for a decade, had been prominent in a major Abenaki raid into western Massachusetts from Fort St. Frédéric in 1747, and had participated in the defeat of Theyanoguin at the Cascades the same year.[80] The general "command" of the Indians was left to Jacques Legardeur Saint-Pierre, prominent explorer, interpreter, and soldier in the Mississippi Valley, and leader of the successful ambush at the Cascades. Although best known for his firm dismissal of George Washington's summons at Fort Le Boeuf in 1753, this expert in Canadian Indian diplomacy was undertaking what proved to be his final assignment as interpreter for the domiciled Nipissing and the few Ottawa and other Algonquian warriors on this raid.[81]

Of the incongruities of the Lake George campaign, none is more striking than Dieskau's instant adoption of guerrilla warfare. He left Montreal amid joy at the utter destruction of Braddock and his European army, and had been in the New World only two months when he agreed to an ambush that killed Iroquois scouts and English colonial frontiersmen under the command of the lord of the Mohawk, William Johnson. Vaudreuil's instructions to Dieskau had emphasized urgency, assuming that his army could still undertake an attack on Oswego in 1755. Vaudreuil emphasized the need to use Canadian and Indian scouts effectively, but there was no quick course in guerrilla warfare in the governor's conventional exhortations.[82] In forming his attack, Dieskau was to consult Legardeur de Saint-Pierre and Louis Legardeur de Repentigny, a lieutenant in the *troupes de la marine* with long experience on the Fort St. Frédéric frontier, including prominence in the devastating 1745 raid on Saratoga.[83] François Le Mercier, an artillery officer who was second in command at the conquest of Fort Necessity the previous summer, also accompanied Dieskau.[84] What subsequent recriminations entirely obscured was that Baron Dieskau had considerable experience with irregular warfare in Europe, experience that made him a sensible choice for his assignment of New France. Baron Dieskau had seen the effectiveness of partisans and irregular troops in eastern Europe even before he came to serve as aide-de-camp to Maurice, Comte de Saxe, in the French army of the 1740s. Saxe added irregular cavalry, hussars, and skirmishers to the French army, using his Grassins regiment to scout, forage, raid, and ambush. This same pattern of irregular auxiliaries had been used in the build-up to the Battle of Fontenoy.[85] Dieskau's order of march, dated August 24 at Fort St. Frédéric, reveals a firm grasp of the latest European conventions for dealing with irregular enemies in wooded terrain. The *troupes de terre* were always screened by Canadian and Indian scouts, and ideally the army moved in three columns, with the regulars in close order in the center and open columns of Canadians and Indians marching *à la Canadienne*, and the whole screened in front, flank, and rear by scouts managed by Legardeur de Saint-Pierre. Dieskau showed foresight in urging that there be no pillaging until the battle was over, though he revealed ignorance in ordering the Indians not to distract themselves with scalping during the battle because ten men could be killed in the time it took to scalp one.[86]

Upon arriving at Fort St. Frédéric, Dieskau found that Commandant Lusignan did not share the panic that reached Montreal from St. Jean less than a week earlier. Before the end of the month, scouts brought in reliable evidence that Johnson's whole force of about three thousand colonial troops had reached Fort Edward, that the fort was nearing completion, and that they had been cutting two roads northward, one toward Wood Creek and the other toward Lac St. Sacrement. Dieskau moved his force forward to Carillon, site of a future fort and a post from which to watch both approaches.[87]

Dieskau decided to attack Fort Edward, based on information received from a prisoner captured by Abenaki scouts near that fort and brought to the commander at Carillon on September 4. The prisoner admitted that some five hundred men were completing the fort, which had only one gun mounted and incomplete entrenchments. Vaudreuil, who grilled this prisoner once he had been brought to Montreal, was convinced that Dieskau had misunderstood, and presumed that the rest of Johnson's army had withdrawn to Albany.[88] Dieskau, who had taken along an interpreter for English, later claimed that the prisoner had accurately told him that the rest of Johnson's army had gone to Lac St. Sacrement to build a fort there. Certainly Dieskau's decision to split his force and proceed with a predominantly Candian and Indian raid joined only by the grenadier companies of his two regular regiments makes more sense if he knew that Johnson was north of Fort Edward. The fifteen hundred men left at Carillon, including five hundred regulars, were a strong base that would have plenty of warning if Johnson moved from the other end of Lac St. Sacrement. Dieskau's bold plan—to cut Johnson's supply lines and to destroy stores, ammunition, boats, and the unfinished Fort Edward—was a raid for which his irregulars seemed perfect, given the need for speed and the limits of available provisions.[89]

Using neither the Wood Creek nor the Lac St. Sacrement routes, Dieskau's *corps d'élite* paddled up Lake Champlain to South Bay, left their canoes under a supplementary guard brought for that purpose, and then struck out in three columns for Fort Edward. This overland route of nearly thirty wooded miles was covered in two days. On the night of September 7, the force had reached Johnson's new road a league north of Fort Edward. Scouts and prisoners confirmed that a nine-hundred-man garrison, which now included four hundred New Hampshire troops who had arrived on September 4 and promptly brawled with the New York militiamen garrisoned there,[90] was still in tents outside the unfinished fort.

When Dieskau outlined his plan of attack, the Caughnawaga contingent rejected it, confirming his view that they had been obstructing the operation throughout. They even demanded that three Mohawk captured by the Abenaki be released.[91] Attacking well-manned forts did not appeal to Indians, and this particular attack could launch a war that would disrupt Caughnawaga trade and endanger themselves and their Mohawk kin, who were equally reluctant to be drawn into Johnson's side of this struggle. These reasons were not, however, the argument used. The sachems argued that the fort was in the Hudson drainage basin and therefore on English territory. This clever use of the French watershed theory was wasted on Dieskau, but he was forced to find an alternative plan. Johnson's volunteer courier, Jacob Adams, had been killed by Indian marksmen before he came anywhere near Fort Edward that night, and his captured message indicated that Johnson was aware of a significant French force in the area. Dieskau's alternative was to attack Johnson's camp at Lac St. Sacrement. Whether the Caughnawaga agreed to attack Johnson because he was invading the Richelieu watershed will never be known, but Dieskau's party set out in the morning up Johnson's road to battle.[92]

III

As the forces under Dieskau and Johnson approached each other on the morning of September 8, 1755, another battle had already begun within each of these armies. The arrival of European regulars and military commanders had increased the variety of soldiers in the North American service of the kings of both Britain and France. Johnson had no regulars except the indispensable Captain Eyre, but had been given an assignment that called for all the equipment, logistics, and tactics of a European siege. His force consisted overwhelmingly of colonial regiments of volunteers, untrained and unwilling to accept the strict discipline that was fundamental to the massed musket fire of regular armies. Johnson also had disappointingly few Iroquois. This kind of campaign had limited appeal, even to Johnson's friends among the Mohawk. Guerrilla raiders defended nothing, but these warriors were supposed to defend an army, a road, and an artillery train; if successful, they were likely to face cannon fire at Fort St. Frédéric. News of Braddock's defeat emphasized the risks for cannon-hauling road builders in the wilderness, as well as the booty available to irregulars who could trap them.

General Dieskau's *corps d'élite* was a more disparate variety of warriors. The grenadiers of his regular regiments were European veterans whose notion of excellence in battle included standing firm under direct fire of muskets or cannons, and whose bayonets were the ultimate instruments of victory. These 220 men and their commander were entirely outnumbered by Canadian militia (600) and Indians (700). Canadian militiamen had seen more service in the militarized society of New France than their New England counterparts, primarily as irregular fighters on the frontiers.[93] The force appeared well chosen for a raid, but the Indians and Canadians had no interest in the seemingly suicidal tactics of the European regulars. The decisive refusal of Indian allies to attack Fort Edward had already destroyed Dieskau's strategy. What had been a spoiling raid for Dieskau became an attack on entrenched enemies, which was not the preferred objective of most of his force. Yet Dieskau began September 8 with evidence that these different methods of warfare could cooperate.

According to his cautious standing orders, Dieskau's force set off for Lac St. Sacrement in three columns. The regulars and their commander marched up Johnson's new road, while the Canadians and Indians flanked the regulars in the dense forest on either side. Progress was slowed to the pace of those on the flanks, so the force was on the road about four hours before two captured American deserters told Dieskau that about one thousand men were coming against him.[94] Dieskau decided to exploit the favorite military strategy of the Indians, an ambush catching the party in a narrow ravine through which the road passed just four miles from Lac St. Sacrement. The western side of the ravine was superb for the purpose, having a thirty-foot embankment topped with a terrace to provide excellent cover for the full mile and one-half of the ravine. On the east side of the road there was wooded cover for three-quarters of a mile on what became known as French Mountain. Having ordered the irregulars into these flanks, Dieskau and his regulars halted at the south entrance of the ravine. The regulars were to fire first, announcing that the enemy was entirely within the trap.[95]

When William Johnson went to bed the night before, he knew that Fort Edward was in some danger and that his courier, Jacob Adams, had been shot. At a council of war held the next morning, it was initially decided to send two parties, each consisting of about five hundred men. One was to go to South Bay, to destroy the enemy's boats, while the other set out to reinforce Fort Edward. Theyanoguin objected to this division, insisting that the whole expedition be sent south together.[96] Colonel Ephraim Williams was put in charge of a thousand militiamen from his own regiment, the second Connecticut regiment, and a rear guard of the Rhode Island regiment. Virtually all the Iroquois at Johnson's camp also joined what came to be called the "Bloody Morning Scout."

Williams' column proceeded confidently, suspecting no danger so early in their march to reinforce Fort Edward. Most of the Iroquois, including the elderly Theyanoguin, who was on horseback, were in single file in front of the English Americans. Williams' own regiment, leading these Americans, marched six abreast down the new road that had seen much traffic but few incidents. Apparently there were no scouts on the flanks at all, an Indian formation for the rapid and confident movement of large strike forces,[97] which was in sharp contrast to Dieskau's grueling insistence on three columns throughout his march.

Theyanoguin and his Mohawk were well within the two jaws of the ambush, and the van of the provincials was marching beneath the unseen Caughnawaga and Canadians on the ridge to their right when a shot was fired. Our only "eyewitnesses," General Dieskau and his second in command, Chevalier de Montreuil, were nearly a mile away. Dieskau, writing a week later, claimed that the Abenaki concealed on his right fired after treacherous Caughnawaga on his left revealed themselves without firing.[98] Other accounts claim that there was an exchange of conventional Iroquois taunts (or even speeches) before the first shot was fired by a Caughnawaga on the ridge or a Mohawk with Theyanoguin.[99] Although sprung prematurely, the trap caught the Mohawk and Williams' regiment.

The French regulars and their commanders were too far away to be involved in the initial exchanges, but ran to catch the fleeing enemy. About thirty Mohawk and four of the officers Johnson had appointed to recruit them died in the initial exchanges, but most of the warriors fought their way out of the trap and did much to cover the retreat. Old Theyanoguin dismounted, but could not escape quickly enough; when his body was found he seemed to have been bayoneted and amateurishly scalped.[100] Williams died leading a party up the embankment to try to dislodge the Caughnawaga. His regiment lost most of its fifty killed and twenty-two wounded in those first moments; many had died without even firing their muskets. It was reported that only one hundred of the militiamen fired at all.[101] With most of Williams' officers killed and little support from the rest of the column, the English colonial detachment was broken. Those carrying the wounded back to Johnson's camp soon found themselves in a general rout: "Our People run into Camp with all the Marks of Horror & Fear in their Countenances, exaggerating the Number of the Enemy."[102]

Those within Johnson's camp had heard the firing when the ambush began, and the continuous and heavy fire that came progressively closer. The camp had been defined by a breastwork of logs cut in clearing the area, but was lower than knee high in places. Johnson had boats hauled up from the lake's edge to reinforce the breastwork and added a number of provision wagons tipped on their sides to create more cover. Captain Eyre had four cannon, including a 32-pounder, positioned to cover the road down which the frightened survivors of Williams' detachment came running. Some of the retreating warriors and volunteers continued to return fire, with their last approximation of a volley occurring within three-quarters of a mile of the camp.[103] At this crucial point in Dieskau's attack, his Indian allies again refused to proceed. When they had been given a choice between attacking a fort or a camp, they had chosen to surprise the camp. Now they saw a barricaded force of two thousand alerted men with four working siege cannon. This was very much like attacking a fort around which there was little cover for attackers except stumps. Indians with loot, prisoners, and casualties would not want to continue in any case, and the Canadians "in general regulated themselves by the Conduct of the Indns. when upon War parties with them." Caughnawaga were upset by the number of their Mohawk relatives caught with the English, by their own losses, and by the death of their Canadian interpreter and prominent irregular, Legardeur de Saint-Pierre.[104] A number of Canadians were reluctant to proceed without the Indians. While Dieskau argued, his hope of running right into the camp with the refugees evaporated and Johnson added to his defenses.

Outnumbered forces were foolhardy, by European convention as well as Indian common sense, to attack protected defenders with functioning cannon. However, Dieskau was daring, and he assumed that the hastily gathered protection could be breached by the irregulars while the cream of two French regiments was sacrificed to draw the cannon fire and to silence that battery. Recognizable to the Americans by their gleaming bayonets, Dieskau's 220 regulars were drawn up in a close-order column 6-men wide and about 300-feet deep. Their task was to charge through some 150 yards of musket and cannon fire and take the cannon. Their steadiness while sustaining one-third casualties won the admiration of their enemy as well as their commander, but the task proved impossible.[105] Although the wagons and boats of the defenders were riddled with shot, the militiamen were effective from behind that protection. The cannon were also handled effectively under Captain Eyre, and one of his gunners boasted that the artillery "made Lanes, Streets and Alleys thro' their army."[106] After repeated attempts to silence the guns, Dieskau shifted the remnant of his regulars in an attempt to break through farther to the right. Here, too, the American colonial musketry held them and the Canadians and Indians for another two hours. Dieskau had as many as one-third of his irregulars serving as snipers throughout the four-hour attack. They killed twelve, including Colonel Titcomb, wounded about forty, including William Johnson, and kept up a musket fire that was nearly continuous. At no point did Dieskau's irregulars penetrate the periphery of the defense. By about four o'clock it was clear his plan had failed, and he had been severely wounded. As his army retreated, leaving him and twenty other wounded men to become prisoners, the defenders chased the French from the clearing but did not venture after them into the woods.[107]

The noise of battle had reached Fort Edward, even if the courier had not. A detachment of about 220 New Hampshire and New York militiamen, commanded by Captain William McGinnis, was sent to reinforce Johnson. After a twelve-mile march, they approached the ravine that had been the scene of that morning's first engagement. At about four o'clock, they surprised a larger group of Canadians and Indians who apparently had left the battle at Lake George early and were variously reported as returning for baggage, resting, or scalping and looting the bodies of those who had been killed that morning. The detachment from Fort Edward routed the group after ferocious fighting, confiscated baggage and loot, and proceeded to Lake George. It is not clear how many Canadians and Indians were killed; McGinnis and ten others were wounded, the captain mortally, five were missing, and two others were known dead.[108]

By European calculations, Johnson's English colonials had won the battlefield, the supply road, and their opponents' commanding officer. Yet the provincial army was in such a state of shock that Montreuil was able to reassemble his army that night. By the following night, his force, including perhaps as many as three hundred wounded, had arrived back at their boats at South Bay. Although Johnson had contemplated destroying those boats forty-eight hours earlier, there was no effort to harass the retreating French, who reached Carillon on September 11.[109]

The English Americans were immobilized; they had beaten off an attack but gained little confidence by doing so. A council of war held the day after the battle decided to appeal for more troops and to "employ all our time in securing ourselves here in the best manner possible."[110] Johnson claimed to be surprised and disappointed that the troops were not invigorated by their victory; instead, the "resolute & obstinate Attack made upon our Breast work in the Face of our Cannon seems to have given our Troops a dread of the Enemy."[111] Perhaps they shared the Indian view that one major engagement was enough. Johnson's army strengthened its camp in anticipation of another attack, and half the garrison was on guard duty. Johnson had been wounded in what was politely designated as his thigh, but his pain was enough to limit his initiative during and after the battle. The protection of Dieskau and twenty other prisoners from angry Mohawk who had lost numerous warriors, including Chief Theyanoguin, was another preoccupation (Figure 5).

FIGURE 5
Benjamin West, *General Johnson Saving a Wounded French Officer* (*Dieskau*)
from the Tomahawk of a North American Indian (ca. 1764–1768).
(Courtesy of Derby Art Gallery, Derby, England)

Burying the dead was a sad and tedious task in the wake of the battle. Those Americans killed in or near the camp were buried a day later. While Johnson's Iroquois allies ventured out to gather plunder, the colonial volunteers suppressed their interest in loot and ventured out only in large burying parties. Many of the dead could not be identified as comrade or foe, since they had been stripped and scalped. The next day, Lieutenant Colonel Seth Pomeroy's party buried 136 more who were known to be their own, including his brother. As if to console his sister-in-law, he wrote her about another soldier who was still dying but had been found two days after the battle with the entire back of his skull missing.[112] Mohawk anger was vented by digging up and scalping Indians who were found buried in the woods.[113] They also found bodies of Indian and white comrades who had been taken prisoner and killed while bound. Understandable outrage at these executions led to claims that the French were giving no quarter, and to Vaudreuil's boasts that the Caughnawaga hated their pro-English relatives so much that they refused to take them prisoner.[114] The prisoners had obviously been taken. They were probably killed during the final phase of the battle of Lake George, when their captors fought Captain McGinnis' unit and could neither guard prisoners nor allow them to help the enemy.[115] Those provincial troops who had lived through September 8 at Lake George lost much of their enthusiasm for action.

If casualties were the measure of victory, neither side did as well as it claimed. Johnson's initial account of his losses was uninformed and too few. The official returns, corrected, read 154 dead, 103 wounded, and 67 missing. Most of those listed as missing had not deserted into woods full of Canadians and Indians; most of the missing were later found dead. Pomeroy was preoccupied with the losses, but overlooked the Iroquois casualties, which brought the totals to 223 dead and about 108 wounded.[116] Governor Vaudreuil was also inclined to minimize the losses, even though he gave all the blame to Dieskau. Montreuil, however, may have included many with minor wounds who were ignored in subsequent counts, including his own. The official French journal of the operation probably minimized Indian casualties in a total count of 149 dead, 163 wounded, and 27 taken prisoner.[117] The reported number of those killed, wounded, and captured was remarkably close on both sides, with those fighting for the English losing 331 and the French, 339.

Johnson's Iroquois allies were soon anxious to go home. He tried to tempt or shame them to stay with the expedition, but bowed to their custom of going home to conduct condolence services for their dead.

They were later sent several of the French prisoners, to take the names and places of some of their dead warriors.[118] Johnson asked that General Shirley be told nothing about the transfer of these prisoners to the Mohawk.[119] Johnson was clearly caught between two sets of values. His courtesies and generosity to Dieskau were in keeping with the best European military conventions. Dieskau was protected, given medical care, lent money, and sent to Johnson's own house in Albany, where he was kindly cared for by Johnson's sister, who had just been widowed by the baron's offensive.[120] As the Mohawk set off with considerable plunder and some condolence gifts, they assured Johnson of their return and hoped that "you may not make up a sudden Peace with the French as was done last war, and leave us in the lurch and Disappointed of venting our resentments upon our enemies."[121] Their parting elicited mixed feelings in the army. It was clear that the Mohawk had "behaved better than the whites" in the Bloody Morning Scout.[122] Yet there was disgruntlement about the amount of the plunder that went, without scrutiny, to the Mohawk, and claims that they had taken things that belonged to American soldiers, including much needed blankets.[123] With the Indians gone, Johnson had to rely on his two companies of colonial rangers for all his scouting. Before the end of the month he heard that the Mohawk had held a council, managed by the influential women elders, which decided that the Mohawk should not rejoin Johnson, and the other Iroquois had sent similar notice. The Mohawk did little scouting for the English armies for years, and American ranger companies were to take their place. Johnson was not about to take offensive risks without the Mohawk.[124]

Johnson was prompt in announcing victory to General Shirley and the other colonial governors, but his letters soon came to haunt him.[125] Shirley was pleased with Johnson's exaggeration that nearly one thousand of the enemy had been killed, that Dieskau had been captured, and Legardeur de Saint-Pierre was dead. All this made Johnson's fretting about defensive preparation in case of a counterattack seem incomprehensible; how could the French recover so quickly from such a rout? Shirley urged Johnson to proceed with the task of taking Fort St. Frédéric. Both Johnson and Eyre had argued for a good fort at the site of the battle to ensure possession if no further progress could be made. Shirley retorted that the fort would not help much with another campaign and did not protect the country. Not only was the Wood Creek approach left open to the enemy, but Dieskau had proved that another approach, via South Bay, was also unprotected from a post at Lake George.[126]

Shirley's reaction had merit, but he did not know the mood of Johnson's army. Like the Iroquois, these men seemed to consider one fierce battle as enough for a soldier in a campaign. Shirley also overlooked the fact that the new road, if it was not protected, could become an avenue into New York for the French. Johnson went on the defensive, blaming his obstinate council of war and disregarding his commander-in-chief. The camp was strengthened so that it had "Some Battlement to Stand behind" and properly mounted cannon by September 16.[127]

Talk of proceeding against the French persisted through the autumn.[128] Fresh reinforcements arrived, but enough wagons could not be found even to keep the camp supplied. It took twenty thousand pounds of provision to maintain one thousand men at Lake George; in the six-day trip from Albany, these supplies were shifted into and out of about a dozen bateaux and some twenty-four wagons.[129] It became clear by early October that twice as many wagons as had ever been working the road were needed to allow the expedition to proceed down the lake.[130] Robert Rogers returned from scouting Fort St. Frédéric and Carillon with discouraging reports of the new Fort Carillon. Work began there before the end of September, and the square earthwork fort with four bastions and a redoubt progressed quickly compared with work at the south end of Lake George.[131] Despite an army of more than four thousand effectives for most of the next two months, and New York politicians insisting that even a failed offensive was better than none,[132] Johnson undertook no initiatives beyond the building of Fort William Henry.

Building a fort proved to be divisive, even though its need was accepted. On the eve of the Battle of Lake George, Johnson's council of war had reversed an earlier decision to build, under Captain Eyre's direction, a fort "capable of commodiously Garrisoning 100 Men." While Johnson and Eyre wanted a fort capable of withstanding "some Artillery," the council had accurately reflected the New Englanders who made up most of the army by insisting that only a picketed fort be built.[133] Johnson still tried to overcome the councillors' "Obstinacy & Ignorance," but found them convinced that their men were unwilling to do the digging for a regular fort. Johnson persisted with his own views, gathered support from the new governor of New York, Sir Charles Hardy, and finally convinced the council of war held on September 29. There he mentioned visiting the unfinished stockade and finding only a dozen men working, although five hundred had been ordered to do so. They finally agreed to build a fort that could hold a garrison of five hundred, and that seven hundred men under Captain Eyre, be detailed to build the fort and be exempt from all other duties.[134] A week later Johnson was still fighting to speed construction, complaining that "averseness to labour & the want of due subordination" were "capital sins of this army. I have made war against them by every method . . . but to me at least, they are invincible."[135]

General Dieskau would have agreed. His ambush of September 8 showed some of the potential of cooperation between regulars, colonials, and Indians, as had the defeat of Braddock that summer. However, the Battle of Lake George had also shown the difficulties of imposing European methods and objectives on Indians and colonial soldiers in both armies. Johnson's colonials were impressed with Dieskau's regulars, but were in no more hurry than the Mohawk to imitate the regulars in assaulting entrenchments at Fort Carillon. Dieskau had stopped Johnson; the Indian perception that one major battle was enough helped stop both armies. The campaign, in which both sides failed, concluded amid recriminations that were not silenced by the noise of axes and shovels. At opposite ends of Lac St. Sacrement, which Johnson had so prematurely renamed Lake George, both armies were digging European fortifications, entrenching European military methods and values.

3

FORT
WILLIAM HENRY
1755–1757

The battle for Lake George had only begun with that bloody September day that left both sides chastened. The woods at both ends of the lake reverberated with the sounds of axes that month; both contenders went on the defensive and built fortifications. The wilderness that had insulated both sides from enemy cannon did so no more. Lake George had become a military waterway that left opposing cannons only a few days apart.

Although armchair engineers have mocked the particular location of Fort William Henry, Captain William Eyre had made an intelligent choice. Amid fears of another French attack, there was no question of disrupting the well-placed camp to use that site, though it was superior as a location for a fort intended to protect boats[1] and defend the new road that led so easily to the Hudson River. To achieve the same objectives, as well as provide a supply base for an advancing army or a defensive point for one in retreat. Eyre chose a sandy, twenty-foot-high hillock to the west, near the lake's edge.[2] French artillery could not be landed at the head of the lake without being under fire from the fort, and the swamp to the east and the west prevented the placing of enemy cannon close enough to be able to blow a breach in the wall. Eyre was also confident that the fort's artillery could prevent an enemy from establishing a battery on the higher ground to the southwest.[3]

A fort was, to a degree, the signature of the army that built it, and the previously noted dispute over the type and size of fort led to two successive buildings on the same site. Johnson and Eyre initially wanted a fort "capable of commodiously Garrisoning 100 Men" and able to withstand "some Artillery," but Johnson's council of war insisted that only a picketed log fort be built.[4] New Englanders felt they had been worked hard in building Fort Edward, and Eyre's professional thoroughness had many colonial critics. A picketed fort was easier to build and easier to burn by a retreating garrison. Eyre and Johnson knew that a picketed fort could be considered only if attack by siege cannon were impossible because defensive cannon could not be mounted on the walls of such a fort. Although any fort was a commitment to fund a garrison, Johnson's council of New Englanders wanted this commitment to be small. They were also not anxious to build or man a fort that so obviously and disproportionately supported New York.

The initial building of Fort William Henry was an obvious display of the limits imposed on a commander, as well as the sufferings tolerated by the soldiers in the "irregular" army Johnson led. The work on the picketed fort in September showed some of the difficulties. Although the New England officers had argued for this expedient, rather than a more substantial fort, neither they nor their men were enthusiastic about the work. Officers who were elected by their men tended to reflect their wishes, and the men were not impressed with this project. Those who worked on this fort were not exempt from guard duty and were not paid extra for heavy labor that was not shared by the whole army. Those who admitted to any carpentry skills were not numerous, and they were divided between work on the fort and building flat-bottomed boats for the intended advance down the lake. Despite orders that five hundred men were to work on the fort each day, Johnson found only a dozen doing so by the end of the month and the fort was far from finished.

Johnson finally won a striking political victory in gaining approval for an earthen fort "in the manner the French build"[5] to garrison five hundred men. The more ambitious building project represented another admission that the Indian warfare he had learned was not central to the war being fought. This fort would allow Johnson's artillery to be used effectively from wall embrasures. While no professional expected a fort to withstand artillery attack indefinitely,[6] this method of construction provided considerable protection from cannon for long enough to allow reinforcement. Americans knew that forts could not prevent frontier raids, but a secure supply base could hasten the taking of Fort St. Frédéric to obstruct those attacks. British regulars knew that solid forts stopped regular armies, at least for the duration of a siege. The fort had to fit the task and the garrison that was to be provided; an overbuilt and undermanned fort was much worse than none at all.

Johnson may have convinced his council of war to approve the more substantial fort as an alternative to aggressive initiatives, but he could not silence the vocal opposition of some officers led by Major General Lyman. The fort was being constructed against the sound strategic judgment of Johnson's commanding officer, William Shirley, and against the earlier objections of provincial officers who had insisted that their men did not want to dig a fort. Others may have shared the thoughts of Private James Hill of Ephraim Williams's regiment on September 30 when "we went to Work on a nother foart and Left of[f] Bilding the Bots in order to Bould a foart what Wod be Cannan Proof, and to tair the tother down for it Was not fit for Nothing bout for Small arms."[7] The only improvement for the men this time was that those seven hundred men assigned to work on the new fort were not to have any other duties.[8]

Fort William Henry, like all earthwork forts, was constructed primarily with shovels. The thirty-foot-thick walls were built in the process of digging a thirty-foot-wide ditch outside. The wall was a gigantic sandbox built of pine logs outside and inside, as well as bracing the structure. After raising the walls about ten feet at full thickness, the builders narrowed them to between twelve and eighteen feet thick, depending on the exposure. The fort's ten guns were mounted on top of the widest part of the wall, to fire through embrasures cut in the parapets. The four similarly constructed bastions that protruded from the corners of the distorted square of the fort also mounted cannon that could blast grapeshot at anyone attempting to climb the connecting walls, called curtains. At the top of the parapets, infantrymen could fire from behind earth and log protection at least twelve feet thick and more than twenty feet above the palisaded center of the V-shaped dry ditch.[9] (Figure 6). Only on the north side, where the steep slope descended to Lake George, was the ditch unnecessary.

With one-quarter of the army assigned to construct the fort, that crew numbered between five and seven hundred early in October, rising to a thousand after all the reinforcements had arrived by mid-month.[10] A shortage of tents and blankets brought hardship and sickness for some of these men. Illness seemed to spread quickly,

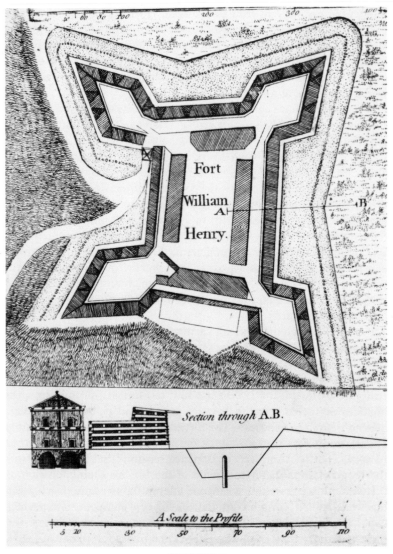

FIGURE 6
Fort William Henry, 1757. From Ann Rocque's
A Set of Plans and Forts in America (London, 1765).
(Photo courtesy of Metropolitan Toronto Library Board, Toronto, Canada)

though some thought it was encouraged by evacuation of those who were thought unlikely to recover quickly, generous and varied food allowances for the sick, and freedom from digging. On October 20, a Massachusetts captain divided the army into five roughly equal components: those on guard duty, those unfit, those busy cooking the rather plentiful stores, those working on the fort "or mountain of sand they are making . . . and the Rest cheating and hulking about some friend sick. Some have overeat themselves and a Great number Confounded Lazy which Dogg about hear and there."[11]

In addition to persistent shortages of axes, shovels, and carpenters,[12] poor morale and discipline proved major hindrances to the completion of the fort. Corresponding with colonial governors, who continued to press him for an offensive, General Johnson railed against his weak officers, whose conduct of courts martial was pathetic, against "the Democratical (if you will alow me the term) Fabrick of this Army," and against the real epidemic of homesickness, which he thought incurable.[13] Deserters received little or no punishment when caught: the most severely treated received fewer than half as many lashes as the soldier drummed out of Fort Edward in August for immorality.[14]

Discipline problems were aggravated by supply problems at the end of October. The additional soldiers who arrived after the Battle of Lake George had not strained the capacity of the food convoys that supplied the fort. However, a three-inch snowfall late in October was followed by rains that raised the Hudson, making the ford at Saratoga unusable and putting supplies even farther from demands.[15] Although the army was put on short rations of bread, reserves were down to two days' requirements. More ominously, the rum was nearly exhausted by early November, and rum had been one of the few effective inducements for obedience.[16]

In addition, just as the beginning of November brought the end of service terms for some Connecticut troops, Johnson received orders from the Massachusetts lieutenant governor not to let any man from that province go without express orders. The first discharges brought increasing discontent for the rest, since they were required to continue work on the fort while they received short rations.[17] On November 9, the more than five hundred remaining Connecticut troops refused duty and threatened to leave. They were retained by promising them a discharge after twelve more good days of work on the fort. Two days later, some twenty New Yorkers deserted and were brought back without being punished.[18] The disintegration of the army was most apparent when a dispute about payment for a jug of beer erupted into a full-scale riot between New York and Massachusetts regiments. Clubs and naked cutlasses were in use before order was restored.[19]

Despite these staggering problems, the flagpole on what was now named Fort William Henry went up November 13, forty-four days after construction began. The fort was usable, though somewhat less frantic work continued on the barracks and storehouses. That same night, Mohawk scouts reported that a French army was within ten miles, and the whole garrison was mustered at 4:00 A.M. to bring in the stores and the ten guns and to build mounting platforms for the latter.[20] This proved to be just another in a series of false alarms made more credible by the knowledge that Fort Carillon had been completed and a French advance camp had been constructed at the foot of Lake George. American rangers had great difficulty getting through the French screen of Indian scouts to gain more detailed knowledge of troop numbers or movements.[21] Four days later, an earthquake "terribly shook that howling wilderness" from Montreal to Albany and Boston, bringing down chimneys in the newly built barracks at Fort William Henry, apparently without being regarded as an ill omen.[22]

The question of who would garrison Fort William Henry had been an issue since before construction had commenced. There had been some talk of British regulars joining the campaign before it ended, or perhaps garrisoning the fort in the winter, but anticipated differences about the ranking and disciplining of regular versus colonial troops made few anxious to see a mixing of the two types of soldiers.[23] Johnson voiced doubts about any of the current force being kept on as garrison. Since colonial enlistments were about to expire, few would volunteer to stay on, and the current officers did not seem appropriate.[24] Although a council of war held on November 18 established that the garrison should be five hundred, and four hundred for Fort Edward, another meeting held a week later and attended by commissioners from the colonies of Massachusetts, Connecticut, and New York cut the numbers to 430 and 320.[25] After the rest of the army withdrew on November 27, Colonel Jonathan Bagley of Massachusetts reported that he had only 206 of the 402 men who had been assigned to garrison Fort William Henry under his command. The two long, two-story barracks, as yet without windows or floors, could more than accommodate that garrison[26] (Figure 7).

Before leaving the fort he had designed, Captain William Eyre prepared revealing instructions for its commandant in case of attack

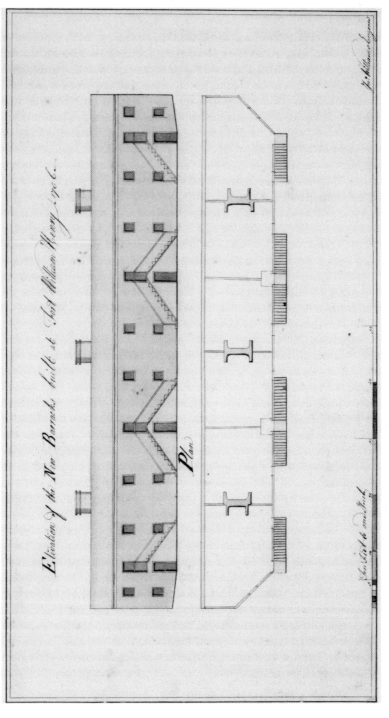

FIGURE 7   Barracks at Fort William Henry, 1756. (© J. R. Maguire)

by artillery. The enemy was to be kept off the height to the southwest with cannon fire. If the lake were frozen, cannon down on the ice could not hurt the fort, and it would be easy to prevent any attempt to drag them up the embankment. An enemy would also be very exposed in seeking access to the height of land on which Johnson's men had fought to defend their camp. From none of these positions, Eyre argued, could enemy artillery breach the walls of the fort, whatever damage a lucky shot might do to guns or men. Matériel to repair gun carriages, ramparts, and parapets were to be stored in the fort, ready for use. With something approaching premonition, Eyre went on to picture an entrenched enemy cannonading a fort and destroying its barracks, while the off-duty garrison was still able to take cover in the casement rooms built into the east wall. The defenders would be ready to battle fires, and the powder would be divided between two magazines that were secure underground at the northeast and northwest bastions. Envisioning a classical European siege, Eyre urged resolution until the enemy cannon were close to the ditch and had blown a hole entirely through the thirty-foot wall. Then, and only then, could a commander think of a surrender that was honorable.

Suspecting that a colonial officer might not know the honors of war which eighteenth-century European regulars awarded to brave enemies, Eyre specified them: "The honours of War are colours flying, Drums a beating, with one or two Pieces of Cannon & Match lighted & so many Rounds, and Days provisions; and the whole to march thro the Breach; But this is never alow'd to any, but those who make an obstinate defence."[27] Here were the European values that, like the fortification, were being imposed on the wilds of the Albany–Montreal frontier. Commandant Jonathan Bagley, who had seen American rangers bring in French scalps and had heard of comrades found scalped around his fort, may have learned something about the honors of war without being confident that these would be observed.

Eyre envisaged scaling ladders as the only possible method for an enemy to attack without cannon, and vigilance was crucial. The flanking guns should be filled with grapeshot, and sharpened brushwood and dirt-filled barrels (gabions) should be ready to strengthen the parapets. As many as one-half of the garrison should be on duty at once during such an attack, maintaining mortar and small-arms fire day and night, but cannon should be fired at night only if an escalade were being attempted. The steep bank down to the lake, so useful against artillery, was not an effective barrier against men with scaling ladders. Eyre suggested that a party with a light cannon might be posted outside the fort, provided that the men could retreat quickly enough.[28] Eyre's instructions for withstanding an attack without artillery sketched what was actually to happen sixteen months later, when he himself was in command of the defense; his instructions concerning an artillery attack foretold something of the more traumatic events of August 1757. These instructions were also a primer on the weaknesses of Fort William Henry, which were debated repeatedly. Two separate inspections of the fort less than a year after completion emphasized that the walls were lower than those threatening positions to the southwest and to the east which Eyre had discussed. One report urged that three feet be added to the height of the west curtain, as well as outworks to give more strength and flanking fire to that vulnerable wall.[29] The other report called for much more extensive improvement, including redoubts to east and west as well as higher and thicker parapets.[30] Lord Loudoun himself went even further, noting that the "running sand" the fort was built on meant that the defensive ditch was always filling in and

> the works are all faced up with Logs bound in, but they have neither been carefull to Pick good Timber for that purpose, nor secured them well at the Ends; and the Sand is so loose, that I am afraid if it were battered with Cannon it would run thro' between the Logs.[31]

This fear, later reinforced by Canadian claims that it could easily be mined,[32] may have caused others to join Loudoun in presuming the fort would fall quickly under cannon fire. More generally, as Montcalm wrote of the newly completed Fort Carillon, this method of construction was cannon proof and as good as masonry, but not durable.[33] Loudoun claimed that this type of fort rotted in five or six years.[34]

By December 1755, the garrisons at Fort Carillon (two hundred French regulars, one hundred Canadians, and forty Abenaki and Caughnawaga) and Fort William Henry (four hundred Americans) settled in for the winter,[35] despite some persisting rumors of an English winter offensive on the lake. The war at this edge of empires had been transformed; the vague boundary between the powers had now been defined as the disputed lake itself, and the forts ensured that no conventional army was going to make speedy progress along this route. The two opposing forts, each backed by another, created a comparatively stable fulcrum that the French exploited in the war of maneuver over the next year. The major French attack of 1756 was on Fort Oswego, with preliminary raids to isolate the post before the end of the winter. On the Lake George frontier, scouting parties raided for prisoners and information during the winter, as they had during the fall, but there were no major attacks.

Fort William Henry was built as the base from which to launch the 1756 English attack on Fort Carillon and Fort St. Frédéric. At the major planning meeting held in New York City in the previous December, English governors and military officers had agreed on the general shape of the coming campaign. A major feint up the Chaudière River toward Quebec City was approved, as were expeditions repeating the three efforts that had failed in 1755—against Fort Duquesne, the French on Lake Ontario, and Fort St. Frédéric. Of these four operations, clear priority was given to the last two proposals. Some ten thousand men were allocated for the push north from Fort William Henry to attack Fort Carillon and Fort St. Frédéric, to build a fort on Lake Champlain, and to construct at least one vessel of force for that lake.[36]

The same meeting had called for more troops from England, but Shirley's plans for 1756 were laid in order to keep the provincial regiments and the regulars separate from each other. The regulars, increased from two to five regiments but still overwhelmingly newly recruited in America, were to be concentrated on the Oswego frontier. The Fort St. Frédéric expedition was, once again, the assignment of the provincial regiments. Massachusetts political leaders could not tolerate William Johnson as leader again, and that assignment went to General John Winslow, a Massachusetts soldier whose recent victory in Nova Scotia continued a long and successful career that has included cooperation with British regulars in the West Indies.[37]

The new fortification of Carillon, as Winslow knew, made any English advance against Fort St. Frédéric harder in 1756. Although similar in size and shape to Fort William Henry, Fort Carillon was built with oak rather than pine, had two substantial outworks on the landward sides and stone barracks for a three-hundred-man garrison,[38] and mounted more and heavier cannon, including eight 12-pounders. It did suffer from its rocky site, however. There was no ditch and, since earth had to be hauled from a distance, the walls were lower and thinner, and one of them was made entirely of wood, as were all the parapets.[39] Those assigned to defend this Lake Champlain frontier were primarily French regulars and Canadian soldiers, numbering eleven hundred, plus an unknown number of Indian warriors. There were some six hundred in garrison at Fort Carillon and at least four hundred in the advance guard at the foot of Lake George.

As was well known to commanders on both sides, an English spring offensive against Fort St. Frédéric would have had major advantages. While Canadians farther north were still mired in mud and unable to move reinforcements or supplies south with any speed, travel would already have improved along New York supply lines. Yet Winslow faced most of the difficulties that Johnson had faced in launching his offensive the previous year. By the end of April, not one of the promised soldiers from the northern colonies had arrived at Albany. For lack of an escort, supplies could not be forwarded to Fort William Henry.[40] By then, an English attack on Fort Carillon could be countered, for the roads between Montreal and Fort St. Jean were usable again.[41] Many English transport problems of the previous year, which resulted in food costing 50 percent more at Fort William Henry than at Albany, were solved by gradually instituting an army-run transport system.[42] Although William Johnson was now concentrating more attention on Iroquois diplomacy, the Mohawk were not coming back in large numbers and scouting was primarily in the hands of colonial rangers drawn from the provincial levies and trained under Robert Rogers.

There were several other recurring difficulties. When the provincial soldiers garrisoning Fort William Henry came to the end of their contracts at the beginning of May, they threatened to go home. Eighty regulars were sent to reinforce them, but a new British law, which put all irregulars serving with regulars under regular army discipline, led Eyre to fear "it more than Probable they will quit it [Fort William Henry] immediately upon the Regulars marching in, As the[y] seem not to be fond of red Coats."[43] Although this difficulty was minor at first, it surfaced repeatedly during the summer, surpassed only by the related issue of the status of colonial officers serving with regulars.

The English offensive of 1756 stalled for numerous reasons, but one that was adequate in itself was the change in command. William Shirley's political opponents, including William Johnson and Thomas Pownall, helped British political and military leaders remove Shirley from his command of the armies in America and from his governorship of Massachusetts the following year. Loss of Shirley as commander was significant, even if his military talents were limited. Through patronage and concern for provincial sensitivies, he had led an aggressive Massachusetts military culture. He could mask and minimize the differences between regular and irregular armies because he had been both governor and commander-in-chief. His successor was appointed by mid-March 1756, and Shirley was informed within a month.[44]

Even a smooth transition of command was disruptive, and the change of command in the spring proved crippling for the campaign. The losing British war effort in America had claimed the military reputations of Braddock and Shirley, and it was to do the same for all three of those sent to run the campaign of 1756. General Daniel Webb arrived in New York on June 7 to serve as interim commander. In keeping with his subsequent reputation for timidity, Webb did not go to Albany to take command, but waited for his superior, Major General James Abercromby, who landed nine days later. Abercromby became temporary commander by June 25 and held the post until Lord Loudoun arrived almost a month later. A two-month hiatus between news of a new commander and his arrival was not tardy, though it came at exactly the wrong time for the 1756 campaign.

All three of the new army leaders were seasoned professionals, men whose views of how John Winslow's seven thousand irregulars should conduct themselves were to clash with the realities. Abercromby was the first of them to ask Winslow whether his army would serve if joined with the regulars. Winslow, supported by his council of war and the orders of the New England assemblies, replied that the army would be "dissolved" by such an occurrence. This position led to explosive letters from both Shirley and Loudoun. The central issue was not that the privates had been recruited to serve under their own officers (which, though true, was not the decisive issue), but that the general officers of the provincials refused to accept being ranked as eldest captains when serving with regulars. This ranking would have meant that eleven experienced regulars outranked any colonial officers.[45]

General Lyman once again led the promising advance northward, leaving Half Moon on July 14. Winslow, whom Abercromby had called back to Albany to discuss cooperation between regulars and provincials, rejoined his seven-thousand-man army at Saratoga and they reached Fort Edward on July 20.[46] They were a month earlier than the previous year, were more than twice as large an army, and were better equipped with artillery. This force was at Fort William Henry before the end of the month. A few days later, Winslow and his staff were called back to Albany once again, this time to face Loudoun on the same issue of officers' rank. It was August 19 before they were back at Fort William Henry, beginning the shipping of stores to a rendezvous down the lake. The next day they learned that Fort Oswego had fallen, and Loudoun ordered Winslow's army not to risk an offensive.[47]

As in the previous summer, bad news from the west had stopped the English offensive down Lake George. One satirist commented on Winslow's effort: "let it not be said, that our Forces, during this Summer, eat the Bread of Idleness: Tho' they durst not fight, they could dig with Safety; and the Season was spent in making Entrenchments at Lake George, and fortifying Fort William Henry."[48] Surgeon Thomas Williams, who was spending his second summer with Massachusetts soldiers at Lake George, was more cutting: "It appears to me that the settling ranks among ourselves may (if gone into according to some gentlemen's minds) be campaign enough for one year."[49] The best that could be said of the campaign was that Winslow's force had strengthened both Fort William Henry and an adjoining encampment to the southwest, and their artillery train had remained. Fort William Henry now had twenty iron cannon, including two 32-pounders and eight 18-pounders, in addition to four small brass cannon and eight mortar and howitzers.[50]

Loudoun gained control of the British campaign just when it had lost all room to maneuver. Shirley's plan had called for an advance against Fort Carillon early enough to divide Vaudreuil's army and take the pressure off Fort Oswego.[51] Montcalm's attack on Oswego was, itself, intended to draw British soldiers from the concentration building to the north of Albany. His success had been too swift and complete to affect British dispositions, but Vaudreuil and Montcalm could relish their victory and its consequences for Iroquois country and the west. They could reinforce the Lake Champlain frontier, confident that this was Loudoun's only possible line of advance.[52]

By late summer, an ominous build-up of forces had occurred at each end of Lake George. Montcalm had more than five thousand men and could call on two thousand more from Montreal. Loudoun's twelve thousand men consisted of Winslow's force and five regiments of regulars, with the possibility of support from as many as twenty thousand militia. He also could use waterways navigable for several weeks after freeze-up farther north.[53]

Winslow's force was, however, dissolving rapidly. Long before smallpox hit the New York frontier in October, the notoriously unsanitary provincial camps there and at Fort Edward were recording numerous deaths.[54] Although Massachusetts commissaries were efficient, those of the other colonies were not able to keep their men supplied with decent food. The campaign was destined to end more ignominiously than the previous year's failure. Fear of a French attack persisted throughout September and, near its end, Winslow mistook one of his own returning scouting parties for a French attack and called for help from Loudoun at Albany. Loudoun petitioned the New England governments for immediate reinforcements; although some twenty-three hundred men were raised, none arrived in the month before the "emergency" was declared ended.[55] For a second consecutive autumn, the governments of New England had been told of a crisis at Fort William Henry, and their response had been a waste of effort. This fort, built despite New England objections, was gaining a reputation for expensive false alarms.

The garrison for the winter of 1756/57 reflected changes in the English conduct of the war. The colonials had wanted the regulars to garrison these forts since the previous winter, so Britain would bear the expense. William Eyre was back to defend his creation with one hundred rangers, now in British army pay, and nearly four hundred British regulars from his own Forty-fourth Regiment. Garrisoning Fort Edward were four companies of rangers and five hundred regulars of the Forty-eighth Regiment. The rest of these regular units and three other regiments of regulars wintered at Albany, while the Forty-second Highlanders were nearby at Schenectady.[56]

The coming of the regulars to Fort William Henry indicated other changes. The type of warfare exemplified by the campaigns of Johnson and Winslow had failed, and Iroquois support had evaporated. In taking over the fort, the British regulars and American rangers were not simply fulfilling the prejudices of the high command. The regulars had found ways to cope with the war here, and retained their position when the next campaign sent provincial troops to serve under them. This transition was also built on a new way of dealing with that other persistent war, *la petite guerre*, of scouting and raiding parties.

II

Throughout the twelve years after 1745, the Abenaki and their Indian and Canadian allies had maintained their dominance in the spasmodic guerrilla warfare of these woodlands. From the destruction of Saratoga in 1745, the private revenge raids witnessed by Pehr Kalm in 1749 and suffered by Susannah Johnson in 1754, to the scouting and scalping parties that harried William Johnson's army as it advanced to Lac St. Sacrement, the overwhelming Canadian advantage in Indian support had grown stronger. Victories over Braddock in 1755 and Shirley in 1756 only increased the number of warriors from tribes as far away as the Mississippi Valley who came to fight the English on the New York frontier. Inviting and joining them were Canadian soldiers and traders with decades of experience in woodland warfare and Indian diplomacy. These, and the French priests who had influence in the villages of the Canadian mission Indians, found recruitment of Indians easy in these years of Vaudreuil's success.

Late in 1755, Canadian scouting and raiding parties had little difficulty gathering information, scalps, and prisoners from the environs of the newly built Fort Edward and Fort William Henry. Those garrisons could be unnerved by as trivial an incident as finding letters from English prisoners in Canada, which unseen messengers had attached to bushes within sight of the fort.[57] However, in mid-winter, when garrisons and scouts on both sides were reduced and travel was minimal, the commandant of Fort Carillon had been known to offer 1,000 livres for a prisoner.[58] Nonetheless, he had better information about his enemies and a better defensive screen of scouts than did his counterpart at Fort William Henry.

Scouting had become a serious problem for the English after casualties in the Battle of Lake George had prompted the Mohawk to withdraw most of their support, though losing that battle had not prejudiced French recruiting among the Caughnawaga or the Abenaki. A few Mohawk still visited Johnson while he was at Fort William Henry in the fall of 1755, but he had difficulty getting them to scout, which remained true the following year.[59] Johnson advised Jonathan Bagley, his successor at Fort William Henry, on dealing with those warriors who would rather drink than scout. "Whenever any of them get drunk the only way is to disarm them & tye them—& not to beat them."[60] Iroquois who visited the fort late in 1756 complained that they had been treated like dogs.[61] The few Mohawk raids of 1756 and 1757 were independent of English efforts to scout, spy on, and harry the French.[62]

William Johnson was forced to start recruiting non-Indian scouts from the provincial troops under his command in September 1755, with very mixed results. Some colonial irregulars were as horrified as the redcoats at the taking of scalps.[63] Most were unfamiliar with Indian culture and guerrilla warfare, and these things could not be learned nearly as quickly as one could turn a farm boy into a passable regular soldier. Given the timidity of Johnson's army after the battle they supposedly won, troubles with newly recruited scouts were predictable. A fifty-man party abandoned a five-day scouting expedition on the third day because they "heard or thought they heard some Party of the Enemy." A sizable later expedition aborted after one of its sentries was found dead, scalped, and left with a hatchet in his head. The lieutenant sent to rally the group failed; the men preferred to be listed on his roll call of named cowards rather than proceed. Another party heard a musket shot and voted to return to Fort William Henry immediately.[64]

Nevertheless, among the brawling New Hampshire frontiersmen, Johnson found men with the necessary experience and disposition. Robert Rogers led a dozen small parties to scout Fort Carillon and Fort St. Frédéric in the winter of 1755/56. Until the French and Indian forces were reduced to their winter garrisons, Rogers had difficulty getting close enough to Fort Carillon to provide solid information. Johnson was left to choose among these incomplete reports, those of a French deserter, and a Mohawk patrol (which had disrupted Fort William Henry with reports of a French attack early in November).[65] Later in the winter, Rogers' somewhat larger patrols on snowshoes or skates ranged north of Fort Carillon to take prisoners, burn buildings, kill cattle, and disrupt communications.[66]

These successes during the winter had led to new responsibilities for the American rangers as the 1756 campaign developed. Rogers was to raise an independent company of rangers, a unit given special pay and put under regular army discipline. Shirley had assigned them "to distress the French and their allies, by sacking, burning, and destroying their houses, barns, barracks, canoes, bateaux, &c." and to attack convoys.[67] Although these offensive raids were made out of Fort William Henry, their primary assignment was not to provide scouting protection, prisoners, or information for its commander. These larger parties still traveled mainly at night, ate and slept without fires, and displayed the ingenuity that built their leader's reputation. Ambushes along the Lake Champlain routes killed several people, and prisoners were taken. For all their well-recorded daring and perseverance, which gave heart to Winslow's soldiers, Rogers' rangers were a minor irritant on what was a comparatively quiet French frontier until Oswego was taken in August 1756.[68]

With the capture of Oswego, Vaudreuil and Montcalm had hurried to reinforce the Lake Champlain frontier, expecting Lord Loudoun to launch an attack while French strength was concentrated in the west. The balance of terror now swung sharply against the English rangers despite the recruiting of Stockbridge Indian scouts and the expansion to four ranger companies. Rogers led a party that was discovered on the west shore of Lake Champlain early in August, and their expedition failed.[69] Joseph Marin *fils*, fresh from leading warriors in the siege of Oswego, joined one hundred Canadians and Indians on another raid that killed or captured all but six of a fifty-man scouting party near Fort William Henry that month.[70] By the fall there were some 760 raiders based at the French end of Lake George, including Abenaki, Huron, Caughnawaga, Mississauga, Nipissing, Ojibwa, and Potawatomi warriors.[71] Lord Loudoun again felt forced to the defensive in the scouting war, and the American ranger companies were confined to protecting the neighborhood of Fort William Henry and Fort Edward.[72]

Most of the French-allied Indians had arrived at Fort Carillon by the end of September 1756 and were active in scouting, raiding, and taking prisoners during the next month.[73] Louis Antoine de Bougainville, who was there with Montcalm, argued that Vaudreuil should never have sent so many Indians at once, for they quarreled endlessly, yet wanted to stay together in large raiding parties. While the Indians bickered for days about a course of action, Bougainville was amazed by the quantities eaten and drunk. Bougainville's prejudices were apparent; the French could not control these allies, especially when they were numerous, and could not stop them from going home when they had taken a scalp or a prisoner. Bougainville was upset when there were many Indians and also when there were none; he wanted "a specified number of these mosquitoes" with the army in rotation.[74] This French gentleman was also horrified at Indian cruelty to prisoners.[75] Most of these tensions were portents of the campaign of 1757 and so was a brief scout by Bougainville, the engineer Jean-Nicholas Desandrouins, and artillery officer François Le Mercier. From the top of what was to become Mount Defiance, they looked south up Lake George and concluded that the English could not obstruct French passage up the lake to Fort William Henry, even by fortifying some of the islands.[76]

III

As Major Eyre's garrison settled in at Fort William Henry for the winter of 1756/57, the guerrilla war continued at a reduced pace. French intentions to attack Fort William Henry in 1757 had already been clear the previous October. Enos Bishop, a neighbor and fellow captive of Susannah Johnson, escaped from Quebec in September and was the only one of three companions to accomplish the overland journey without guns, hatchets, or enough food. He reported hearing that Montcalm had orders to take both English forts.[77] A French regular captured by Rogers' rangers at the end of October allowed that "if Mo[ns] Montcalm does not change his mind, they will come and attack Fort William Henry in the Spring."[78]

Although Loudoun kept his rangers close to the forts, one significant exception was made. Needing information on French activities at Fort Carillon and Fort St. Frédéric, Loudoun ordered Rogers forward. Seventy-four men, not including eleven who became disabled and were sent back, made this the largest party Rogers had ever led. Size and equipment of the force indicated that the purpose was to take more than one prisoner. When the snowshoe-clad rangers emerged from the bush on the west side of Lake Champlain on January 21, they saw a sleigh heading north from Carillon to Fort St. Frédéric. This perfect target drew the rangers, but suddenly nine other sleighs appeared. Seven prisoners were taken from three of the sleighs, but the others escaped to alert Lusignan, commandant at Carillon.

Rogers soon discovered the danger of his position, for his prisoners admitted that nearly 250 Canadians and Indians had just arrived to help the 300 French regulars garrisoning Carillon. After a brief halt to dry their guns, the rangers and their seven prisoners set out in single file through the woods west of Lake Champlain. Each prisoner was guarded, Indian fashion, by the soldier who had taken him, and Rogers' orders were to kill the prisoners in the event of an attack.

The attack exploded at the front of the column as they cleared a rise, and Rogers' men killed their prisoners and returned the fire. The rangers were driven back by eighty-nine French regulars under Captain M. de Basserode of the Languedoc regiment and an equal number of Canadians and Ottawa, including Charles-Michel Mouet de Langlade, the Canadian-Ottawa prominent in the destruction of Pickawillany and Braddock's army.[79] The rangers had the advantage of snowshoes and retreated to high ground, which they defended until nightfall. Rogers then dispersed his force, abandoning the severely wounded whom he reported as among fourteen killed in action.[80] General Abercromby commended the rangers and recommended that they be paid the bounty for the prisoners they had taken and then been forced to kill.[81] The border between conventional war and Indian raiding was blurred again.

One of those abandoned without a word after that terrible five-hour fight, which began with him killing his own helpless prisoner, was Thomas Brown, a ranger from Captain Thomas Speakman's company at Fort William Henry. Brown had been wounded three times, but crawled away from a fire that night before two other severely wounded comrades were attacked. Brown saw one of them scalped alive and the other, Robert Baker of the Forty-fourth Regiment who had volunteered for this assignment, carried off as a prisoner after being prevented from stabbing himself. Brown began four years of captivity when he was captured by Ottawa the next day. He was interrogated by a French interpreter and then joined Baker, whom he helped on their forced trek to Fort Carillon.

Lusignan once again hosted English prisoners belonging to Indians. Brown, Baker, and four others were held separately in the guardhouse and interrogated. An interpreter threatened them with hanging for having killed their prisoners the previous day, but later admitted that this was only to frighten them. Lusignan would not have executed prisoners of his Indian allies, and the killing of prisoners held by an exposed force under attack was not deemed murder, either there or when Indians had done the same during the last phase of the Battle of Lake George. More characteristically, Lusignan had Brown's wounds dressed, sent him a quart of claret, and transferred him to the hospital. Although his Indian captors tried to take Brown away, he and the other five captives were kept at Fort Carillon until March 1. Brown saw this as a kindness, as was no doubt the intent, but Lusignan knew that the Indians would stay until their captive had recovered and, in the meantime, the commandant held these six prisoners, who had been in Fort William Henry and could provide information useful in the impending attack on that fort.[82]

This battle had involved some 250 men, an increase in the scale of woodland warfare on this frontier, but was soon to be dwarfed by the winter attack Vaudreuil planned on Fort William Henry. The exact purpose of the French raid was disputed then, as part of the growing rift between Montcalm and Vaudreuil, and is debatable now. Montcalm had submitted a plan "surprising Fort George [Fort William Henry], and burning, at least, the outer parts of the fort with 800 men."[83] Montcalm had wanted this raid led by a senior regular officer, François-Charles de Bourlamaque. Vaudreuil decided to double the size of the force and put his brother in charge, yet later claimed that his purpose remained to conduct a spoiling raid rather than a siege of the 474-man garrison at Fort William Henry.[84]

François-Pierre de Rigaud de Vaudreuil, the governor's younger brother, was a short, thin, tough thirty-six-year-old career officer in the *troupes de la marine* whose military accomplishments had included leading the successful siege of Fort Massachusetts in 1746, and leading the van in the conquest of Oswego ten years later. He was given a force of 650 militiamen, 300 *troupes de la marine*, 300 Indians, and 250 French regulars chosen by Montcalm to display sufficient endurance to combat Canadian bragging. At the expense of the king of France, these men were all superbly outfitted for winter travel in woolens covered with moccasins, Indian leggings, and a hooded great-coat. Over these they wore a blanket and a bearskin. Each man also had three knives, a tomahawk, snowshoes, skates, and iron creepers to walk on ice. These soldiers left Fort Carillon looking like Indian hunters, each pulling a small hand sleigh loaded with gear and a twelve-day supply of provisions. Provisions were precious in Canada that winter, especially since the colony was feeding the captured Os-wego garrison of eighteen hundred; food limited the attack to a raid or very short siege.[85]

The alarm was sounded in Fort William Henry at 2:00 A.M. on March 19, when axes were heard to the north and a light was spotted down the lake. Before dawn, Rigaud's party attempted to burn a sloop and some bateaux.[86] There was heavy firing to cover another attempt at burning the boats during the day, and that night the attackers finally succeeded in burning all the boats and a woodpile.

A parley, strangely previewing that summer's events, occurred on the next day. Rigaud sent Le Mercier, the regular artillery officer who had been with Dieskau on this ground two years before, to negotiate. Le Mercier was blindfolded by a young British engineer, Adam Willi-amson, before being led into the fort. The defenders were offered the honors of war, including the security of officers' effects, provided "some things only be left by the Officers to please and gratify the Indians." They should have no "Apprehensions of Mischief from the Savages," for Le Mercier claimed to have sufficient regulars to protect the English from the Indians. The garrison would be escorted wher-ever it wanted to go. Should the garrison resist, Le Mercier warned, there would be calamity for it. If the fort fell, "the Cruelties of the Savages cou'd not altogether be prevented," however compassionate the French might wish to be.[87] Eyre refused to surrender, and the attacking army was told that the defenders believed that there were a thousand Indians attacking and "they expected to be Equally ill Treated whether the Fort was surrendered upon Articles of Capitula-tion or . . . taken by storm."[88]

Thereafter, the attacks were at night, but Eyre's regulars and rangers were vigilant and their grapeshot-loaded cannon deterred the scaling ladders, just as Eyre's earlier instructions had predicted. The attackers burned storehouses, including one loaded with provisions, as well as huts and a sloop under construction. The fighting lasted for four days before the attack was abandoned. The garrison found three wounded men whom they took as prisoners, and claimed to have killed several other attackers while seven of their own were slightly wounded. One of the prisoners admitted that, after the failure of the parley, it was understood that the garrison was to be given no quarter."[89]

The builder and commandant, recently promoted to major, could be satisfied that Fort William Henry had passed its first test. For Eyre and the English, this was a success at a time when victories were few. However, a watchful regular garrison in a fire-resistant earthen fort, with twenty mounted cannon, had done nothing exceptional in resisting attackers without cannon and numbering little more than three times the garrison strength. Montcalm and Bougainville considered Rigaud's raid a failure and so did some Indians who returned to Fort Carillon empty-handed.[90] Governor Vaudreuil claimed that the purpose of the expedition had been to spoil English preparation for an offensive on that frontier and that the parley and scaling ladders were just part of a successful ruse in accomplishing that purpose.[91] The difference between a wooden stockade and a well-defended earthen fort was made clear to all; it would take more than a splendidly equipped raiding party to capture Fort William Henry.

4

SIEGE

Governor Vaudreuil was determined to take Fort William Henry in 1757 and made no secret of it. Throughout the winter, the English heard of the planned attack from Iroquois who had been to Montreal, from French soldiers taken prisoner, and from English prisoners who had escaped from Montreal. Reports were so frequent that at least one suspicious American observer was convinced that the attack must be intended elsewhere.[1] Vaudreuil planned that Montcalm's army would destroy both Fort William Henry and Fort Edward, carrying munitions back to Fort Carillon and unleashing Indian raids on Albany and Schenectady. He assured the new secretary of state for the navy, François-Marie Peyrenc de Moras, that such a strike would force the English to abandon any thought of an attack on Quebec.[2]

Vaudreuil's first major achievement of 1757 was the gathering of unprecedented numbers of Indian warriors for the campaign against Fort William Henry. His established belief in the military value of Indian warriors and their methods had been confirmed, during his first two years as governor of New France, by the major victories against Braddock and against the garrison at Fort Oswego. The victory over Braddock's army had been due largely to some six hundred Ottawa from Michilimackinac and Detroit, as well as their Huron and Potawatomi allies. Most of the Indians who protected Fort Duquesne had not been locals defending their own lands, though some Shawnee, Delaware, and Mingo warriors fought in defense of their comparatively new homelands in the upper Ohio Valley.[3] This signal victory over Braddock, and its rich booty, helped lure some five hundred warriors down from the *pays d'en haut*, or upper Great Lakes, in the spring of 1756, but most were turned back by reports of smallpox at Forts Niagara and Frontenac.

At Montcalm's quick victory at Oswego, the 260 Indians with his army were overwhelmingly Abenaki, Algonkin, Iroquois, and Nipissing, who came from the mission villages around Montreal.[4] Only forty Menominee, and some twenty-two Ojibwa, arrived from the *pays d'en haut* to participate in the siege of Oswego. The formal surrender of that eighteen-hundred-man English colonial garrison was followed by a "massacre" of at least thirty wounded prisoners by unnamed Indians and purchase by the French of other prisoners held by the Indians. The French recorded their horror at these violations of the formal surrender terms, but tolerated the actions of the Indians, which were done "without our being able to prevent them or having the right of remonstrating with them."[5] Warriors learned that the French would pay to reclaim English prisoners; some of these warriors would be at Fort William Henry the following summer.

Embellished tales of the conquest of Oswego spread to the upper Great Lakes, portraying the victors as swimming in brandy.[6] Several hundred Ottawa, Ojibwa, and Potawatomi, members of that powerful anti-Iroquois confederacy known as the "Three Fires," came down to join the winter garrison at Fort Carillon in the fall of 1756.[7] Vaudreuil held a major conference at Montreal in December that brought Iroquois visitors from New York together with Caughnawaga, Nipissing, and Algonkin from the mission villages, some Potawatomi and Ottawa from Detroit and Michilimackinac, as well as a roster of Canadian guerrillas who interpreted for the Indians they had raided with. This meeting was to encourage recruiting for the Fort William Henry campaign, to impress the visiting Iroquois, and especially to warn the Mohawk, who had stayed away. The Ottawa and Potawatomi chanted their enthusiasm in a war song asking the French; "Father, we are famished; give us fresh meat; we wish to eat the English."[8]

Recruiting in the *pays d'en haut* early in 1757 was phenomenal, more successful than Vaudreuil could have hoped. Some of the Ottawa and Potawatomi warriors who had been to Montreal in 1756 went home to recruit, encouraged by the commandants of the French trading posts of the upper lakes and by the recent victories.[9] A thousand warriors from the *pays d'en haut* eventually joined the attack on Fort William Henry. Hundreds more were with the flotillas of war canoes as they came down from Lakes Superior and Michigan to what became a great gathering near Detroit in early June 1757. Some warriors turned back after hearing of the prevalence of smallpox in New France. Several hundred decided to follow another promising warpath southward to Fort Duquesne, to raid the frontiers of Pennsylvania, Maryland, and Virginia.[10] One thousand warriors were not diverted or distracted, but completed a voyage of as much as fifteen hundred miles to arrive in Montreal by early July 1757.

Most, though not all, of these warriors from the upper Great Lakes were, to some degree, within the economic and military hinterland of New France, but the personal and cultural connections were limited. Although there were missions established at Detroit and Michilimackinac, no priests accompanied the warriors. A few of the Ottawa from Detroit and from Michilimackinac were thought Christian enough to have Abbé Jean-Claude Mathevet formally assigned as their chaplain during the campaign, but his primary responsibility was with the domiciled Nipissing.[11] He was the only missionary linked to any of the Indians from the *pays d'en haut*. The priests soon found themselves struggling to protect the faith of their catechumens from what would be a massive Indian display of traditional martial values.

The only French influence over these visiting allies was exercised by Canadians with warrior reputations. To influence the 337 Ottawa, drawn from seven separate bands in what was later to become Michigan, Montcalm's staff counted on Charles Langlade. He was the nephew of attending war chief Nissowaquet and was renowned among his mother's Ottawa and his father's Canadians for his exploits against the Fox, the Miami, and the English. Joining him was Charles-Joseph Noyelles de Fleurimont, who had spent several years at Michilimackinac and made his warrior reputation against the Chickasaw.[12] These two men, and two other Ottawa-speaking interpreters, were the valuable but limited links between Montcalm and this largest contingent of allies from the *pays d'en haut*.

Influencing the nearly three hundred Ojibwa (Chippawa) would be at least as difficult for the army's leaders. Some from this loosely associated nation were *Saulteaux* from as far west as Pointe Chequamegon on Lake Superior, and nearly half were from three much nearer but less committed bands of Mississauga, who had been English allies in the 1740s but had been forced back to the French alliance by severe Ottawa reprisals in 1749. Some supposedly drunken dissidents in the

Toronto band of Mississauga planned to burn Fort Rouillé (Toronto) early in the summer of 1757. After being threatened by a patrol of French regulars from Fort Niagara supported by the Potawatomi, they joined the Fort William Henry campaign instead.[13] This whole disparate Ojibwa contingent was bound to Montcalm's intentions only by two lesser-known Canadian officers, who spoke their language, and one civilian interpreter.[14]

The French felt a closer rapport with two other tribes from the *pays d'en haut*, represented by smaller delegations, the Potawatomi and the Menominee. Bougainville, who called the Potawatomi of lower Michigan "the wisest and most obedient of all the Indians," counted eighty-eight Potawatomi with the army at the end of July. The Menominee (Fols Avoies) from Green Bay had participated in the taking of Fort Oswego, and 129 of them returned to help New France in 1757, led by warriors bearing their clan names, The Elk and The Cat.[15] Both of these tribes were anxious to raid with Louis Coulon de Villiers, an officer with the *troupes de la marine* who had served at St. Joseph and won at Forts Necessity and Oswego.[16] Each tribe was assigned an interpreter, but more important were Villiers, fellow-warrior Joseph Marin *fils*, and Chevalier de Langis, another officer who would distinguish himself and his Indian companions in this campaign.[17]

The lure of coup and loot had been broadcast well beyond the major Algonkian-speaking tribes of the French allies in the upper Great Lakes. Forty-eight Siouian-speaking Winnebago came from what is now Wisconsin, as did some Sauk, Fox, and Iowa from farther west. The ten Iowa were the first of that tribe ever to visit Montreal.[18] A few Miami from St. Joseph were there early and left in anger, but seventeen of them reappeared just in time for the siege. The Nipissing brought three neighboring warriors who spoke an unfamiliar Algonkian dialect and were known as *Têtes de boule*.[19] Five Delaware from Tioga (near Athens, Pennsylvania) were the first to come to Montreal from that large, disillusioned tribe of former English allies.[20] These smaller groups brought more than their share of bitter rivalries with several of the major tribes. The limits of French persuasion on these strangers was obvious. Marin and Langis were cavalierly designated in Bougainville's list of the Indians as "officers attached to" all of them, including the Potawatomi and the Menominee. A single member of the Reaume family of Michilimackinac traders was equally optimistically called the interpreter for seven different tribes.

The Indians from the *pays d'en haut* were an exceedingly disparate and volatile element in Montcalm's army. Smoldering hostilities like those between the Chequamegon Ojibwa and the Fox made them entirely unwilling to cooperate. Suspicions of new allies and of former enemies adopted by allies added to resentments like those of the Mississauga and the Miami against the Ottawa. Rivalries for military reputation and booty, in addition to simple misunderstandings, were inevitable even if alcohol had not been available. For some of these tribes there were no French interpreters, no Canadian officers who had previously fought with them, and no French missionaries who were familiar with them.[21] None of the Indians from the *pays d'en haut* were subjects of New France. They were unpaid allies who came for coup and plunder, expecting Montcalm's army to feed and arm them and, in some cases, care for their families.[22] Most warriors reached Montreal before the end of June, contributing to the governor's satisfaction as well as his concern. While a shortage of provisions had delayed the commencement of Montcalm's campaign, suddenly that shortage, and concern for the tranquility of Montreal, were grounds for a speedy launch of the expedition. As July began, the first regiments of French regulars were sent south from Fort St. Jean, soon to be followed by the assembled Indians from the *pays d'en haut*.

Recruiting of the "domiciled" Indians was, understandably, delayed until the others had left for Fort Carillon. A recruiting party including Montcalm, Bougainville, Rigaud, and St. Luc de la Corne set out first for the Lake of the Two Mountains (Oka), just west of Montreal. Nipissing, Algonkin, and Iroquois tribesmen lived in separate sections of this single village, with one church and two Sulpician missionaries. Montcalm explained his purpose, offered cattle for a war feast, and then attended the evening gathering of chiefs of the three tribes in the council house. The Nipissing took precedence here; Chief Kisensik led the negotiations, and the famous warrior Aoussik, recently returned from raiding at Fort William Henry, led the war dance that provided 171 men for the campaign. St. Luc de la Corne, an experienced Canadian trader and famed irregular who was appointed "general" of all the Indian forces in part because he spoke five Indian languages, was particularly responsible for the fifty-three Nipissings, who also were accompanied by an interpreter and Abbé Mathevet. The forty-seven Algonkins in the army had the same missionary, and the officer chosen for his influence with them was the ubiquitous Chevalier de Langis.[23]

The recruiters went on to the Caughnawaga settlement of "French Mohawks" at Sault St. Louis the next day. Somewhat more elaborate and more Christian ceremonies were observed there, with comparable negotiations and a war feast. Montcalm's aide-de-camp and secretary, Bougainville, again danced a novice's war dance in place of the commander, but this time he was adopted into the tribe. The Caughnawaga showed no sign of reticence to fight their Mohawk kin; the 258 Caughnawaga who joined the expedition represented almost all the adult males in their village.[24] Earlier efforts to lure Iroquois from New York had been more disappointing, bringing only eight Onondaga and only three from the mission station of La Présentation. The Seneca, who were the New York Iroquois most inclined to the French, together with some Cayuga, had gone again to the Ohio campaign rather than fight their Mohawk confederates. In all, there were 363 Iroquois warriors with Montcalm, accompanied by their blood-brother Chevalier de Longueuil,[25] two interpreters, and Abbé Picquet. The fifty-two Huron from Detroit and Lorette were formally counted with this Iroquois contingent, although given their own interpreter.

The recruiters did not have to visit the Abenaki, who had migrated from Acadia and were settled as four bands near Montreal, probably because the Abenaki had been fighting their own war with the English throughout the previous peace. These Abenaki sent 245 warriors for Montcalm's campaign, to which were added 60 warriors from neighboring Acadian tribes. Chevalier de Niverville, who had military experience on all of New France's frontiers and had been with the Abenaki in raids in Nova Scotia, in Massachusetts, and in Dieskau's attack of 1755 was, throughout the campaign, regarded by the French high command as the man with the most influence with these eastern Indians. The Abenaki were also accompanied by an interpreter and joined by their young Jesuit missionary from St. François, Père Pierre Roubaud.[26]

Roubaud, who joined the Abenaki encampment at Fort St. Jean in the middle of July, was already worrying that his catechumens were attending the boisterous intertribal war dances of other mission Indians. Roubaud and the two Sulpician missionaries attempted to counter these influences with morning Masses for the Abenaki, Algonkin, Nipissing, and Caughnawaga before they broke camp and paddled their flotilla of war canoes up Lake Champlain to Fort Carillon.[27] There they joined the rest of the army, including those unChristian and even anti-Christian warriors from the *pays d'en haut*, who had already been scouting and raiding in the neighborhood of Fort William Henry.

II

The no-man's-land between Fort Carillon and Fort William Henry had belonged to the French-allied Indians in the spring of 1757. Successful raids ensured that the best information flowed north, like the waters of Lake George. A major raid in April by Ottawa and Potawatomi warriors, led by Aoussik and Charles Langlade, had taken four scalps and three prisoners. Chevalier de Langis had led two separate Caughnawaga raids that yielded a total of seven prisoners.[28] Prisoners revealed that there were no British initiatives on the New York frontier, not even repairs to the Fort William Henry outbuildings damaged in March.[29]

The success of these raids may have prompted a significant shift in perspective for the French regular officer in charge of Fort St. Frédéric, Chevalier de Bourlamaque. By the end of June, he was giving little or no direct reward for prisoners or scalps. Instead, Indians were encouraged by generosity with arms and equipment and major feasts before and after the raids. This may have reflected a regular officer's disdain for scalping, and showed that he wanted no prisoners to eat provisions and spy on his preparations for the coming campaign. Bourlamaque may also have found that Indians who brought him prisoners did not raid again, but stayed near the fort, waiting to take their prisoners home in triumph. The feasting provoked envy in the regulars and militiamen who were on short rations, and Bourlamaque's reduced interest in prisoners may have encouraged harsher Indian attitudes toward them.[30]

A major Indian raiding party, consisting of two hundred Indians from the *pays d'en haut*, ten Canadians, with twenty-five Abenaki and Caughnawaga scouting, left Fort St. Frédéric on June 30. As they entered Wood Creek, they were ambushed by Captain Israel Putnam's fifty-five-man party of American rangers from Fort Edward, who killed a Canadian and mortally wounded several Indians.[31] The next day, in pursuing Putnam's retreating scouts, the raiders captured three of the rangers (two Mohican and a wounded American). Bourlamaque reported to Montcalm, who was still in Montreal recruiting mission Indians, that two of the prisoners had been brought in, but the Indians "tore the other apart, and, as he was good, they ate him." He added that Montcalm would not get either of the living prisoners: "The Englishman will die, and the Mahican, whose flesh is not appetizing, will be burned."[32]

The torturing of prisoners by Indian raiding parties, whether or not they had suffered casualties, could commonly occur due to individual temperament or tribal custom, but the eating of prisoners was very unusual. The Ottawa were the only tribe reported as eating prisoners in this campaign, either as an unceremonial display of ferocity or as a source of meat.[33]

These Mohican had been prisoners of the Indians, so there was no interference by the French or the Canadians. Vaudreuil, who usually sought court recognition for Canadian officers who accompanied Indian raiders, mentioned only the dead Canadian by name in his report to the minister of marine and said nothing of the eating of a prisoner. Montcalm and Bougainville were aware of the practice and wrote home about it with dark humor. Montcalm had written to his mother earlier, mentioning that the burning of prisoners had become unfashionable but that Indians had burned one in the Ohio Valley that year so that none would forget how.[34] Bougainville mentioned that Shawnee and Delaware raiders in the Ohio Valley

> have eaten an English officer whose pallor and plumpness tempted them. Such cruelties are frequent enough among the Indians of La Belle Rivière. Our domesticated Indians, softened by the glimmerings of Christianity which they have received, are no longer cruel in cold blood, but one cannot say, however, that their character is changed.[35]

On the very day that this war party had set out for Wood Creek, Bougainville wrote from Montreal in genuine apprehension about the Indian allies

> demanding broth which is to say blood, drawn 500 leagues by the smell of fresh human flesh and the opportunity to teach their youths how to cut up a person destined for the cook pot. These are the comrades who are our shadow day and night. I shudder at the ghastly spectacles which they are preparing for us.[36]

Although the French commanders of the attacking army voiced forebodings of cannibalism and cruelty to prisoners, they indicated more helpless resignation than calculated cynicism.

There were tensions in the Canadian and Indian camp about a mile north of Lake George, where Marin was recruiting for another major raid in mid-July. Ottawa ferocity toward captives could not hide the fact that their last raiding party had been defeated at Wood Creek by a much smaller force of American rangers. A French captain of the

Béarn regiment stated in his journal for July 14 that "a soldier has been killed last night by an Indian,"[37] without identifying the Indian or the camp. He may have been a scout for the English, as was the one who scalped a French sentry ten days later, but the killing may have been the result of a fight within the camp. Drunken fights did occur, like that between a Mohican adopted by the Abenaki and a Caughnawaga, but most warriors were wary of disputes that could easily become fights to the death.[38] When Marin's six hundred warriors learned they were to raid between Fort William Henry and Fort Edward, they objected that they were being sent to slaughter, as there were three thousand men at the head of the lake. When about four hundred Menominee, Potawatomi, and their neighbors, together with eighty French and Canadians, finally set out on July 16, the Ottawa were so upset about missing the honor of participating in this strike that Montcalm had to placate them later with promises that they could soon "hunt a bit of meat."[39] Ottawa outrage and disgust reached new heights when one of their reconnaissance canoes was mistaken for the enemy and fired upon, leaving one of their chiefs dead and another wounded.[40]

Marin, who had been successful in a raid near Fort William Henry the previous August, took his party by the Wood Creek route without encountering any opposition. The trees that had been felled into the creek by Canadians to obstruct a planned English invasion a decade earlier, and that had delayed Pehr Kalm in 1749, were gone; the raiders' canoes met only a set of rapids as they traveled all the way up to the abandoned site of Fort Anne. Half of the Indians refused to approach Fort Edward, reminiscent of Dieskau's differences there with the Caughnawaga two years earlier, but the rest proceeded easily down a trail that soon became the thirty-foot-wide wagon road which Colonel Lyman's axemen had cut in 1755. This discovery amazed the French command, since this undefended route could easily be used to separate Fort William Henry from the support of Fort Edward.[41] Marin's raiders surprised ten guards protecting a timber-cutting detail about a half-mile from Fort Edward on the morning of July 23. Survivors reached the fort, and a larger party came out to exchange heavy fire with Marin's men for about ten minutes before the latter withdrew. In the initial attack, Indians from the *pays d'en haut* had used bows and arrows, the quite killers. Since most tribes had long since replaced bows with guns, these arrows with unfamiliar markings held a special terror, which the garrison at Fort Edward promptly shared with their fellows at Fort William Henry and with the colonial newspapers.[42]

Entirely unknown to one another, three groups of warriors were heading north that day toward the camp near Fort Carillon. Marin's reunited group retraced its route via Wood Creek, bringing scalps and three prisoners, two of whom reportedly died of their wounds on the way.[43] Colonel John Parker, leading five companies of his New Jersey Blues and a few New York militiamen, left the wharf at Fort William Henry in twenty-two whaleboats, heading down the lake to the falls to destroy a sawmill and take some prisoners. The third group, which escaped notice then and since, were Mohawk, apparently conducting their own raid on the French camp at Fort Carillon.

The Mohawk arrived first, surprising a patrol of fifteen grenadiers from the Guyenne regiment within 150 yards of the tents of the French regulars at the falls and only two miles from Fort Carillon. The raiders killed two, whom they scalped, and wounded two others. Pierre Rigaud, who was in the Indian camp more than a mile farther south on the road to Lake George, immediately sent two parties to find the intruders. Sieur de Villiers took 150 men with him to set an ambush on the Mohawk trail, in vain. The larger party, headed by a Canadian ensign named de Corbière, was sent along the north shore of the lake to what was thereafter known as Sabbath Day Point, to cut off a retreat by way of the lake.[44]

The Mohawk had stirred up the French camp and escaped, but the leading scouts of de Corbière's pursuit party noticed several unidentified boats on the lake at nightfall. Runners returned to the camp at the portage, where some five hundred Indians and fifty Canadian reinforcements scrambled into birch canoes and bateaux. Warriors brought these canoes ashore near Sabbath Day Point and hid with them in the brush, while scouts watched Colonel Parker's whaleboats anchor in the lake for the night. A strategy for the ambush was agreed on among the war chiefs (thirteen of them Ottawa; five Ojibwa; five, Potawatomi; and The Cat of the Menominee), together with Langlade, Joseph-Hippolyte Hertel de Saint-François,[45] and de Corbière. At daybreak, Parker's whaleboats were under way again. In the morning mist, three of the boats became separated from the others. These three drew some fire from the shore, and the others hurried to their assistance. Waiting until all the whaleboats had passed Sabbath Day Point heading north, the Indians then launched their canoes unseen from the south side of that point. By the time the war whoops announced the attack, Parker's whaleboats were already trapped; their retreat to Fort William Henry was blocked by an armada of canoes manned by some six hundred Ottawa, Ojibwa, and Menominee warriors. Only four of the twenty-two whaleboats, including the one containing Colonel Parker, managed to escape.[46] Some men tried to surrender to warriors who were not yet prepared to take prisoners, some whaleboats were overturned by Indians, and others were run ashore by men desperate to escape the slaughter.

In the initial attack and subsequent chase, about one hundred of Parker's terrified men were shot, drowned, or hunted down in the forest once they reached the shore. Perhaps as many as a hundred returned to Fort William Henry in the whaleboats or over land, but they represented less than 30 percent of the expedition.[47] Once the victorious Indians felt that the battle was over, or rather that the campaign was over, they took more than 150 survivors as prisoners. Their success had been overwhelming; the warriors had inflicted an immense number of casualties, while only one warrior had been slightly wounded.[48]

For Père Roubaud, who already had special plans for Sunday July 24, his third day in the Indian camp near Fort Carillon was unforgettable. Some of his Abenaki catechumens made their confessions and received their first communion that morning, and Roubaud preached his first sermon in Abenaki, pleading with them "to do honor to their religion by their conduct in the presence of so many Idolatrous Tribes, who either were not acquainted with it or blasphemed it. . . ."[49] Later that morning, excitement filled the camp at the sight of a flotilla of canoes decorated with scalps; Marin's contingent was returning. Onlookers might be proud, envious, or shocked to count thirty-two scalps and one prisoner. The initial tale told, to the admiring camp and to Montcalm, was of a pitched battle with the whole of the garrison at Fort Edward, and the thirty-two scalps were those taken in haste from a small fraction of the dead British. Before the day ended, the truth was out. There had been thirteen English killed, including six regulars, while the attackers lost one Canadian and dropped a couple of the freshly taken scalps in the retreat.[50] In an atmosphere of intense intertribal rivalry, a considerable achievement had been made to seem even greater by cutting scalps into two or three pieces.

Both Marin's triumph and Roubaud's pleas were largely forgotten by late afternoon with the return of the first victors and victims of the rout at Sabbath Day Point. Sight of an approaching bateau, with Ottawa warriors and their five bound captives, sent the whole camp scurrying to get clubs. Roubaud talked a few Abenaki out of participating, only to be pleasantly surprised by the sudden cancellation of the traditional gauntlet ceremony. As Roubaud reported it later, a fierce Ottawa chief, at the persistent urging of the French officer commanding the bateau, shouted menacingly from the boat: "These prisoners belong to me; I wish you to respect me by respecting what belongs to me; Let us have no ill treatment, of which the whole odium would fall back upon my head."[51] These first five prisoners were taken into Fort Carillon and interrogated separately, and Roubaud visited one of them there before they were returned to their captors. Meanwhile, the other 150 prisoners were brought ashore by their conquerors.

Roubaud's three-mile walk back from the fort to his tent among the Abenaki and Ottawa brought him to a repulsive sight. Files of terrified prisoners, now slaves with ropes around their necks, were being paraded by jubilant warriors whose spirits were higher because of captured rum and purchased brandy. As he approached his own tent, Roubaud saw a large fire around which a group of Ottawa were eating a prisoner. "The saddest thing was that they had placed near them about ten Englishmen, to be spectators of their infamous repast." Roubaud failed to influence either a young brave or an old warrior and retreated to his tent, his only solace being that none of his Abenaki had participated. The next morning, the offensive feast was resumed, and the three missionaries moved their tents away, fearing that the sacrifice of the Mass on the site of "so many abominations" might allow the idolatrous to "take advantage of our most solemn ceremonies in order to make them the substance, or even the ornament, of their mockery."[52]

Montcalm and Bougainville knew that at least three prisoners were being eaten in the Indian camp. They seemed to regret what was happening, but regarded the Indians' prisoners as the Indians' business.[53] Their aloofness could not be sustained, however, because many of the victorious Indians were determined to go home. A warrior who took a scalp carried proof of conquest without encumbrance, but a warrior who took a prisoner had to guard him, and hence could no longer be a warrior. Individual braves, or war chiefs in some tribes, were responsible for any prisoners they took, since there were no Indian "prisoner-of-war camps."

Montcalm became involved in an afternoon of puzzling and frustrating bargaining in order to keep the triumphant tribesmen from the *pays d'en haut* with his army. Some chiefs wanted to leave, "saying that it was tempting the Master of Life to continue to expose themselves to the dangers of war" after their recent wonderful accomplishment. Montcalm wanted the Indians to send their prisoners to Montreal, but some of the warriors wanted to go with their slaves to ensure that they were well treated. In his journal, Bougainville wondered how these Indians could visit with their slaves, give them white bread, and argue that the governor would not treat them well enough, whereas, at the same time, other tribesmen were eating prisoners. The agreement struck on the afternoon of July 25 has not survived, so it is not known what promises encouraged the chiefs to stay. Perhaps it was at this point that the first eighty of some two hundred Ottawa and Mississauga warriors left for home, with or without their prisoners. The remaining chiefs from the *pays d'en haut* learned enough about New France's trade in prisoners to demand new negotiations with Montcalm, who was busy preparing for the advance up Lake George. At a midnight council with Montcalm, the chiefs insisted that each warrior or war chief's band be given receipts for its slaves, that Governor Vaudreuil give the slaves white bread and blankets, and that all slaves be returned to their owners unless the latter wanted to sell them.[54] The next day, Montcalm was finally able to send the prisoners to Montreal.

Montcalm held a major two-day council with all the Indian chiefs at their camp, beginning on July 26 by reviewing with them his planned attack on Fort William Henry and the Indians' part in it. The mission Indians replied first, with the Abenaki, Algonkin, and Nipissing spokesmen approving the plans. The Caughnawaga, who played intertribal diplomacy masterfully, had no senior chiefs present, and their junior spokesman promised to report the plan to the elders, confident that they, too, would approve. La Motte of the Menominee and the old Ottawa chief Pennahouel, who had once been an enemy of the French but had just participated in another of many victories as their ally, endorsed the plan in the name of the Indians from the *pays d'en haut*. At the request of the Indians, the departure of the first contingent was delayed a day.[55]

On the more ceremonial second day, the grand council that met to bind the nations together with a belt of six thousand beads was so crowded with French onlookers that the Menominee, Sauk, and Fox could not initially find room in the circle. Nipissing chief Kisenik once again opened proceedings on behalf of the domiciled Indians, thanking those from the *pays d'en haut* for coming to defend the lands of others from English invaders and commending the recent victory: "It covers you with glory, and Lac St. Sacrement, stained red with the blood of Englishmen, will forever attest this exploit." Montcalm urged unity and the belt was thrown into the assembly, where it was picked up by tribal orators exhorting all to accept it. Pennahouel urged all to remain throughout the enterprise and disparaged those who had left after the slaughter at Sabbath Day Point.[56]

The war belt, which tradition gave to the tribe with the greatest number of warriors present, when to the Iroquois of Caughnawaga, Oka, and La Présentation without question.[57] Their spokesman addressed the Indians of the *pays d'en haut* particularly, with praise for the unity shown, thanks for their effort, and exhortations that they take the belt. Pennahouel then accepted the unexpected offer of the belt, though there were intertribal discussions later to determine who should keep it.

The planned approach to Fort William Henry was endorsed, involving an advance contingent on foot to secure a landing place for the flotilla. The number of Indians participating and the casualties were to be monitored according to Indian custom. Each warrior presented a small stick on joining his expedition and hoped to pick one up again after the battle. The Caughnawaga, who traveled the lake regularly to visit kin or trade at Albany, volunteered to scout for both forces. As the western Indians' customs did not include a final war song, this conclusion to the proceedings was omitted in deference to these welcome allies.[58]

The Indian allies had dominated the preliminary stages of the campaign, which ended with Montcalm's war council of July 26 and 27. The raids had hurt the English and brought prisoners who revealed more than the state of Fort William Henry. The complete English ignorance of French preparations, particularly evident from the interrogation of members of Parker's expedition, surprised the French command. Most of the Indian allies had agreed to remain with the army after their victory over Parker, in anticipation of an even more impressive conquest to be measured in scalps and prisoners. As far as Montcalm was concerned, the major contribution of the Indians had been the effective insulation, from English scouts and patrols, of his regular army concentrating at Fort Carillon. Perhaps Lord Loudoun, brooding aboard HMS *Winchelsea* off Halifax, gave the Indians something closer to their due. Upon hearing of the Parker expedition's fate, Loudoun wrote to the secretary of state, "from their having permitted the Enemy to get the Superiority of the Lake, without which they could not have got up Artillery, I look upon that Place and Garrison, as lost, with the whole Troops there."[59] Lieutenant Colonel George Monro, having been denied information about French movements that were protected by aggressive Indian scouting parties, had gambled most of his little fleet and lost.

Despite all Montcalm's efforts to attract and hold Indian support-ers, both he and Vaudreuil knew what Rigaud's raid had confirmed: Fort William Henry could be captured only by an army conducting a conventional siege centering on massed cannon fire. Vaudreuil had asked the French court for eighteen hundred men and provisions in addition to forces to match anything the British were to send to America in 1757. Although the well-informed French court knew that the British were sending some eight thousand regulars to America, Vaudreuil was sent only eighteen hundred additional men. He was assured that the British would focus on the Cape Breton fortress of Louisbourg and was encouraged to keep a defensive posture on the Lake Champlain front.[60] Nevertheless, Vaudreuil and Montcalm pro-ceeded in hope of reinforcements and provisions from France, but before the arrival of either.

The core of Montcalm's army was 6 battalions of regular *troupes de terre*, numbering 2570 men, already at Fort Carillon when he arrived on July 18. The La Reine and Languedoc battalions, which had con-tributed grenadiers to Dieskau's last battle two years earlier, were noticeably under-strength, at 369 and 322 men, respectively. The Guyenne (492) and Béarn (464) battalions were also beginning their third campaign in New France. The Béarn battalion had participated in the easy siege of Oswego the previous year, as had the newly arrived La Sarre battalion (451). The Royal Roussillon battalion (472) was spending its second summer on the Lake Champlain frontier. The first two French ships of 1757 had arrived at Quebec at the beginning of July, bringing news that two additional battalions of the Régiment de Berry had been sent to Louisbourg. For Canada, there were only twenty-six artillerymen of the Corps Royal who were in time for the siege, and four hundred new recruits for the regulars who were not sent on to Fort Carillon.[61] Provisions, which were the most serious shortage, did not arrive in time. Aside from the men at Louisbourg, virtually all the French regulars in New France were concentrated at Fort Carillon.

Complete dominance of French-regular thinking in this phase of the campaign was evident in the brigading of the *troupes de la marine* and the Canadian militia at Fort Carillon. The *troupes de la marine* had been raised and officered as companies of fewer than seventy men each. The officers were the toughest and most aggressive irregulars in New France, advancing in rank on merit, with very little purchasing of commissions or promotions. The soldiers were mainly recruited in France and trained in Canada. In the interservice rivalry with the better paid French regulars, these more versatile but less drilled soldiers of the navy were being slighted. Montcalm transferred most of their leading Canadian officers to the Indian contingents, and some officers and men were brigaded with the Canadian militia. Only one-fifth of the *troupes de la marine* were organized into a separate brigade of 524 men, who were to perform as regulars and to be officered by those thought least fit for guerrilla raiding.[62]

The Canadian militia was raised in various-sized companies from specific parishes for emergency service without pay. They went on war parties, sometimes manned defense works, and were used to supply frontier forts or to build roads. The six brigades (2546) into which the attending militia was reorganized matched the regulars in number and represented about 20 percent of the colony's manpower. The army also included some three hundred Canadian volunteers and nearly two hundred officers and men of the colonial engineers and artillery under the leadership of Michel Chartier de Lotbinière and François Le Mercier, respectively.[63]

Cannon were recognized by both sides as crucial to an effective siege of Fort William Henry. The previous autumn at Quebec City, there had been experiments with cannon mounted on a platform over a pair of bateaux.[64] In May, teams of horses, oxen, and men had hauled thirty-six cannon and four mortars, including some pieces captured from Braddock and from Oswego, over the portage at the falls of the Richelieu.[65] As Montcalm's army prepared to attack from Carillon two months later, these same pieces had to be hauled up the longer and more difficult portage to Lake George. The horses and oxen were not used because there was insufficient food for them to be able to do such heavy work and because some of the oxen had been killed and eaten by Indian allies. The Canadian militia manhandled the artillery as well as the 247 bateaux, provisions, and ammunition over four miles of rugged, newly cut road that was repeatedly washed out by heavy rains and included a crossing of the fast waters between the falls.[66] This frantic work, including night hauling by as many as five hundred men, ended with July. Bougainville, who had seen all twelve days of it, admitted that "the hardships cannot be imagined, and it is impossible to give a fair idea of it."[67] Due to the Indian and Canadian raids, numerous scouts, and the decimation of Parker's expedition, the strenuous and vulnerable work of moving the artillery train up to Lake George was accomplished without effective English scouting, to say nothing of disruption.

The day before portaging was completed, a detachment of nearly three thousand men, led by the able Brigadier François-Gaston de Lévis, set out along the rugged west side of Lake George. Caughnawaga and the Canadian volunteers were the advance guard, and the rest of some eight hundred Indians served as flank guards for two columns of militia and *troupes de la marine* who were, in turn, flanking the grenadier companies of the regulars. This line of march was reminiscent of Dieskau's. In three days, they scrambled over the densely wooded hills and swamps to the agreed rendezvous site at Ganaouské Bay (Bolton, New York), established a defensible camp, and lighted the three fires that guided Montcalm's fleet without alerting Fort William Henry.[68]

On Sunday July 31, one day after Lévis' detachment had set out, 150 Indian canoes left from the north end of Lake George. As they passed Sabbath Day Point, Père Roubaud noticed derelict whaleboats on the beach and the mutilated, unburied bodies of the unfortunate New Jersey Blues killed one week before. The Indian fleet, manned by over eight hundred warriors, proceeded to an agreed rendezvous about half-way between their embarkation point and Lévis' intended camp.[69]

Despite a storm, Montcalm's main fleet took less than twelve hours to cover the distance that Lévis' detachment had struggled for three days to cover on foot. Thirty-one "pontoons," each composed of 2 bateaux fastened together under a platform carrying a carriage-mounted gun or mortar, were in the middle of some 247 bateaux bringing the final contingent of 3842 regulars, militia, and *troupes de la marine*, together with the provisions for the whole army and a field hospital. Leaving about two o'clock in the afternoon of August 1, the bateaux were met two hours later by the Indian fleet, which led the marine force that began landing at Lévis' signal fires shortly after midnight. Nearly eight thousand men had moved two-thirds of the way up Lake George without encountering any resistance. Despite orders against firing guns, lighting fires, or sounding hunting horns, the confident French did some of each.[70]

Lévis' men set out again on foot about noon on August 2, and the fleet followed at their pace. A bay suitable for anchoring the artillery pontoons had been noted within six miles of Fort Willian Henry, and Lévis established a well-positioned camp three miles closer, giving plenty of protection for landing the army, stores, and artillery. The Indian canoes kept close to the shoreline, but soon reached the last point of land hiding them from the view of those in the fort. The Indians camped there to await orders. After nightfall, two of the remaining English whaleboats were noticed scouting the lake surprisingly close to the camp. As the Indians prepared to attack them, a sheep bleated, warning the English scouts that the French army was near. The whaleboats fled, and numerous Indian canoes were launched across the lake in pursuit. The whaleboats reached the eastern shore, and the pursuers killed five and captured three of the thirteen scouts, while losing two of their own men. Before being killed by Nipissing tribesmen to avenge the companions who had died in the incident, these prisoners described to the French officers the state of the defenses at Fort William Henry.[71]

III

In the four months since Rigaud's raid, Fort William Henry had figured much less prominently in the military plans of the English than of the French. William Eyre's garrison had been relieved by five full companies of the Thirty-fifth, or Otway's regiment, supported by two ranger companies. The fort was commanded by the steady and experienced Lieutenant Colonel Monro. Although a veteran regiment, the Thirty-fifth had been full of new recruits when it arrived in North America the previous year, and Loudoun was doubtful of its worth. He did not miss them in his assault force for Louisbourg;[72] these regulars were intended to mislead Vaudreuil into holding a considerable French force at Fort Carillon.

Reports from Canada had been mixed that spring concerning an offensive from Fort Carillon. Peter Labarree, captured with Susannah Johnson and her family by the Abenaki in 1754, was one of four escaped captives who made their way into Fort William Henry late in May. Loudoun told Prime Minister William Pitt of Labarree's poignant story of his neighbors the Johnsons, captured in peacetime and still held after paying their ransom. Labarree and his companions, who left Montreal on May 7, reported that two regiments and three hundred Indians had gone to Fort St. Frédéric and Fort Carillon, and the talk was that "if we attacked Cape Breton, that would not prevent their Attacking our Forts, if we went to Quebeck, they must apply their whole Force to defend it."[73] As Loudoun prepared to leave New York for Louisbourg the following month, he learned that a ranger sergeant had escaped from Canada bringing news that the French were concentrating their troops at Quebec. Loudoun heard what he had hoped for and advised General Daniel Webb, commanding from Fort Edward, to establish an entrenched post at the north end of Lake

George and invest Fort Carillon.[74] What neither the escaped prisoners nor their listeners realized was that food shortages in Canada had delayed the campaign. Most of the French regulars had remained dispersed, and militia recruitment had been delayed until the last moment.

Nevertheless, Monro and his garrison, recently enlarged to over 1500 with the arrival of 113 regulars from two independent companies in New York, 551 from New Jersey, and 231 from New Hampshire, had some indications that a major force was advancing in the month before Montcalm arrived at Carillon. A French prisoner brought to Fort Edward by scouts on June 16 admitted that an army was to attack soon. At the end of the month, two more starving escaped prisoners from Canada staggered into Fort William Henry, talking of two others who were so famished they had surrendered at Fort St. Frédéric. These arrivals also reported that an eight-thousand-man army was coming against the English forts.[75] Two days later, four deserters from Fort Carillon, Germans who claimed they had been recruited for the Dutch but then sold to the French, reported that five battalions of regulars with cannon and mortars were expected to assemble soon to attack both Fort William Henry and Fort Edward.[76] However, during the first three weeks of July, six separate English scouting parties returned without taking a single prisoner or learning more than that "they have a large number of troops" at Fort Carillon.[77] It was the failure of these scouting parties to penetrate Carillon's screen of Indians that had prompted the sending of Colonel Parker's expedition down the lake to disaster.

The garrison that overflowed Fort William Henry was shaken by the news of the destruction of Parker's expedition on July 24. Members of the shattered New Jersey Blues welcomed the survivors, and tales of that defeat spread through the garrison. Adam Williamson, a young engineer with the Royal Artillery, recorded that two men came in from Fort Edward to tell of the thirteen men there who had been scalped the previous day by Marin's raiders. Williamson noted that some of these victims had been shot with arrows, and he was disappointed that a relief party had "pursued the Enemy but to little purpose only recovering two or three of the Scalps the Enemy had taken & some trifling things belonging to he Indians."[78] General Webb arrived to inspect Fort William Henry the next day, accompanied by engineer Major James Montrésor, Captain Thomas Ord of the Royal Artillery, and Lieutenant Colonel John Young of the Royal Americans.

The preparations of the next three days determined the defense thereafter. "A Sort of Council of War," which included colonial officers, decided three central questions. First, it was agreed that there were not sufficient boats to oppose the French on the lake. As a participant, Colonel Parker could provide plenty of evidence that Montcalm's Indian allies had command of the lake: Monro had only five whaleboats and two sloops left. Webb subsequently forwarded six more whaleboats, and twelve ship carpenters and their assistants worked frantically on several oared galliotts that were never finished. When asked the second question, how many men were required "to defend the Fort and oppose the Ennemy in case of a Descent," the officers reached the crucial issue. The fort itself had neither room nor work for more than five hundred men. The decision to use two thousand men allowed reinforcement and relief for the garrison, while establishing a fortified camp to control ground that otherwise favored the French. No attempt was to be made to oppose a French landing along the shoreline with trenches, breastworks, or *abattis*. The third question was posed to prompt an answer confirming the second. Asked to choose between constructing two camps, one on each side of the fort, or concentrating on a single camp to the east, the officers chose one camp near the scene of William Johnson's successful defense two years earlier. Troops were shifted to that site on July 28, and the frantic work of preparing a defensible breastwork began. They abandoned the existing camp on the high ground to the southwest, rightly judged inaccessible for the French cannons. At the fort itself, the roof of the magazine was protected by more sand, the east bastion raised by one log, an exterior storehouse demolished, and the dry ditch cleared. This general disposition showed the caution Webb became famous for, but it was also the result of the Indian raids. The cannon of Fort William Henry, with the heaviest guns positioned to cover the lake, were to be the first and last line of defense.[79]

Webb sent out rangers under Captain Israel Putnam to scout the lake in three whaleboats on July 28. Putnam encountered three canoes bearing white flags about halfway down the lake, feared a trap, and returned with a report of many enemy and boats on both shores of the lake. What he saw could not have been a major portion of the attacking army, but Webb was finally convinced that a major attack was imminent. Webb promptly hurried back to Fort Edward the next day, raising suspicions about his personal bravery. He called up the New York militia and sought other colonial reinforcements on July 30, the same day Lévis' advance force left the portage at the other end of the lake. Webb told Loudoun, writing on August 1, that he intended to move the rest of his army to contest a landing or engage in a pitched battle. The next day Webb sent a detachment to reinforce the garrison at Fort William Henry to a total of 2372 men. This additional contingent included some 812 men of Colonel Joseph Frye's Massachusetts regiment, 57 New York troops, and 122 Royal Americans, all under the command of Lieutenant Colonel Young. Included were six whaleboats and an artillery train consisting of six small brass cannon for the entrenchment.[80] Webb intended to send more help, as was indicated in a letter sent by his aide to Monro on August 3, claiming Webb "is determin'd to assist you as soon as possible with the whole army if requir'd" and ending with "sincere wishes for your safety till we can come to your assistance."[81] Webb wanted massive militia support for any advance against what he took to be an eleven-thousand-man army; camp gossip at Fort Edward as late as August 7 claimed, erroneously, that Monro had written that all were in good spirits and that Webb should not send help until "he Could Cume with a party strong a nought to Drive of[f] so great an army of frinch."[82] Montcalm's Indians had been so effective against English scouts that Webb's mobilization was to be very tardy.

Most of Lieutenant Colonel Young's detachment arrived at Fort William Henry too late on August 2 to set up camp properly. During the night the camp was alarmed by gunfire from the Indian attack on the two whaleboats scouting the lake. Two hours before dawn, five of the thirteen men of the boat crews came out of the woods, bringing news of death, capture, and the loss of two more whaleboats.[83] In the next hour the attacking fleet began working its way closer, in plain view and spread impressively across the lake, exchanging token out-of-range cannon fire with the fort cannon. The garrison fired the two huge 32-pounders, which was the agreed alarm signal to Fort Edward. In the first of three letters for help written to Webb that day, but not sent until nightfall, Monro noted that "we know that they have Cannon," an ironic indicator that weak previous intelligence had not been trusted even on this essential point.[84]

Lévis' detachment, now including all the Indians with the army but none of the grenadiers, meanwhile worked its way through the woods to encircle Fort William Henry and cut communication with Fort Edward. Lieutenant Colonel Monro, who commanded in the English entrenched camp, sent a hundred Massachusetts troops to contest control of the road, but they were soon driven back with heavy losses.[85] Although the defenders had stockaded the 150 head of oxen and 50 horses that had hauled in the cannon, boats, and supplies the night before with Young's contingent, the animals were captured by the Indians of Lévis' advance guard. Besides providing some fresh meat for the undersupplied attackers and occasioning a gesture by the Indians to repay Montcalm for twenty-five draft animals they had butchered earlier when Montcalm had needed them, this coup also added significantly to the transport crisis at Fort Edward over the next few days.[86]

Montcalm decided the general shape of the attack when he visited Lévis' advance guard, which afforded a good view of the thoroughly protected fort and camp. The fort mounted eighteen cannon, including a dozen that fired shot ranging from nine to thirty-two pounds. Only four smaller cannon were of brass, which was less likely than iron to disintegrate with continuous firing, but the iron ordnance also included thirteen smaller swivel-guns, two high-trajectory mortars, and a howitzer that fired exploding shells. The camp, where two years earlier Johnson's men had conducted an effective defense on even shorter notice, now had a breastwork of logs and stones to protect nearly two thousand men who were firing ball and grapeshot from six brass guns, four iron swivels, and plenty of small arms, in addition to the protective fire of the fort's cannon.[87] Montcalm had no trouble deciding against an immediate assault or against a siege from the elevated but unsuppliable position of his advance guard.

The siege was to be a conventional European cannon duel, for which trenches were begun about seven hundred yards from the fort on the west side, shielded by wooden gabions filled with dirt, and fascines of bundled wood embedded in dirt from the trenching. The large cannon in Fort William Henry were directed toward disrupting construction of the battery and trenches, and the cannon of the fort's east curtain and bastions were helping to counter persistent Indian small-arms fire on the camp. Seven Indians were reported killed or wounded in the first day's action, and the English camp suffered about thirty casualties.[88]

Montcalm's call to surrender, sent in under a flag of truce later in the day, was a mix of conventional military courtesy, warning, and threat. Montcalm correctly announced that he had superior forces and cannon, but neither had been seen in use as yet and Monro could not be sure of the claims. Montcalm emphasized that "I have it yet in my power to restrain the savages, and oblige them to observe a capitulation, as hitherto none of them has been killed, which will not be in my power in other circumstances." This offer showed his lack of awareness of Indian losses already sustained, and later became a helpful document for Montcalm, but it may also have represented an exaggerated belief in his own power over his Indian allies. Adam Williamson might have recalled that the message echoed one sent to the commander of the same fort less than five months earlier, before a siege which proved unsuccessful. Monro courteously dismissed the invitation, since he knew that a fortified garrison was expected to be able to hold off an attack by three times its number for a few days until reinforcements arrived. He reported the day's proceedings to Colonel Webb calmly, understating the losses of the first day, but concluding, "I make no doubt that you will soon send us a Reinforcement."[89]

The main French camp had been established on the west side of the lake, just beyond the range of the cannon of Fort William Henry (Figure 8). Early on Thursday, August 4, Montcalm decided on the deployment required to answer those cannon, and he put Bourlamaque in charge of the details of the siege. The fort's northwest bastion was to be the prime target of the first two batteries. Staying about two thousand feet from this target, the French built a road and an initial trench reaching nearly one-third of a mile from the artillery landing place across the line of fire. This would allow the first French cannon to be landed and hauled to a battery to be built just within range of the fort. A second battery was to be built nine hundred feet farther along that parallel, to provide cross-fire on the same target. Clearing trees and digging sandy trenches while under cannon fire from the fort were the assignments for shifts of Canadian militiamen who dug throughout the entire siege.

The defenders in the fort could see the attackers at work, but lacked the men to oppose them with anything other than cannon and mortar fire. This slowed the French a little, but also caused the English concern when the first of their mortars exploded in the northwest bastion. Although there were no serious injuries and the mortar was promptly replaced by the only howitzer in the fort, this and the split muzzle of one of the 18-pounders were indicators of problems to come. Iron artillery suffered metal fatigue and was weakened as it heated, necessitating smaller charges of powder. To avoid explosion, it was recommended that iron cannon be allowed to cool after every twelve firings. Tearing the flammable roofs off the barracks, undertaken two days before any French cannon was fired, was also depressing.[90]

The most severe fighting of this second day of the siege was around the entrenched English camp. Indian marksmen harassed those in the encampment constantly, despite some effective mortar fire from the

FIGURE 8
Map of the siege of Fort William Henry, August 1757.
From Ann Rocque's *A Set of Plans and Forts in America* (London, 1765).
(Photo courtesy of Metropolitan Toronto Library Board, Toronto, Canada)

fort and numerous sorties to force them back and protect the water supply. Monro did not hear from Webb, whose discouraging reply was captured and held by Montcalm, but that night Monro again wrote to his commander at Fort Edward. He complained of the Indian small-arms fire, noted that the French regulars had stayed out of range and were still preparing batteries, and assured Webb that he "would there-fore be Glad (if it meets Your Approbation) the whole Army was Marched."[91] Webb did not receive this letter; instead, his latest infor-mation came from a Canadian militiaman taken prisoner between the forts. The prisoner's claim that there were eleven thousand men in

Montcalm's army was accepted by Webb, meaning that he would need a comparable relief expedition, which he did not have.[92]

That night was relatively quiet, since the fort's cannon were not fired. The men with Monro in the camp kept fires burning all around the perimeter, and there were no attacks. Near the French camp, the entrenching crew worked throughout the night while others landed the first of the artillery. On August 5, the third day of the siege, the fighting seemed much like that of the previous day for the English. The fort's gunners continued to bombard the new French trenches, driving back the La Sarre and Royal Roussillon regiments, which were protecting the trenches from a possible sortie. In this cannonading, both of the fort's 32-pounders burst and the last of the 18-pounders exploded, wounding several men. Those in the camp were able to replenish provisions and stores from the fort, but felt themselves under constant attack from the Indians.[93]

Meanwhile, the mood was changing in the French camp and among its Indian allies. The Caughnawaga warrior Kanectagon, who had set out to take a prisoner two days earlier, returned triumphant on August 5.[94] General Webb had sent a party of three rangers with his message for Monro, and Kanectagon had killed one, captured the second, and scared off the third. The jacket lining of the dead ranger yielded Webb's discouraging letter, dated noon of August 4 (Figure 9). In this famous note, Webb conveyed inaccurate intelligence on the size of the invasion force and urged Monro to consider terms. To exploit this unexpected psychological advantage promptly, Montcalm doubled the manpower preparing the batteries and trenches that night.

The Indians were becoming impatient with orders and saw themselves as having led in three days of fighting while waiting for Montcalm's cannon to fire. Many had left their positions to visit the French camp. Some adapted trenching to their own purposes much nearer the English camp, and others stalked the enemy from its own garden.[95]

One adaptation in Indian behavior toward prisoners deserves particular notice. Père Roubaud, who was scurrying through the woods south of the fort vainly seeking his Abenaki faithful, came upon a captured Mohican who was tied to a tree. Probably a Stockbridge Indian serving in a ranger company, this short and corpulent prisoner, whom Roubaud thought ugly and deformed, was the victim of vicious beatings by passers-by. After seeing one of the prisoner's eyes nearly torn out of its socket by a blow to the head, Roubaud chased off the spectators "with a tone of authority" that surprised himself.[96] That the Mohican was tied to a tree by a captor who was not protecting his own

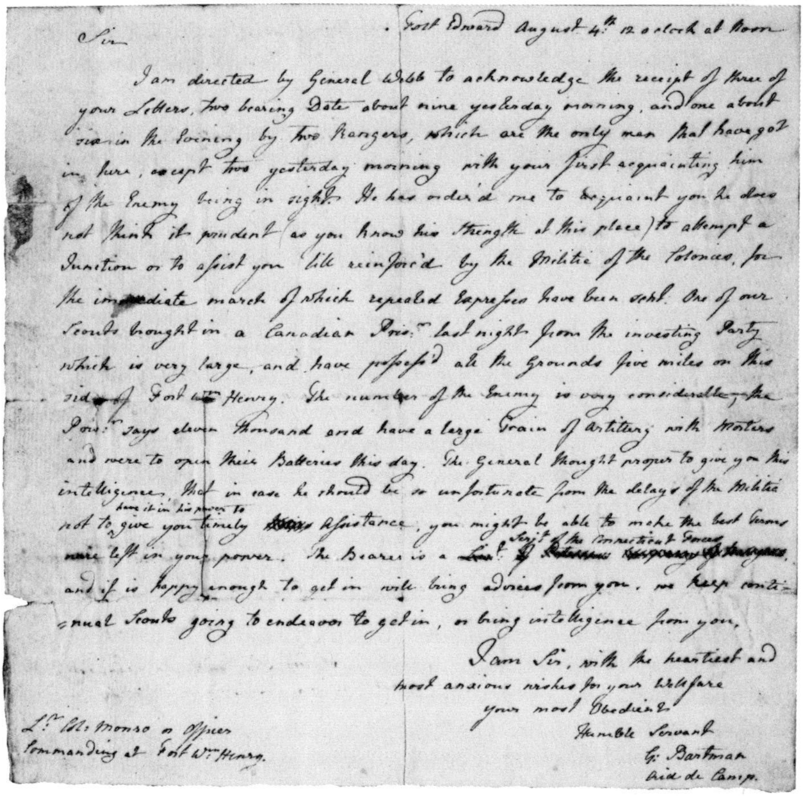

Fort Edward August 4th 12 o clock at Noon

Sir

I am directed by General Webb to acknowledge the receipt of three of your Letters, two bearing Date about nine yesterday morning, and one about six in the Evening by two Rangers, which are the only men that have got in here, except two yesterday morning with your first acquainting him of the Enemy being in sight. He has order'd me to acquaint you he does not think it prudent (as you know his strength at this place) to attempt a Junction or to assist you till reinforc'd by the Militia of the Colonies, for the immediate march of which repeated Expresses have been sent. One of our Scouts brought in a Canadian Prisr. last night from the investing Party which is very large, and have possess'd all the Grounds five miles on this side of Fort Wm. Henry. The number of the Enemy is very considerable, the Prisr. says eleven Thousand and have a large Train of Artillery with Mortars and were to open their Batteries this day. The General thought proper to give you this intelligence, that in case he should be so unfortunate from the delays of the Militia not to have it in his power to give you timely assistance, you might be able to make the best Terms were left in your power. The Bearer is a Serjt. of the Connecticut Forces and if is happy enough to get in will bring advices from you. We keep continual Scouts going to endeavor to get in, or bring intelligence from you,

I am Sir, with the heartiest and most anxious wishes for your Welfare your most Obedient Humble Servant

G. Bartman
Aid de Camp.

Lt. Col. Monro or Officer Commanding at Fort Wm. Henry.

FIGURE 9
Bloodstained intercepted letter from General Webb's aide-de-camp to Colonel Monro, August 4, 1757.
(Courtesy of The Huntington Library, San Marino, California)

prisoner is suggestive. Although the captor wanted more from this engagement than this single prisoner, he chose not to kill and scalp him. Others insulted and hit the prisoner, but did not kill and scalp him either. The suffering Mohican, with the strange Jesuit unwittingly standing guard over him for an unknown captor, was proof that some Indian allies were accepting Montcalm's argument about staying with the campaign until its end. The scene also demonstrated that, in this large intertribal army, it was difficult to protect prisoners destined for later adoption, torture, or sale.

Montcalm called a general council of the Indians to complain about their failure to stay at their posts and do systematic scouting. He objected to what he regarded as the foolishness of warriors exposing themselves unnecessarily, which had resulted in fifteen deaths.[97] Montcalm offered belts and strings of wampum "to get them back again on the right path, to wipe out the past and to brighten the future with the light of good fortune." Then Montcalm explained the contents of Webb's letter and how he intended to use it. Although pleased with the gifts and the news, the Amerindians also voiced their grievances with the conduct of the siege. The chiefs were not being informed of measures taken. Indian advice was not acted upon, without any explanation of why it was being ignored. They were not consulted on scouting arrangements, but "as though they were slaves, it was attempted to make them march without having consulted with their chiefs and agreed with them." Montcalm promised to do better, and the meeting ended amicably with the announcement that the cannon would begin firing the next day.[98]

The fort announced the beginning of August 6 with two howitzer shells and a single heavy shot at 6:00 A.M., and it was answered by nine cannon and a mortar in the first battery of Montcalm's artillery. French artillerymen found the range quickly, and the French cheered when the flag in the fort was shot down. The symbolism immediately became deadly when a carpenter, attempting to repair the flagstaff, had his head shot entirely away by a subsequent shot. The French mortar trained on the camp caused several severe injuries in addition to disabling one brass gun. Defenders noticed that some of the arriving shot had British royal markings, having come to Canada by way of Oswego or the Monongahela, as had some of the cannon. A message from Webb arrived rather miraculously that afternoon, transmitted verbally by two rangers who could not satisfy Monro as to its full meaning. It included something about William Johnson and some Indians. When Monro wrote Webb later in the day, he pleaded for more artillery. Four cannon had burst during the preceding day, and the camp had been forced to send two of its remaining 12-pounders into the fort.[99]

After another night of hard digging to repair damage done by fire from the fort and to complete the platform for the left battery, Montcalm's artillerymen began August 7 with a three-hour bombardment using a total of seventeen cannon, two mortar, and two howitzers. The fort was now clearly outgunned. According to Adam Williamson, the young engineer inside the fort, "most of the shells fell in the Fort," and other defenders remembered "many instances of their bursting among his [Monro's] men, and, being filled with deadly missiles, caused a great destruction of life."[100] Others noted that some of the French cannon had a remarkable range of thirteen hundred yards, bringing the encampment under direct fire. Apparently the fort itself was standing up well, and the attackers were focusing their artillery on the garrison inside.[101]

After three hours of brisk firing, Montcalm called a halt in order to exploit his psychological advantage. Bougainville was sent forward with a flag of truce that was red, since the French flag had a white ground, and an escort of fifteen grenadiers. The English ordered him to halt at the glacis, where he was blindfolded and led into the fort by Adam Williamson. "It was no Summons only a complimentary letter to the Commandant informing him of their having taken an express from General Webb." Webb's despairing three-day-old letter had been with Montcalm for two days, but was the latest and most specific news available to Monro and confirmed the obvious fact that no relief had arrived. At this time, Monro could not know that his letter of the previous morning had managed to reach Fort Edward and had been answered by a letter claiming that Webb was coming with five thousand men and an artillery train. (This letter apparently took three very long days to deliver, arriving late on August 9, without falling into French hands).[102] During the truce, the French continued to work on a major approach trench, engineers reconnoitered the ground to the southwest of the fort, and, while "the Enemy made a Shew of all their Indians, about 1200," Canadians and other Indians with de Villiers entrenched a position behind a small grassy knoll near the English encampment. Bougainville, who remained blindfolded throughout his visit to the fort and the encampment, was returned safely to his escort, and the recess was over.[103]

The truce had no overwhelming effect on the defenders, though it must have suggested that Montcalm was firmly in charge of his army. The Indians had made English desertion all but impossible throughout the siege. The truce may have allowed a couple of regulars to plan their desertion, but it was not encouraging to other potential deserters when these two were each wounded several times as they headed for the French camp that night.[104] Montcalm learned more about the disintegration of the fort's artillery from these men, but he suspected they were spies.[105] While most of the English journals exude bravery and defiance, one does suggest growing anxiety: "Colo. Monro published his orders to all in the Fort that if any person proved cowardly or offered to advise giving up the Fort that he should be immediately hanged over the walls of the Fort."[106]

The French bombardment was incessant for the rest of the day, with the exploding howitzer shells causing the most havoc, both in the fort and in the camp. The commander of the fort garrison, Captain John Ormsby of the Thirty-fifth, was among the severely wounded. An artilleryman reported that a ten-inch howitzer shell hit the ammunition box on one of the bastions, and the explosion killed or wounded sixteen, "one of wch was a Provential Officer that never was heard of, but part of his coat was found."[107] Metal fatigue continued to disarm the fort's iron artillery, as two more cannon burst.

The fiercest fighting was for the grassy knoll that had been captured by the de Villiers patrol during the truce. Eighty Massachusetts troops established themselves among some logs and were reinforced by two hundred provincials and regulars in what proved a vain attempt to drive the attackers back. Perhaps as many as fifty English defenders died before the venture was abandoned, and the Canadians and Indians had twenty-one casualties "in this useless affair."[108]

After that day, and after a night of continuing bombardment and fixed-bayonet alarms among his troops in the expectation of an assault, Monro wrote to Webb complaining that his letter of August 4 had aided the enemy. He also disputed Webb's exaggeration of the French forces, which "every one here is of opinion was greatly Magnified; if they really had those Numbers, they might have demolished us at once, without Loss of time." Even Monro's tenacity was showing its limits. The letter began "The Fort & Camp still hold out, in hopes of a speedy Relief from you, Which we hourly Expect, and if that does not happen, we must fall into the hands of our Enemies."[109]

Daybreak of August 8 revealed another night of astonishing progress of the French and Canadians, who had dug an approach trench some 250 yards down a hill and bridged a swamp to the foot of the fort's garden. Despite heavy English cannon and musket fire, this work continued throughout the day under cover of parapets and wooden canopies. They made this bridge passable for artillery and began a battery for nine more cannon. Despite the heaviest night of firing from the fort, aimed directly at these new works, the digging continued.[110]

Lévis' scouts alarmed the French camp by reporting a relief column approaching from Fort Edward late that afternoon. Lévis concentrated his Canadians and Indians on the road, and Montcalm hurried to reinforce Lévis with the La Reine battalion and the grenadier companies of the three other regular regiments. The activity caused a stir among the English, too. Monro readied the men in the camp for action, though none of them knew whether it was the beginning of a final assault by the French or preparation to break out in support of the relief force they desperately wanted to see.[111]

The report proved false; no relief force had left Fort Edward after all.[112] Monro's letters throughout the siege emphasized that help was expected, and Webb's as yet undelivered letter of August 6 claimed that he was preparing to move forward with the nearly five thousand men under his command. But Webb knew that neither the construction of Fort William Henry nor its regulars had been highly valued by Lord Loudoun. At this point, Webb believed that the defenders faced some eleven thousand men, who could be positioned between his relief force and the fort. To expect to relieve the garrison at Fort William Henry with five thousand men, most of whom were newly raised militia, would have been very optimistic. To march an army of regulars and American militia (with only 150 Indian supporters) hauling a field train up a sixteen-mile road controlled by innumerable enemy Indians would have been daring, if not suicidal. To risk such a defeat and to sacrifice the defense of Albany and the rest of the northern frontier rather than attempt to hold the French with a reinforced Fort Edward, would have been foolhardy.[113] Webb could be accused of many things, but not of being optimistic, daring, or foolhardy.

As Monro's hopes for reinforcement faded on the evening of August 8, Webb wrote his last letter to the embattled commander, a letter that was intercepted and never reached Fort William Henry. Webb had just finished a day of detailed planning of emergency defensive works for Fort Edward, done with the aid of the newly arrived popular commander of the Royal American battalion, George Augustus, Viscount Howe.[114] In his letter to Monro, Webb complained of the slowness of the militia he had called for (only a week earlier), but said that the expected arrival of one thousand of them the next day would let him proceed to Monro's assistance. Perhaps Howe's arrival had encouraged him, for Webb now seemed ready to risk the expedition. "We wish most heartily that you may be able to hold out a little longer." On receiving this letter, Monro was to have sent back several couriers with estimates of "what you judge the Enemy's numbers to be, and how long you think you could hold out against the present Cannonading."[115]

That evening, when Monro had no reason to hope for such a letter, he sent an engineer, probably Adam Williamson, to examine the state of the fort. The fort itself was intact, though both the northeast and northwest bastions had lost the top three feet of timbers and the casements had been somewhat damaged by exploding shells.[116] The English artillery, ammunition, and other stores were nearly exhausted, "besides, the men had been without rest five nights, and were almost Stupified."[117] The fort, designed by Captain William Eyre, had withstood three days of cannonading, exceeding the expectations of both the American doubters and the British military skeptics. The garrison of fort and camp had behaved better than Loudoun, Webb, or even Monro could have expected. Yet it was increasingly clear that the struggle was soon to end, one way or another. Monro called a council of war for the next morning.

5

"MASSACRE"

Before dawn on August 9, the senior officers defending Fort William Henry met with their commander, as agreed the night before, to discuss capitulation. During the night, the French had completed their third battery, at the foot of the garden, so that eighteen-pound cannon were ranged parallel to and within 150 yards of the fort's weak west wall. This was close enough to make both fort and entrenched camp untenable. Duty officers from the fort reported that another of their mortars had exploded earlier in the morning, killing or wounding a total of thirteen men. The intensifying French bombardment could not be answered by the remaining five small cannon, one mortar, and single howitzer, all running out of ammunition. Reviewing this evidence, the engineer's report, and the last discouraging letter received from General Webb, the British and colonial officers were unanimous in advising Monro to negotiate honorable terms of surrender.[1]

A flag of parley raised over the fort brought silence to the cannon soon after 6:00 A.M., and Captain Rudolphus Faesch, a Swiss officer in the Royal Americans who had served in the French army, was sent out with a small guard drawn from his own company.[2] Faesch's wounded lieutenant colonel, John Young, followed on horseback to the French camp to negotiate. Montcalm, who had refused the honors of war to the Oswego garrison because of its lame defense, answered that the defenders would be given the same favorable terms as those given the British defenders of Minorca in 1756.[3] This was the first and last time the French offered an English garrison a parole of honor in North America.[4]

At a time when military honor was a cultivated art form, the terms of this surrender were most generous. Bougainville later confided in his journal, and in Montcalm's, that the garrison could easily have been taken as "prisoners at discretion," as had been done at Fort Oswego the previous year. The prospect of feeding two thousand additional men was one deterrent; the other was the humanitarian consideration (or was it a subsequent deception to defend Montcalm's reputation?): "one could not have restrained the barbarity of the Indians, and it is never permitted to sacrifice humanity to what is only the shadow of glory."[5] Consequently, the whole garrison was to march to Fort Edward the next morning, with drums beating, with colors flying, and with soldiers and officers retaining their arms and baggage. As a special mark of recognition for its "brave and honorable defense,"[2][6] the garrison could take one cannon in the procession, which was to be escorted by a detachment of French regulars and some of the officers and interpreters who fought with the Indians. In return, the defeated agreed not to bear arms against the French or their allies for eighteen months. It was also agreed that all French "officers, soldiers, Canadians, women, and Indians" taken prisoner in North America were to be returned to Fort Carillon within three months. The sick and wounded English who could not be transported to Fort Edward were to be in the care of Montcalm, and to be returned when well. Nothing more was demanded, except an officer as a hostage for the safe return of the French escort taking the column down the sixteen-mile road to Fort Edward.[7]

Ultimately, terms derived from the latest European etiquette of war were only as meaningful as they were to an Ottawa or Potawatomi warrior. Indians were around the fort during the negotiations, calmly walking off with the few remaining horses they found there.[8] Lieutenant Colonel Young conveyed the worry to Montcalm before the final signing. Montcalm was concerned as well, remembering the scandal of the murder of wounded prisoners after his conquest of Oswego the previous summer and recalling his own warning penned to Monro six days earlier, advising surrender before the Indians lost men and thereby became more difficult to contain than their diversity made inevitable. Montcalm decided to hold a general council of chiefs before signing the terms, even though this course admitted that the

Indians were allies and not completely under his command.[9] Accompanied by Young, Montcalm endeavored to explain the terms to those chiefs who assembled. He could not know how accurately, how completely, or with what editorial comments these terms were being translated for some sixteen hundred Indians of thirty-three tribes by eight interpreters, four missionaries, and a dozen Canadian irregulars who were listed as "Officers attached to the Indians" in the formal roster of the attacking army.[10]

The assembled chiefs did not object to the terms and agreed to restrain their young warriors, but politeness may have been read as acquiescence. Even if these Indians discounted their own earlier rhetoric about eating and drinking enemies, they still claimed the right to pillage the fort and the entrenched camp after the English had left. Stores of war and provisions were, however, to be the property of the Canadian government, and the personal effects of the English officers and men were to be respected. The Indians were free to take what they thought fell between those categories.[11]

At noon, a French detachment arrived at the gate of the fort, where a brief ceremony of transfer was held, and the 450 English duty soldiers marched off to their entrenched camp. At this point, a number of Indians ran in through the gate and gun embrasures in search of their promised booty. Members of the retreating garrison heard cries of "Murder" and "Help" from within the fort, where thirty sick and forty severely wounded had remained behind, some in the comparatively well-protected but isolated casements under the ramparts.[12] Père Roubaud, who did not explain how a missionary came to be inside the fort so quickly, reported that a few of these unfortunate English were attacked and killed. Although other Indians scoured the fort without much success, Roubaud saw one warrior who "carried in his hand a human head, from which trickled streams of blood, and which he displayed as the most splendid prize that he could have secured."[13] Roubaud, writing later, presented this as a foretaste of barbarities to come. Some of the seriously wounded, including Captain Ormsby, were saved, probably by the forceful intervention of the entering French garrison. Indians watched with suspicion and derision as the English soldiers carried their belongings and as wagons hauled the officers' baggage.[14] The French had some difficulty protecting the military stores and provisions from the Indians.[15] There were complaints that the French took the best for themselves and that the Indians had been deceived by the surrender terms. One English officer heard an Indian chief "violently accuse the French general with being false and a liar to them, that he had promised them the plunder of the English, and they would have it."[16] Anger would be intensified by the envy directed at those few warriors who had a trophy to prove they had been active in a great battle. The English, now gathered in the adjoining camp they had defended so well, gained no clear picture of what had happened in the fort, but could imagine.

Some Indians had already been inside the English entrenched camp before the capitulation was signed, and it is unlikely that they had been at Montcalm's council of chiefs or had heard the terms explained by them. At noon, Montcalm had posted a guard of two hundred French regulars inside the camp.[17] Monro ordered the destruction of all liquor in the camp, but reports vary on how thoroughly and by what methods the liquor disappeared. That afternoon, English officers entertained their French counterparts with an impressive spread of delicacies, served with wine and beer.[18] Indians were inside the camp throughout the afternoon, acquiring what they could and being considered troublesome and dishonorable thieves by both the English and the French. There was persistent difficulty about the English officers' baggage. European officers carried what any warrior would have regarded as an enormous amount of personal baggage. Some American officers, judging from their claimed losses, patronized the Albany clothiers in order to assert their status with multiple uniforms of velvets and silks in scarlet, blue, or green, topped with lace-trimmed beaver hats.[19] Even warriors who exactly understood the terms of the surrender could presume that much legitimate booty was being unfairly protected as personal belongings. Some English officers offered money to Indians to leave their belongings alone. Other confrontations turned nasty, and Montcalm was called to settle matters. He used "entreaties, threats, flattery, conferences with chiefs, the intervention of officers and interpreters who have any authority with these barbarians."[20] He left for his own camp about nine o'clock that night, after the Indians had been cleared from the camp. It was announced that the parolees would leave the camp at first light,[21] but this display of French confidence masked well-founded fears.

Near midnight, an escort of two hundred French regulars picked from the La Reine and Languedoc regiments assembled quietly at the entrance to the camp. Monro, with Montcalm's prior approval, had ordered the march to Fort Edward that night in the hope that trouble with the Indians could be averted. In addition to his twenty-three hundred men pledged not to fight Frenchmen or their allies, including Indians, Monro was overseeing dozens of women, children, and other camp followers whose position had not been specified in the capitulation. It was one thing to trust French honor, but it was quite another to assume that all the Indians were aware of the terms, would not take them literally, and would not despise them, as their *coureurs de bois* translators may have encouraged them to do. Even without Indian anger, vengefulness, or inebriation, what could these soon-to-leave parolees expect from warriors who had spent weeks canoeing a thousand miles to fight for the martial trophies that were their only pay, were passports to manhood for some, and assurances of higher esteem for others.[22]

The grenadiers led three companies of Monro's own Thirty-fifth Regiment out of the entrenchment, followed by the other three companies of the same regiment. The marching orders were suddenly countermanded because the Indians had noticed the preparations. A British artillery officer explained, "The Marquis de Montcalm signifieing that the Savages not satisfied with the Plunder they had got in the Morning, intended to attack us on our March, and that it was more advisable we should remain until the Morning, when we should have an Escort of Four Hundred and Fifty Men."[23] A late-night discussion among senior French officers, Canadian officers, and interpreters had heard that two-thirds of the Indians were not in their camps. It had been decided that the morning departure was better, that those with influence with the Indians would attempt to have them withdraw, that Canadian officers respected by the Indians would stay in the entrenchment until the departure, and that chiefs of each nation would accompany the column in the morning.[24]

The attempt to leave at midnight only added to the anger of the Indians. They could not fathom French behavior in wasting their victory and protecting their enemies from their allies. They resented the European conspiracy, which had defrauded them of their agreed share of the loot in the fort and now, apparently, plotted to trick them out of the timely search for spoils of war within the entrenchment as well. At the end of a very long day, Colonel Joseph Frye of the Massachusetts regiment noted, "All the Remainder of this night the Indians were in great numbers round our lines and seemed to shew more than usual malice in their looks which made us suspect they intended us mischief."[25]

The long day for the English became an even longer night. They did not unpack the belongings they had gathered for the midnight departure and spent their sixth consecutive night with little sleep, this time without cover and presumably without liquor.[26] Fears based on events and reports of the previous day were multiplied for many by the tales remembered from calmer campfires, or terrors that had been read in those captivity narratives popular in the British colonies. If many had previously believed that the Indians did not attack at night, as some senior officers did, the continuous Indian activity around the camp was disturbing. In his effort to curb the Indians, Montcalm had assigned all those known to have any influence with the Indians to spend the night in the camp to prevent trouble.[27] Some of these men were known by sight to some of the parolees.[28] If the rumored identifications were as frightening as the truth, the terror must have been palpable. Here, for the protection of the English, were men like Joseph Marin de la Malgue, who had twice led raids on Saratoga, had distinguished himself at Oswego, and had destroyed one detachment outside Fort William Henry in August 1756, and another outside Fort Edward only weeks ago.[29] For British regulars like Captain James Furnis and engineer Adam Williamson, who had survived the defeat of General Braddock, it would have been small comfort to know that they were being protected now by Jean Daniel Dumas, the official victor over Braddock, and Charles-Michel Mouet de Langlade, who not only was prominent there, but also had allowed gross violations of surrender terms at Pickawillany in 1752 and had been active in the defeats of both Rogers and Parker earlier in 1757.[30] Officers among the parolees were warned that the Indians would have to be gratified from the baggage, and "if any resistance was made by which a single Indian should be killed, it would not be in the power of Mr. De Montcalm to save a man from butchery."[31] Fear was an easy victor over exhaustion.

As the eastern sky lightened to end that tense night, the English assembled by unit for the march, anxious to be gone, yet apprehensive. The Indians, who had stayed out of the English camp during the night by agreement reinforced by orders to the French pickets, were returning over the breastworks. Colonel Frye found them "in a worse temper (if possible) than last night, every one having a tomahawk, hatchet, or some instrument of death."[32] After gaining few trophies at the surrender of the fort, and nearly being tricked out of everything portable by the attempted midnight departure, the few dozen Indians who came in first were more than "curious."[33] Initially, demands again focused on the officers' baggage. The small French escort arrived outside the entrenchment and flanked the western exit, which sloped down to meet the road to Fort Edward. The Royal Artillery and the Thirty-fifth Regiment, leading the developing column, began to leave.[34] Colonel

Monro complained to the French officers about Indian harassment, particularly of Lieutenant Colonel Young's belongings in the nearby company of Royal Americans, and sent his complaint to Montcalm. French officers with the escort advised the English to give up their packs, which was ordered.[35]

As the British regulars began to move, increasing numbers of Indians became more insistent. In poignant conformity with the restrictions concerning loot, several Indians took away the horses that had been granted to pull the solitary brass cannon that symbolized the bravery of the British and the martial civility of the French. Captain Furnis of the Royal Artillery was with the regulars at the front of the intended column and reported that he and those near him gave up their packs. Indians not only were taking packs, but also began stripping officers and men of their clothing, swords, muskets, as well as drums, halberds, and fifes. The chance of conveying orders was fading amid the growing din, even if the terrified men had been able to obey. The regulars managed to assemble their line of march on the road outside the entrenchment. Those who still had their weapons were now ordered to carry them "clubbed." This demeaning gesture in European military etiquette was to avoid provoking the Indians by displaying bayonets, or provoking the French with any breach of parole.[36] These regulars appear to have been flanked by most of the small French escort and would fare comparatively well in the ensuing violence.

Inside the encampment, the provincial troops suffered more. Miles Whitworth, a surgeon in Colonel Frye's Massachusetts militia regiment, later testified that he had remained with seventeen wounded men from his regiment, even after turning them over to the French surgeon the previous afternoon. The men were unable to join the march on the morning of August 10. The special night guard that the French had placed over the huts of the wounded was withdrawn without replacement as the English began to leave about 5:00 A.M. Indians entering the camp dragged the seventeen wounded out of their huts and immediately killed and scalped them in plain view of the horrified surgeon and soldiers of the colonial regiments. Whitworth testified that several Canadian officers, among whom he recognized St. Luc de la Corne, and French pickets posted nearby did nothing to help the wounded.[37]

Meanwhile, other warriors were dragging Indians from the ranks of the American rangers and provincial regiments and forcing them over the breastworks. The English eyewitnesses, having seen what happened to the sick and wounded, presumed inaccurately that all these

Indians would also be scalped or tortured in accordance with a military tradition that did not include immunity in return for promises not to fight for eighteen months.[38] Blacks and mulattos among the English soldiers and camp followers were also hauled away. They, too, were treated better than the witnesses presumed.[39] Both Indians and Europeans believed that blacks were property, and Montcalm's Indian allies therefore regarded them as loot.[40] Although the Massachusetts regiment did not have women with it, witnesses from that group described violence against regular soldiers' wives and camp followers who were to be in the rear of the column.[41] All these initial targets, the Indians, the blacks, the soldiers' families, and the wounded, suggest that someone conveyed the exact terms of the surrender to at least some of the Indian allies of the French, but did not, or could not, convey its spirit. As at Oswego, the wounded were Montcalm's personal charge, and their murder was read as his personal disgrace by one culture and as a minor matter by another. The initial burst of violence struck terror and produced clothes, watches, money, and arms, some of which were soon conveyed to the nearby Indian camp along with some of the first captives.[42]

The Indian camp had been superbly placed for the siege, and this also proved true for the subsequent slaughter. Chevalier Lévis had severed communications between Fort Edward and Fort William Henry by establishing de la Corne's camp of some fifteen hundred Indians and Canadians squarely across the road to Fort Edward. The camp was a chain of tribal campfires, some within five hundred yards of the gate of the entrenched camp, out of which the terrified provincials now attempted to leave in some semblance of order. Some of those Indians who had taken black or Indian prisoners out of the entrenchment, as well as others leaving with scalps, packs, guns, or kettles, ran back to their camp to display their prizes and announce to the others that the time for plunder had come. The trophies prompted many more fellow-warriors to hurry to the entrenched camp.[43]

The provincial regiments now struggled to leave the entrenchment. What the Massachusetts colonel described as "at last with great difficulty, the troops got from the retrenchment,"[44] Jonathan Carver, of the same regiment, remembered as being stripped of coat, waistcoat, hat, buckles, and money by three or four Indians who threatened him with their tomahawks. Carver was then near the exit of the entrenched camp and begged the protection of one of the French pickets there. Assigned to stand guard, the sentinel could not have protected Carver and hundreds of others, even if he had wished to; "he only called me an

English dog, and thrust me with violence back again into the midst of the Indians." As Carver struggled to rejoin his company, he was harassed by other Indians who jabbed him with spears.[45]

Most of the English were out of the entrenchment when they were struck by the most ferocious of the attacks. Hundreds of warriors, on learning that scalps and prisoners had been taken in the entrenchment, emerged from their camps to look for their share. Someone began the dreaded war whoop that was an intertribal signal of attack.[46] Warriors clambered over the deserted breastworks to join Indians already inside. Missionary Roubaud, who arrived minutes later, said of English stragglers still in their camp: "Woe to all those who brought up the rear, or to stragglers whom indisposition or any other cause separated however little from the troop. They were so many dead whose bodies very soon strewed the ground and covered the inclosure of the intrenchments."[47]

Having dispatched those left behind, the warriors raced out of the entrenchment in pursuit of those gathered outside. Camp followers and the New Hampshire militia were hit first, since they were at the rear, but soon there were Indians around the whole English contingent. Families of the regulars, who had been in the garrison for months, were among the first to be attacked by warriors who were after the more prized soldiers beyond them.

The Massachusetts regiment, positioned near the rear of the column, provides our only witnesses of the actual slaughter. The colonel, reporting to his House of Representatives, remembered that no sooner were the troops out of the entrenchment "than the savages fell upon the rear, killing and scalping."[48] Ensign John Maylem remembered the "hell whoop" followed by death everywhere for men, women, and children. Maylem wrote his account as a long poem dated seven months later. He mentioned "The harmless Babe (torn from its Mother's Arms and dash'd, impetuous, on the Wave-worn Cliff!)," already a common feature of New England captivity narratives for nearly a century.[49] Another Massachusetts officer claimed that as the English were leaving the entrenchment, French soldiers taunted them with what the Indians were going to do to them, and the column became disorderly. At that, "the Indians pursued tearing the Children from their Mothers Bosoms and their mothers from their Husbands, then Singling out the men and Carrying them in the woods and killing a great many whom we say lying on the road side."[50] Jonathan Carver, a volunteer in the same regiment, remembered that, after the war whoop, the Indians began killing indiscriminately. Lamenting the impossibility of describing the "horrid scene," Carver wrote that "men, women, and children were dispatched in the most wanton and cruel manner, and immediately scalped. Many of these savages drank the blood of their victims, as it flowed warm from the fatal wound."[51]

Apparently Père Roubaud arrived during the slaughter, which he said was begun by a few Indians in the entrenchment. He mentioned no war whoop, but said the first killings were "the signal which made nearly all of them so many ferocious beasts. They struck, right and left, heavy blows of the hatchet on those who fell into their hands." But the carnage ended more quickly than its fury indicated, after "hardly more than forty or fifty" men had been killed. It is not clear whether this number included those dead inside the entrenchment or whether he was including women and children.

At the first attack on the rear of the column, a halt was called and eventually obeyed by the Massachusetts regiment. Their colonel reported that, once the men knew what was happening farther back in the column, they pressed forward again in confusion. With some standards missing, a din of screams and whoops, and units mashing together, the provincial regiment disintegrated. The colonel admitted in a private letter that the attack drove his men "into Disorder, Render'd it impossible to Rally." He held some remnant of his regiment together until it reached the Canadian advance guard, less than a mile down the road from his place in the assembled column. These French refused him protection and urged him to take to the woods, which he did.[52] Ensign Maylem and Private Carver, as well as an unidentified provincial officer, also mention French refusals to help, from sentinels at the camp and from men of the small escort for the column. Maylem saw "naked flying Troops" scattering, and Carver and twenty of his fellows decided to take their chances on their own, broke ranks, and headed for the woods.[53] At the front of the column, Royal Artillery Captain Furnis observed panic among the regulars, and "all Efforts proved ineffectual to prevent their running away in a very confused and irregular Manner."[54] Père Roubaud gave a more general description of what was now "a crowd of unfortunate people who were running at random, some toward the woods, some toward the French tents, some toward the fort, others to every place that seemed to promise an asylum."[55] Indians, who preferred the more individual style of combat and valued prisoners more than scalps at the end of a campaign, now gave chase.

What is clear from all the sources, and especially from Roubaud, is that the indiscriminate killing lasted for only a very short time. If all sixteen hundred warriors had attacked the column with hatchets for as little as sixty seconds, the results would have been very few survivors, since there are no indications of significant resistance by people who had been effectively disarmed.[56] The change from slaughter to a gigantic scramble for prisoners was, according to Roubaud, due to the "patience" of the English.[57] As he had noted earlier in describing the taking of prisoners among the survivors of the Parker expedition, Roubaud saw the Indians as wanting to take prisoners if it was safe to do so.[58] Those leaving the Fort William Henry encampment were without functional weapons and aware of the terms of their parole, and some were husbands and fathers unable either to flee or to fight.

As the Indians began taking prisoners, the first senior French officers arrived from Lévis' camp, led by the Chevalier himself. Lévis put some spirit into the escort and scurried around attempting to protect the English, with the result that some of the escort were injured by Indians. Montcalm also came running from his camp nearly a mile away, accompanied by several of his officers. According to Roubaud, Montcalm tried exhortations, threats, and promises and finally resorted to force. He grabbed a nephew of Lieutenant Colonel Young from an Indian. In saving the youth, Montcalm sentenced several other prisoners to immediate death. Some captors, who saw what the angry Montcalm did, now chose to take a scalp rather than give up a prisoner.[59] Montcalm did not stop the "massacre"; nor did he stop the taking of prisoners. He arrived after the killing had ended and did not have the military resources with him to intimidate the Indians. He demonstrated outrage, courage, and determination to remedy the situation, and he proceeded to recover prisoners by various means. Foremost among these was to call on the officers attached to the Indians, the missionaries, and the interpreters to negotiate with individual Indians for the recovery of prisoners.[60]

Captain Jean-Nicholas Desandrouins, an engineer with the French regulars, was wakened by the tumult that was nearly a mile away from the main French camp. He dressed quickly, borrowing a blue infantry mantle so as not to be mistaken for one of the English, and hurried less than four hundred yards where he came upon an Indian apparently in search of a place to hide his captive. Desandrouins grabbed the Indian by the wrists, but found the prisoner so disoriented and demoralized that he did not even run. Another French officer completed the rescue, and Desandrouins then heard the first of many complaints from very disgruntled Indians.[61]

Desandrouins reveals something of the process of recovering prisoners. He was particularly concerned about the British artillery officers and engineers whom he had met the day before. He spoke with officers attached to the Indians and with missionaries and managed to gather three artillery officers, one Dutch, one Swiss, one English—all nearly naked. Through Abbé François Picquet, the famous Sulpician missionary to the Iroquois, Huron, and Micmacs, Desandrouins found Adam Williamson. Williamson was stark naked "and in a pitiful condition." Picquet was also able to retrieve Williamson's dress uniform. There is no mention of what Picquet or Desandrouins paid or promised, if anything. Even when these refugees were sheltered in his tent, Desandrouins was chasing off Indians seeking booty, and learning from interpreters that the disappointed warriors were cursing Montcalm.[62]

Père Roubaud told more of the process. When the killing had ended, the prisoners had been hauled away, and the worst of the disorder was over, he hurried to the fort. There he found a crowd of English women seeking help in reuniting their families. He learned from a French officer that a Huron was in the French camp with a six-month-old English child. Apparently this Huron and several of his fellows had pitched a tent in the French camp, and there Roubaud found the infant playing with the necklaces of his captor. The Huron refused to give up the child for a sizable sum and chided the priest in French that the infant could be baptized if it did not survive on tallow. The Huron offered an exchange for an Englishman, which did not help Roubaud. Finally, after a conversation in Huron that Roubaud could not understand, the captor offered to exchange the child for an English scalp. Roubaud hurried off to the camp of his Abenaki and asked the first one he met for a scalp. He was readily given not one scalp, but a choice of several. Despite knowing about the money to be made selling prisoners, this Abenaki had taken scalps instead. Roubaud reported that a crowd of French and Canadians followed him as he ran back to the French camp brandishing the scalp (and giving unjust support to those who thought Jesuits demonic). His transaction completed, Roubaud then had some anxious minutes of fatherhood before he found the child's mother in the Canadian camp and its father in the fort.[63]

Transactions like Roubaud's indicate the limits of efforts to negotiate for prisoners. While he had spent more than an hour retrieving one child by negotiation, other captives were recovered more quickly by French confiscation. One was James Furnis, who, like many of the regulars in the front of the English column, had run down the road toward Fort Edward. After running some three miles, he was caught by two Indians. The captors had to bring Furnis back to the lake and their canoes; but, as they did so, they were confronted by a French guard who, like Desandrouins, simply confiscated their prisoner. Furnis was not the only one being escorted back to the fort by a French officer and twenty men.[64] When he arrived there, Furnis found others who had been prisoners of the Indians as well as some who had surrendered themselves to the Canadian advance post discovered by the English as they fled along the road. While some colonial soldiers reported French unwillingness to help them, which in some instances at least was an unrealistic hope, others were protected by Canadians in Lévis' advance guard, by the French garrison in the fort, and in the Canadian and French camps. Estimates of the total number of English rescued by the French range from above three hundred to nearly five hundred, and it is possible that the lower estimates counted only soldiers and the higher estimates included camp followers.[65]

John Maylem was among those whom the French did not regain at Fort William Henry. He was captured about a mile and a half from the lake by three Indians. (Three captors may seem excessive, but both Furnis and Carver mention being grabbed by two warriors who would presumably share a prisoner.) Maylem was quickly disguised as an Indian and taken to a fleet of some twenty canoes at the edge of Lake George, where he found fifty other prisoners, all wearing Indian war paint. This was both a symbol of adoption and a cunning disguise in the face of French efforts to recover prisoners. Maylem's contingent of prisoners was moved quickly from the head of the lake, though they took seven days to reach Montreal, indicating that some of the Indians may have avoided French posts along the way.[66]

Almost all the Indians left quickly on August 10. Their campaign was terminated because they had the prisoners they had come for, and they intended to take them home in triumph. French efforts to recover the prisoners must have reminded the Indians of those long arguments of July 25, when Montcalm had talked them into giving him their prisoners for safekeeping. The warriors could easily see these French efforts to regain the English as a ploy to keep the Indians with the campaign and also as evidence that the French could not be trusted to keep their word concerning those prisoners already sent to Montreal with the French (as proved to be the case). Some thirteen hundred Indians had gone by the end of the day, leaving only the Abenaki and Nipissing.[67] Gone were not only the far-west tribesmen, but also the converted whom Abbé Picquet had ministered to. Some left in anger and indignation at having been robbed of their promised rewards, while others may have been weighed down with plunder and may have taken as many prisoners as they could guard and feed on the way home. Certainly the Indian contingent that carried away Maylem and about fifty others had done well, even if there might also be anger with the treatment they had received from their French allies. Maylem was convinced that about one hundred other prisoners had been taken directly to Indian villages, presumably by tribes residing near Montreal, rather than being carried into the city, as he was. He became one of approximately two hundred prisoners who would later be the subject of protracted negotiation between Governor Vaudreuil and the Indians from the upper Great Lakes.[68]

Those English soldiers who escaped completely at Fort William Henry ran to Fort Edward. The regulars of the Thirty-fifth and Royal American regiments, who had headed the column, lost their possessions and coats to the Indians or abandoned them in flight. Furnis, who had run along behind the other regulars, complained that "all Efforts proved ineffectual to prevent their running away in a very confused and irregular Manner."[69] Although only recently commissioned, Furnis reflected the military view shared by the French regulars that English disorder had aggravated the incident. The English had bolted down the road to Fort Edward, past the camps of the Indians and Canadians, most of whom were already at the entrenchment. Most of the regular officers and some of their men surrendered again to the advance guard of the Canadians, but most of the privates ran on, as did a few officers. Captain Furnis' batman had been luckier than his master. Having stopped to help Furnis out of his boots, Edward White raced on to Fort Edward. He was not the first to reach safety there.[70]

The paroled garrison had been expected at Fort Edward. A runner had arrived about 7:00 P.M. on August 9 with word of the surrender, and its terms had been conveyed by two French officers who deserted and were brought in to General Webb on the morning of August 10. Webb had arranged for an escort of five hundred men to meet what was presumed to be a protected column, "but at 7 o'clock we saw about 30 of our People coming running down the Hill out of the woods along the Road that comes from William Henry, mostly stript to their Shirts and Breeches, and many without Shirts."[71] Between 10:00 and 11:00 A.M., a larger group, which Colonel Webb described as "a part of the remains of the Army," arrived "in the most distressing Situation." Senior officers were noticeably absent among these early arrivals, and there were only three commissioned officers, none ranking above captain, and a few color sergeants.[72]

The first reports, by winded and frightened men who had just raced sixteen miles, were truer than seemed likely from their variety. The regulars near the front of the column had been stripped of most of their belongings and outer clothes, and had witnessed the killing of the wounded. Others from farther back in the line reported the treatment of blacks, mulattos, and Indians in the English column.[73] Still others told of the slaughter of women and children. A young private of Colonel Frye's regiment, fortunate to be posted at Fort Edward rather than Fort William Henry, wrote in his diary that

> this Day when they Came to march the Savage Indiens Came upon them and Stript them of their Packs and Cloths and the most of their Arms then they Pickt out the negrows Melatows and Indiens and Dragd them Away and we Know not what is Become of them then they fell to killing of our men At A most Dredfull manner they Ravesht the women and then Put them to the Slaughter young Children of the Regular forces had their Brains Dasht out Against the Stones and trees.[74]

Some of his regimental fellows were incorporating the presumptions of well-known captivity narratives into their account of the horror they had seen. As the refugees straggled in over the next few days, aided by a cannon fired at two-hour intervals, it became clear that only about ten out of more than eighty women had managed to reach Fort Edward, and that the refugees numbered only about six hundred.[75] It was not unreasonable for men who had fled what they thought was a furious massacre by well over a thousand warriors to presume that some seventeen hundred people had been either killed or taken prisoner.

Men who had made the unsoldierly flight from Fort William Henry also had vital personal reasons why they could not minimize their ordeal. Just one month before, a colonial private in the Royal Americans had been shot there for desertion. On a single day of harsh discipline at Fort Edward, two more Royal Americans were to be "Shot by a Platoon of ye Companys they belong too" for desertion, and three men of the New York regiment received six hundred lashes apiece. The lashing was then suspended, but the three would soon receive the other four hundred of the thousand lashes that were their exemplary punishment for desertion. In such a brutal military atmosphere, men who scurried into Fort Edward with suspiciously few officers needed a very good reason. Of some thirty-four regular officers, only three are known to have run to Fort Edward.[76] More provincial officers were among the refugees, though there was only one "that had not lost the most of his clothes, and all his Regimental Rigging." If the French advance guard had refused to protect the provincial officers, as Colonel Frye had been refused, more of them might be expected to reach Fort Edward on their own, as Frye did two days later.[77] Jonathan Carver's account of repeated efforts to return to his unit and of fifteen hundred killed or taken was a view of the situation from the perspective of a survivor whose terror had burned the event into his memory. It was what he would have reported when he arrived at Fort Edward on August 13, having spent three nights in the woods.[78]

These appalling first accounts spread a great fear through the northern American colonies. Arrival of the refugees led a Massachusetts sergeant at Fort Edward to declare, "This & Yesterday are ye Two Most Sorrowful Day[s] that Ever were Known to N England."[79] The garrison at Fort Edward had already been tense. They had heard the siege guns firing at Fort William Henry as they prepared for a likely attack on their own fort by what was thought to be an army of eleven thousand. The call for militia reinforcement had been issued too late, and the colonies were not responding nearly as quickly as the senior military officers at Fort Edward and Albany hoped. Those militia who had arrived were so nervous that a report of Indians in the neighborhood led to a wholesale musket barrage by twenty-five hundred men, accidentally wounding three militiamen.[80]

Fear was also promulgated by the political and military leaders. New York Lieutenant Governor James De Lancey, once an arch opponent of defense on this frontier, sent Massachusetts Governor Thomas Pownall rumors that Fort Edward had been attacked.[81] As soon as he learned that Fort William Henry had surrendered, De Lancey also ordered all French prisoners and "Neutralls" in New York City jailed for their own safety, with a company of militia to guard them.[82] Writing from Albany on August 10, Deputy Quartermaster-General Gabriel Christie urged Governor Pownall to rush Massachusetts militia to Fort Edward: "Let us save that, Sir, otherwise New York itself may fall, and then you can judge the fate of the Continent." In a postscript, he added that the French were at Fort Edward: "For God's sake Exert yourselves to save a Province." The next day, both

De Lancey and Christie wrote Pownall again, still full of urgency, though noting that Fort Edward was not yet besieged.[83] Thomas Pownall, arriving in Boston as the new governor of Massachusetts on the day Fort William Henry was attacked, had responded energetically to Webb's first call for help, dated July 31 and received August 6. Amid the flurry of frightening dispatches that followed, he tried to curb the publication of the news and had the council consider evacuating the entire western quarter of the province, destroying everything that could not be carried away.[84] All sheriffs were to watch those Acadian refugees living in the province and to detain any who were "demeaning themselves undutifully to his Majesty." Three regiments were, illegally, hastened toward Fort Edward, though commanders in western Massachusetts were apprehensive that stripping the frontier of defenders could invite attack and that "We have a resolute Powerfull Enemy flush'd with success to oppose, and only a raw militia (and I fear despirited now) to meet them."[85] Pownall hoped that the desperate situation would let him gain a new and tougher militia bill.[86] His maiden speech to the Massachusetts House of Representatives reminded them that "the war is no longer about a Boundary whether the French usurpations shall extend to this or that mountain, this or that River, But whether the French shall wrest from British hands the Power of Trade? Whether they shall drive us out of this Continent."[87]

Connecticut had responded to Webb's appeals by raising some five thousand militiamen and marching them to Albany. They arrived after Fort William Henry had fallen and accomplished nothing before they were dismissed on August 25. The cost of this futile effort was estimated at nearly £15,000.[88]

The New Hampshire government's response to the initial call for reinforcements had been very negative. Noting that it was 350 miles from Portsmouth to Fort William Henry, Governor Benning Wentworth's council argued that more men could not be raised and that those at Charlestown could not be sent without leaving the province entirely exposed. They decided to prepare two hundred men to support any place in New Hampshire or Massachusetts that might come under direct attack. At a special convention of the assembly on August 15, Wentworth delivered a stirring address urging the need to rally rather than become "the abject Slaves of Popery & Tyranny." That same day, he learned that Fort William Henry had fallen and that there had been no siege of Fort Edward. He would still press for a stronger act against desertion, citing "the almost total desertion" of

New Hampshire militia under Lieutenant Colonel Nathan Whiting on the Connecticut River. These troops had apparently been the origin of the rumor that Fort Edward had been besieged. Loudoun's request for reinforcements in September prompted Wentworth to mention men unable to bear arms because of the terms of the capitulation, adding that "near one third part of Coll° Messerves Regiment that were posted at Fort William Henry were either killed or Captivated."[89]

At sea off Halifax, Nova Scotia, Lord Loudoun was already preparing to conclude his unsuccessful attempt on Louisbourg when he received Webb's news of Fort William Henry's capitulation and the Indian attack on the parolees. Loudoun suggested that Webb consider abandoning Fort Edward, destroying bridges, roads, and boats, and even sacrificing Albany if necessary. He urged the governors of New England to provide irregulars to harass Montcalm's lines of communication, and ordered Webb to avoid battle until Loudoun himself arrived with more regulars. Having studied Indian military practices only from afar, Loudoun seemed to understand them better than Webb or Montcalm. Loudoun had not yet heard of the sequel to the battle of Sabbath Day Point when he assured Webb that the Indians would not stay with Montcalm's campaign: "I have never heard of any Instance of Indians remaining of either side, after they have either lost any of their People, or got any Booty, but they have constantly returned Home."[90] This knowledge was not much comfort to Loudoun or Webb, for they, like Sir Charles Hardy at Halifax, Governor Horatio Sharpe of Maryland, Governor Robert Dinwiddie of Virginia, and Governor Vaudreuil in Montreal, all assumed that Montcalm would continue south and would be hard to stop.[91]

The *New York Gazette*, before suspending publication because the printers were called up for militia duty, offered the news of the siege until Thursday, August 4, and emphasized the urgent need for assistance. Surmising that the fort had probably fallen, the paper continued: "If so, Fort Edward falls of Course, and where they will stop is hard to determine. And will not this, O my Countrymen yet rouse you, in Defense of your Lives, Liberties and Fortunes!" If volunteers from the city did not provide an example, then destruction would be imminent.[92] Colonel Webb complained that the New York militia "continue to go back as fast, if not faster than they came up," and De Lancey promised to investigate desertion, common in all the militia except those from the county of Albany. One captain named thirty deserters out of the forty men in his company.[93] Whether they left Fort Edward "from cowardice or disgust or whatever other motive," they had deserted Fort Edward while Montcalm's army was in possession of Fort William Henry.[94]

When the New York papers resumed publication, their conflicting reports included a major story printed by government order. This was the most extensive newspaper version of the slaughter, offered in the most graphic prose. "Indian blood hounds" were said to have killed and scalped many officers and men, and killed or captured the blacks and Indians. "The throats of most, if not all the women, were cut, their bellies ript open, their bowels torn out and thrown upon the faces of their dead and dying bodies: and, it is said, that all their women were murdered in one way or another." The gruesome details gathered, invented, or improved on by this "authority" included the view that all the children had been taken by the heels and had their brains dashed out against stones or trees. Readers were reminded of the murder of the wounded in Braddock's army and in the defeated garrison at Oswego, and were told that the survivors of Parker's expedition were not likely to be spared. Nor were readers to forget the innocent who were daily killed and captured along the frontier. The tirade ended by urging that no French prisoners be taken, no capitulations negotiated, and no quarter asked. Every armed man was to sell his life as dearly as he could.[95] This panicked version of the Fort William Henry tragedy survived in American legend.

By August 11, General Webb had intimations that the French were not advancing to Fort Edward. French deserters, who continued to come in surprising numbers, told Webb that the French were intent on burning Fort William Henry—one sign that they were not continuing the campaign—and that "the Indians were going off displeased," which pointed in the same direction.[96] Webb wanted these deserters moved beyond local vindictiveness quickly and sent a captured Canadian lieutenant to be clothed and protected in the fort at Albany so "he may not be liable to be ill used by the people."[97]

The militia reinforcements at Fort Edward may have peaked the next day, when some 4239 men were reported to be there. They represented only a small fraction of the militiamen who were on their way to this third annual, futile, and expensive effort to help Fort William Henry.[98] Those who reached Fort Edward by August 12 witnessed their own reprieve, as the "large smoke" in the sky to the north by day and the brighter northern sky at night for the next three days were convincing signals that the French were not coming.[99]

Having sent the cannon, stores, and provisions back to Fort Carillon, Montcalm's engineers carefully detonated and entirely destroyed Fort William Henry. All that was left that was useful were the half-grown turnips in the fort's garden, some of which were pulled in September by an English scouting party from Fort Edward, and the rest were harvested a month later by French boat crews from Fort Carillon.[100]

6

AFTERMATH

On Sunday evening, August 14, 1757, a party of about thirty men, carrying a red flag of truce, approached Fort Edward. The detachment was led by Lieutenant Savornin of the La Sarre regiment and included Joseph Marin *fils*, several Indians, and Lieutenant Hamilton of George Monro's Thirty-fifth Regiment, who was carrying letters from Montcalm for Colonel Webb and Lord Loudoun.[1] Montcalm's letters were to arrange for the return of English "officers and prisoners," who had received protection from the French after the incident at Fort William Henry.

In accordance with Montcalm's proposal, about five hundred of the missing soldiers, wives, servants, and sutlers were escorted halfway to Fort Edward the next day by an ample party of four hundred French grenadiers and Canadian volunteers.[2] Monro was on horseback, the wounded Lieutenant Colonel John Young was on a stretcher, and Ezekiel Stevens of Derryfield, New Hampshire, was among those wearing French bandages on his head. He had survived being "tomahawked" and very thoroughly scalped, and wore a hat for the rest of his long life.[3] The procession marched down the road, which was still littered with gruesome evidence of the tragedy. They could not be sure how many had died there. "Near Thirty Carcasses, however, were actually seen; and from the frequent stenches they met, had reason to imagine many more lay scattered about."[4] This fragment of the defeated garrison arrived at Fort Edward five days later than originally planned, dressed in a miscellany of clothes given, bought, or recovered by the French. The parade was orderly, accompanied by that brass six-pound cannon that was the symbol of honor. All the regular officers of the Thirty-fifth, the Royal Americans, and the independent companies were now accounted for. Only Captain Ormsby, who had been sent to Montreal by Montcalm because of his injuries, and Captain Faesch, who went along as witness to the return of the parolees, had not returned.[5]

Montcalm had assured Webb, Loudoun, and the French court that the Indians were to be stopped at Montreal and the rest of their prisoners recovered and returned by way of Louisbourg and Halifax. Montcalm had promised that all the men taken from the Fort William Henry garrison would be returned, and his draft letter for Vaudreuil to sign had specified that those taken from the same garrison in the defeat of the Colonel Parker expedition would also be returned, though it later became clear that they were to be returned by way of an exchange in Europe.[6] These humane assurances reflected Montcalm's concern for the parolees, and his wish to save the terms of the capitulation. Whatever Governor Vaudreuil thought of these arrangements, he was forced into action to recover any prisoners whom the Indians brought to Montreal. All of this was easier said by Montcalm than done by Vaudreuil.

Most of the far-west Indians arrived back at Montreal with their prisoners by August 15, the same day Montcalm's army finished burning Fort William Henry and escorting the five hundred rescued English to Fort Edward. After pitching camp on the green outside Montreal that afternoon, some of the warriors killed, cooked, and ate one of their prisoners within full view of the others as well as the horrified townsmen. This killing, apparently without elaborate preliminary torture, was similar to the earlier fate of three soldiers from Parker's expedition. In the earlier instance, it is possible that the killing had been done in ignorance of the price that prisoners could fetch in Montreal. This later killing may have been an expensive and deliberate act of defiance, meant to mock and exploit the sensitivities of the French and to initiate negotiations. Jean-Baptiste-Gregoire Martel, usually remembered as the unscrupulous government store-keeper in Montreal, won the grateful praise of at least two captive Massachusetts officers for his efforts to win liberty and provide comforts for the prisoners.[7] He was unlikely to have been the only sympathetic Montrealer, but some others were busy buying plunder with brandy "and the English die a hundred deaths from fear every day."[8]

Governor Vaudreuil wisely ignored Montcalm's absurd suggestion that the Indians be imprisoned for insubordination. Instead, he scolded the Indians for violating the terms of the capitulation, and then offered them two barrels of brandy per prisoner. The offer was flatly refused. Abbé Picquet recorded an Indian's logical response: "I make war for plunder, scalps, and prisoners. You are satisfied with a fort, and you let your enemy and mine live. I do not want to keep such bad meat for tomorrow. When I kill it, it can no longer attack me."[9] In the course of the next two weeks, Vaudreuil negotiated the release of what he claimed were nearly all the prisoners brought to Montreal, each at an estimated cost to the king of France of 130 livres in goods and thirty bottles of brandy.[10] There is no evidence concerning the payment of the Indian claim checks for the 157 survivors of the Parker expedition; these prisoners were already in Vaudreuil's hands.

The Indians from the *pays d'en haut* left for home from Lachine wearing new clothes and carrying "gifts" of tobacco, vermilion, and lace as well as brandy. If they had left Fort William Henry in haste in order to be home before the waterways froze, as Montcalm claimed in defending his decision not to go on to Fort Edward, those same Indians had then wasted two weeks carousing and negotiating at Montreal before heading west.[11] They were unhappy with the entire campaign, or at least they left that impression with the commandant at Fort Niagara, Captain Pierre Pouchot. Pouchot had encouraged the warriors to join that summer's campaign and had fed some of their wives and children while the warriors had been with Montcalm. Some of the peculiarities of Pouchot's own account of the incident at Fort William Henry seem derived from the reflections of the returning warriors who brought him the news first. He recorded that the attack had developed from efforts to snatch equipment. This and the stripping of the English was "perhaps incited . . . by their French interpreters, who could not bear to see the English depart without their getting any spoils, as they gained in Braddock's affair." Pouchot's comment that Montcalm could have accomplished a great deal more if he had valued the far-west Indians more highly can easily be attributed to the grumblings of disappointed warriors. Their complete victory over Parker, so valuable by any military measure, had been offset by what they saw as the subsequent French collusion with the enemy after the siege. The returning Indians had fewer prisoners or scalps to display than their success warranted, and they had little remaining plunder.

Before long they also discovered that they were bringing with them a devastating epidemic of smallpox.[12] They did not return in comparable numbers to help New France again.[13]

The domiciled Indians of New France were also disgruntled, though they had less to complain about. These warriors were experienced at trading prisoners, and they were also able to bring prisoners home in triumph before adopting some and selling the rest. Few of these mission Indians had been involved in the capture of survivors of the Parker expedition and therefore did not suffer by what may have been the confiscation of those prisoners by the Canadian governor. The mission Indians had also been exposed to smallpox regularly for generations, so their acquired resistance and survivors' immunities lessened the ravages of the disease in their communities. Nonetheless, the domiciled Indians of Canada were reluctant to become involved in later campaigns. The Abenaki were "hunting" when Montcalm visited them to recruit early in the summer of 1758. As Montcalm began the defense of Fort Carillon that July, he could not believe that only sixteen Indians were with him out of the eight hundred warriors he estimated were domiciled in Canada. His remark also indicates that a very high proportion of their community must have participated in the taking of Fort William Henry. Those Indians who arrived too late for the defense of Fort Carillon were insulted by Montcalm and left in anger.[14]

The withdrawal of Indian support for New France came before Montcalm's conventional European defensive strategy began replacing Vaudreuil's mix of regular and guerrilla war in New France in 1758.[15] Indian reluctance became evident before the English victories of that year at Louisbourg, Fort Frontenac, and Fort Duquesne. Indians' support for Canada was severely curtailed by what they saw as disloyal and dishonorable French conduct at Fort William Henry.

For their part, the Canadians and the French were also unhappy with their Indian allies in the Fort William Henry campaign. Indian appetite for provisions, and their slaughter of draft animals at Fort Carillon, caused understandable resentment among all those on short rations and especially among the Canadian militiamen, who had to be assigned to manhandle the cannon and boats. Indian booty, especially the riotous drunken fortnight funded by the sale of prisoners, was undoubtedly resented by the unpaid Canadian militia and the underpaid *troupes de la marine*, who had been outmaneuvered in their own traditional quest for loot by Montcalm's importation of novel humanitarian terms of capitulation. In addition, one Canadian *habitant* was killed by an Ottawa before that tribe finally left Montreal.[16] The French regulars' contempt for what they regarded as dishonorable behavior after the capitulation, inhumanity to the prisoners, and violation of the dead was supplemented by concern that the terms of the capitulation would be voided by this Indian behavior. Like the Indians, the French regulars felt betrayed by unreliable allies. Both had been cheated out of what they took to be the most honorable part of their victory.

Serious Canadian disappointment with the Indians from the *pays d'en haut* was recorded by Peter Schuyler, the popular and prominent colonel of the New Jersey Blues, who was taken in the surrender of Fort Oswego. Schuyler was a wealthy prisoner of war who had considerable personal freedom in Quebec City throughout the Fort William Henry campaign. To gather the largest contingent of warriors the Canadians had ever assembled, he noted, "there is not a Tribe within their knowledge but what they Laboured with 6 Months before to furnish them." The Indians, it was claimed, proved "so very expensive, exhausted so much provisions," and "could not be stinted to Allowance, takeing everything at pleasure, and destroying three times the Quantity of Provisions they could eat." It was also charged that half of the Indians were of no use militarily and that they "did so much Damadge to the Inhabitants that they will not be fond of Collecting such a Number again." Finally, it was noted that "there was more difficulty and more Pains taken to get them out of Canada, than to bring them into it, being verry much Discont[ent]ed with their share of Plunder & reward."[17]

II

In the wake of the slaughter at Fort William Henry, the killed were counted as missing by hopeful comrades and family,[18] and the missing were presumed killed by those recalling the whole horrifying incident. Ten days after his own return, Monro calculated the losses of the regulars in the siege and those missing thereafter. Of the 971 regulars, 20 were killed in the siege, and 27 were wounded, which was six times the reported casualties of the French regulars.[19] Those whom Monro listed as "missing" can be presumed to have been captured or killed in the Indian attack. All were privates except for three captains, a sergeant, and two drummers. The regulars captured and killed in the incident included 11 percent of Monro's own regiment, 13 percent of the regular independent companies and rangers, and 31 percent of the Royal Americans—129 soldiers in all.[20]

No comparable evidence was available on the American provincial troops. Monro, reporting only on the siege, said, "No Regular Accot Could be got from the Provincials but their Numbers Kill'd Could not be Less than Four Officers & about 40 Men. And very near as many Men Wounded."[21] Monro was right about the colonials wounded in the siege, but his account of those killed was high unless he was including the wounded who were butchered on the morning of August 10.[22] Determining those provincials who were killed or captured that day, rather than in the siege, was simply impossible. In writing to the speaker of the Massachusetts House of Representatives, Colonel Joseph Frye reported that "my Regimt is Rent to Pieces." Some of his missing officers and men had been returned to Fort Edward under French escort on August 15. However, by the end of the month there were still five out of forty-five officers missing, supporting the impression that the provincials were more roughly treated by the Indians and less protected by the French.[23] Frye still had no account of the number of missing enlisted "sentinels."

Provincial troops could regard themselves as discharged by the terms of the capitulation, and nearly three-quarters of them escaped both slaughter or captivity and made their way home in small groups. Neither they nor their officers would ever know the number of actual casualties. Members of Colonel Frye's regiment were provided with food and lodging on their way home and maintained at full pay for the remaining two months of their enlistment, as were the New Hampshire troops. They were, however, charged for their missing guns, understandably considered "a great Hardship & Discouragement" (Figure 10)."[24] If these New Hampshire and Massachusetts soldiers were representative, approximately 992 American provincial troops who survived the siege and the Indian attack were home before Vaudreuil had finished negotiating for the release of their missing comrades (Table 1).

By the end of August 10, over five hundred parolees became trophies, as prisoners or as scalps, for the sixteen hundred Indian allies of the French. Almost all the captives who regained their freedom in the fall of 1757 were redeemed in the last two weeks of August by Governor Vaudreuil.[25] Captain Rudolphus Faesch of the Royal Americans, the official witness to the redemptions, was carrying some 1200 livres that Montcalm had lent him to help care for the prisoners. Faesch had set out for Montreal on August 14 in an Abenaki flotilla of canoes that

TABLE 1
Fort William Henry Parolees, 1757

Unit	Men Paroled Aug. 9	Returned by Aug. 31	Returned Sept 1 to Dec. 31	Killed and Missing Dec. 31
Regulars				
Thirty-fifth	586	523	36	27
Sixtieth	118	82	13	23
Artillery	29	27	1	1
Independents	218	190	9	19
Total	951	822	59	70
Provincials				
Massachusetts	792	563	102	127
New Hampshire	221	154	19	48
New Jersey	289	[205][a]	34[b]	50
New York	55	[39][a]	3	13
Total	1357	961	158	238
Total	2308	1783	217	308

[a]Estimates [in brackets] are based on the fortunes of the 1013 provincial soldiers of New Hampshire and Massachusetts. See Appendix.

[b]All thirty-four New Jersey soldiers returned with Captain Thomas Shaw are included, assuming that those from the Parker expedition were matched by New Jersey parolees sent home via New York (HL, LO 4897, 4944).

Sources: Huntington Library, Loudoun Papers 4267, 4313A, 4661, and 5249(6), and see Appendix.

also carried his new friend Père Roubaud. Faesch was in Montreal until September 4, and then went on to Quebec, where both smallpox and "the purple flux" were raging. Captain Ormsby, who had been badly burned in the siege, and about fifty other sick and wounded from the Fort William Henry garrison were judged still unable to make the voyage back to the British colonies.[26]

Three vessels sailed from Quebec on September 27, taking redeemed prisoners to Halifax by way of Louisbourg. The brig *St. Dominique* carried Captain Faesch, 2 Massachusetts officers, with 135 men recorded as of the defeated garrison, plus 5 women and 3 children listed as with Monro's Thirty-fifth Regiment.[27] Aboard the sloop *St. Charles*, Faesch counted two officers, fifty-eight men, six women, and a boy. Included among these were two couples who had been reunited: William and Elizabeth Heaburn; and Francis and Marguerite Innes, accompanied by their son Alexander.[28] Captain Thomas Shaw of the New Jersey Blues, captured at Sabbath Day Point, shepherded ninety-four other former prisoners aboard an accompanying schooner.[29] By the time these vessels arrived at Halifax in mid-

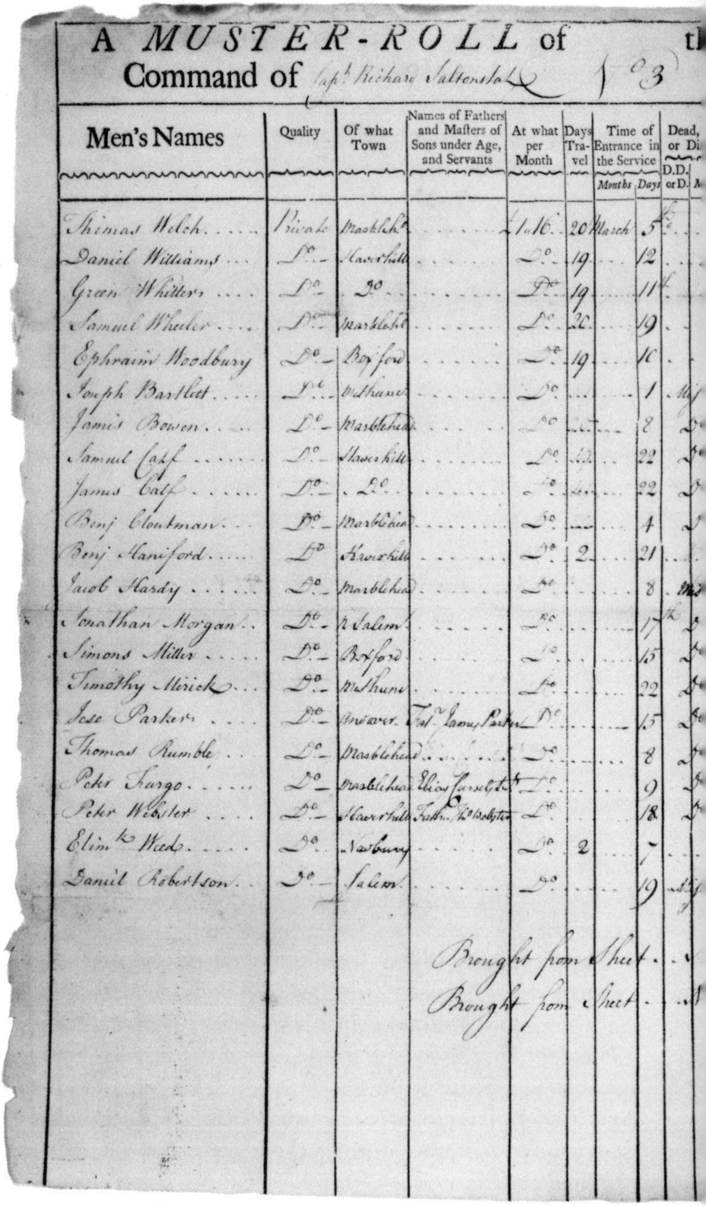

A MUSTER-ROLL of th[illegible]
Command of Capt. Richard Saltonstall No 3

Men's Names	Quality	Of what Town	Names of Fathers and Masters of Sons under Age, and Servants	At what per Month	Days Travel	Time of Entrance in the Service: Months	Days	Dead, or Di[illegible]: D.D. or D.
Thomas Welch	Private	Marblehd		£1.16	20	March	5	
Daniel Williams	Do	Haverhill		Do	19		12	
Green Whittier	Do	Do		Do	19		11	
Samuel Wheeler	Do	Marblehd		Do	20		19	
Ephraim Woodbury	Do	Boxford		Do	19		10	
Joseph Bartlett	Do	Methuen		Do			1	Mi[illegible]
James Bowen	Do	Marblehead		Do	[illegible]		8	Do
Samuel Calf	Do	Haverhill		Do	[illegible]		22	Do
James Calf	Do	Do		Do	[illegible]		22	Do
Benj Cloutman	Do	Marblehead		Do			4	Do
Benj Haniford	Do	Haverhill		Do	2		21	
Jacob Hardy	Do	Marblehead		Do			8	Mi[illegible]
Jonathan Morgan	Do	N Salem		Do			17	Do
Simons Miller	Do	Boxford		Do			15	Do
Timothy Mirick	Do	Methuen		Do			22	Do
Jese Parker	Do	Andover	Fathr James Parker	Do			15	Do
Thomas Rumble	Do	Marblehead		Do			8	Do
Peter Fargo	Do	Marblehead	[illegible]	Do			9	Do
Peter Webster	Do	Haverhill	Fathr Wm Webster	Do			18	Do
Elimk Weed	Do	Newbury		Do	2		7	
Daniel Robertson	Do	Salem		Do			19	[illegible]

Brought from Sheet

Brought from Sheet

FIGURE 10
Part of muster roll of Captain Richard Saltonstall's Massachusetts company, indicating those missing in the action at Fort William Henry (Courtesy of the Massachusetts Historical Society, Boston, Massachuset

…mpany in His MAJESTY's Service under the

[1757] *Viz.*

Time of Return from Captivity		Until what Time in the Service		Whole Time of Service		The whole of Wages due to each Man			For Arms not returned			What each Man received of the Captain			What each Man received of the Commissary of the Regiment			What each Man received of the Commissary-General.			Ballance due to each Man		
Months	Days	Months	Days	Weeks	Days	£.	s.	d.	£.	s.	d.	£.	s.	d.	£.	s.	d.	£.	s.	d.	£.	s.	d.
…	…	Octobr	24	33	3	15	0	10½	2	10	—		2	11		6	7	—	—	—	12	1	4½
…	…	Do	23	32	2	14	10	7	2	10	—	—	—	—	2	19	5	—	—	—	9	1	2
…	…	Do	23	32	3	14	11	10½	2	10	—	—	2	—	3	5	9¾	—	—	—	8	14	0½
…	…	Do	24	31	3	14	2	10½	2	10	—	3	11	10	2	3	2	—	—	—	5	17	10½
…	…	Do	23	32	4	14	13	2	2	10	—	—	—	—	1	1	5½	—	—	—	11	1	8½
…	…	Augt	9	23	1	10	8	3½	2	10	—	—	—	—	—	—	—	—	—	—	7	18	3½
…		Do	9	22	—	9	19	3½	2	10	—	2	8	2	—	0	6½	—	—	—	4	11	7
…		Do	9	20	1	9	1	3½	2	10	—	—	—	—		18	3½	—	—	—	5	13	…
…		Do	9	20	1.	9	1	3½	2	10	—	—	—	—		2	9½	—	—	—	6	9	1
…		Do	9	22	5	10	4	3½	2	10	—	1	5	4	1	14	7	—	—	—	4	14	6½
…r	7th	Jany	4	41	3	18	12	10½	2	10	—	—	—	—	—	1	2½	—	—	—	16	1	8
—	—	Augt	9	22	1	9	19	3½	2	10	—	—	—	—	—	2	9½	—	—	—	7	7	1
…		Do	9	20	6	9	7	9	2	10	—	1	14	6	—	11	6¾	—	—	—	4	11	8¾
…		Do	9	21	1	9	10	3½	2	10	—	—	—	—	—	2	9½	—	—	—	6	18	1.
…		Do	9	20	1.	9	1	3½	2	10	—	—	—	—	—	2	11½	—	—	—	6	8	4
…		Do	9	21	1	9	10	3½	2	10	—	—	—	—		2	2½	—	—	—	6	18	1
…		Do	9	22	1	9	19	3½	2	10	—	1	3	3¾	1	2	9½	—	—	—	5	3	9¾
…		Do	9	22	…	9	18	—	2	10	—	1	7	8	1	4	2	—	—	—	4	16	2
…		Do	9.	20	5	9	6	5½	2	10	—	—	—	—	—	2	2½	—	—	—	6	14	3
…y	11th	March	11th	52	6	23	15	9	2	10	—	—	—	—	—	2	11½	—	—	—	21	2	9½
—		Augt	9.	20	4	9	5	2	2	10		1	5	4	1	0	7½	—	—	—	1	0	2½
					£	250	—	5½	52	10	—	16	1	¼	18	4	7	—	—	—	£163	4	10¼
…		…		…	—	501	12	1¼	67	10	—	8	10	5½	34	13	7¼	…	…	…	390	18	0½
…		…		…	—	411	16	8¾	70	…	…	9	3	9¾	42	1	3	1	18	6.	288	13.	2
					£	1163	9	3½	190	—	—	33	15	3½	94	19	5¼	1	18	6	842	16	¼
																					190		
For Arms rang Deducted from Each man																					1032	16	¾
Deduct for 3 Month pay to the Captt & Lieut																					39		
																					£993	16	¾

October, at least four of the freed captives had died and twenty were sick with smallpox, prompting the army commander there to establish a hospital for them.[30] The rest of the released prisoners were sent on to Boston, New York, and Philadelphia to find their way home or, in the case of the regulars, to rejoin their regiments. Freedom had come for the 304 prisoners, including 11 women and 4 children, who had reached Halifax safely.

It is difficult to know how many of those aboard these three vessels were actually from the capitulation at Fort William Henry. Once prisoners arrived in Canada, they became indistinguishable in the flood of English military prisoners, most of whom Vaudreuil was sending to Europe. French military success produced prisoners who ate Canadian provisions and revealed secrets; they were better exchanged in Europe for French prisoners. In the fourteen months to November 1757, Vaudreuil claimed to have sent 1320 English prisoners to Europe, including some parolees from Fort William Henry.[31] To get home much more directly, an unspecified number of survivors from the Parker expedition joined the flag-of-truce fleet for Halifax by answering to the names of parolees. There is evidence that some prisoners taken at Oswego the previous year were included in this group as well.[32]

One of the freed prisoners brought by this fleet who was certainly not of the Fort William Henry garrison was Susannah Johnson's husband, Lieutenant James Johnson, who was finally ending three years of captivity. By the new year he was home again with Susannah, who, with her two youngest children and her sister, had just arrived by way of England. They had reached New York in December 1757, where they met Colonel Schuyler, who was on parole, and learned of James's release and Schuyler's redemption of Sylvanus, which had served only to move him from Abenaki to Canadian control.[33] James, who had been forced to leave two of his children in Canada, was never to see them again. He died seven months later in the Battle of Ticonderoga (Fort Carillon).[34]

As of the end of 1757, over three hundred of the former Fort William Henry garrison were still "missing," plus an unknown number of wives, sutlers, and other camp followers (Table 2). The fate of these "missing" cannot be known with precision, but a surprising amount of evidence has survived concerning the New England soldiers involved, who constituted more than half of the group. These "missing" can be considered as consisting of four groups: those living in the Indian villages of Canada or the *pays d'en haut*; those sold privately to

TABLE 2
Fate of Soldiers "Missing" from Fort William Henry.
An Estimate

Unit	Missing January 1758	Returned 1758–63	Died Captive	Last with French	Killed and Unknown
Massachusetts	127	14	17	22	74
New Hampshire	48	9	6	8[a]	25
Total	175 (100%)	23 (13%)	23 (13%)	30 (17%)	99 (57%)
Others[b]	133	17	17	23	76
Total	308	40	40	53	175

[a]Derived from Massachusetts figures and Appendix. Colonel Peter Schuyler's accounts for assistance to New Hampshiremen have not survived.

[b]Assuming that 133 other soldiers missing in January 1758 had fates similar to the 175 New Englanders.

Sources: See Appendix.

Canadians; those held by the Canadian government; and those who had been killed in the "massacre."

The number of prisoners held in the Indian villages will never be known, but seems to have been at least 38 of the 308 captives still missing at the end of the year.[35] Two Indian soldiers with the Massachusetts forces remained missing, but Joseph Joseph, a Plymouth Indian, was held captive in a Canadian Indian village throughout the war, proving that not all Indian captives were killed, as was claimed in initial reports. Other captives known to have been held beyond the initial triumph ceremonies of the mission Indians included Jonathan Bailey and Elijah Denbow, but they promptly escaped to Montreal and Quebec, where they were held prisoner until 1759. That May, Denbow, of the New Hampshire regiment, finally escaped with eight others (including Major Robert Stobo as well as ship's carpenter William Clark, his wife, and three girls) by canoe, captured shallop, and then captured schooner, down the St. Lawrence to English-held Louisbourg.[36] Benjamin Goodnow had been carried off by the Caughnawaga, with whom he lived for two years before escaping to General Jeffrey Amherst's army at Crown Point, an experience almost exactly like that of indentured servant Francis Finney of Plymouth, Massachusetts. Another year passed before William Warren escaped from the Abenaki at Saint François overland to Crown Point, and Joseph Joseph was not released until after the fall of Montreal in September 1760. The last Fort William Henry soldier known to return from Indian captivity was Joshua Rand of Charlestown, Massachusetts. He had been smuggled past Montreal by his Ottawa captors and spent four and one-half years with them above Michilimackinac, and another twenty months making his way home, finally arriving in December 1763.[37]

A second group of prisoners were the black and mulatto soldiers who were treated as property and were held in New France until its fall. Perhaps it is not coincidental that St. Luc de la Corne was a leading Canadian slaveowner, as was Governor Vaudreuil.[38] Well-informed Indians had picked at least five slave-soldiers out of the assembling column of provincial troops at Fort William Henry. These prized captives had not been killed, as initially reported, but sold. Caesar Nero, slave of John Gilman of Exeter, New Hampshire, did not exchange his new slavery for his old until the conquest of Montreal in September 1760. In that capitulation, Amherst insisted that black and Indian slaves taken as prisoners be returned.[39] The same was true for Jock Linn and Caesar, slaves of Nathaniel Whittemore and Jacob Bigelow of Massachusetts. Mulatto Jacob Lindse, another slave of Jacob Bigelow, never returned; nor did a black known as Canada Cuggo.[40] As if the litany of the injustices they had suffered was not long enough, these slaves, and indentured servants like Francis Finney, were not eligible for assistance from the governments of Massachusetts and New Hampshire. The compensation for their suffering, translated into lost work and training, was paid to their masters.

No prisoners under the direct control of Vaudreuil are known to have been held for the duration of the war, though some exchanges were frustrated by his reaction to the unwillingness of the English to return all their prisoners in accordance with the capitulation terms. The French capitulation at Fort Frontenac late in 1758 required an exchange of prisoners, but Vaudreuil was not quick to comply with the terms because Major General James Abercromby had not fulfilled the terms of the Fort William Henry capitulation.[41] Prisoners whom Vaudreuil returned in the resulting exchange included one parolee, John Steel of Massachusetts, as well as young Sylvanus Johnson, now fifteen, ransomed from the Abenaki and sent home after four years of captivity during which he had forgotten his mother tongue.[42] Aaron Conkaney, of Samuel Thaxter's company (Figure 11), lived with the Abenaki of St. François for over a year before being "sold to a french man for a hundred and fifty Livers and put to hard Service." In May 1759, he was confined to prison where he developed a sore leg and "was Cut open Severil times by the Doctors almost from my knee to my foot." Released from prison and brought to Crown Point by a flag

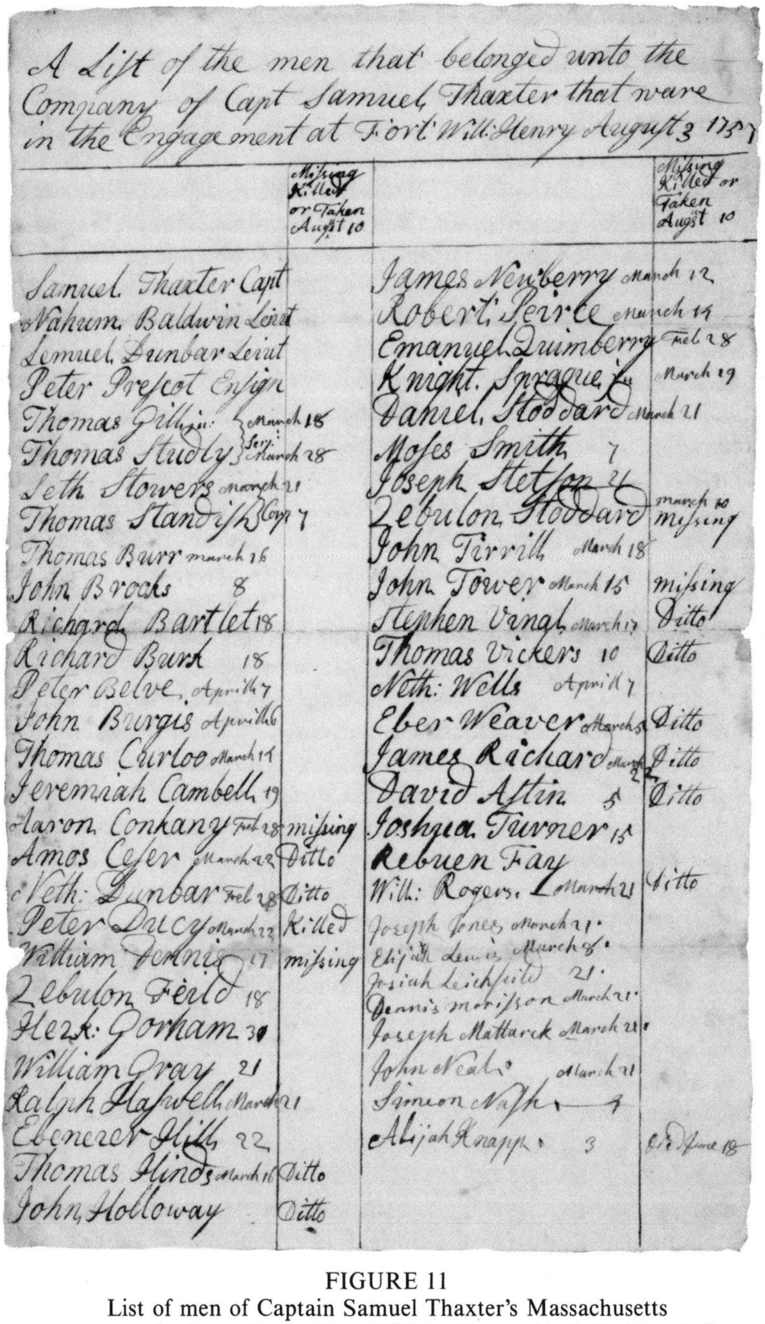

A List of the men that belonged unto the
Company of Capt Samuel Thaxter that ware
in the Engagement at Fort Will Henry August 3 1757

Name	Missing Killed or Taken Augst 10	Name	Missing Killed or Taken Augst 10
Samuel Thaxter Capt		James Newberry	march 12
Nahum Baldwin Lieut		Robert Peirce	march 14
Lemuel Dunbar Lieut		Emanuel Quimberry	Feb 28
Peter Prescot Ensign		Knight Sprague	March 19
Thomas Gillin	March 18	Daniel Stoddard	March 21
Thomas Studly Sergt	March 28	Moses Smith	7
Seth Stowers	march 21	Joseph Stetson	24
Thomas Stand[ish] Corp	7	Zebulon Stoddard	march 20 missing
Thomas Burr	march 16	John Terrill	March 18
John Brooks	8	John Tower	March 15 missing
Richard Bartlet	18	Stephen Vinal	march 12 Ditto
Richard Burk	18	Thomas Vickers	10 Ditto
Peter Belve	April 7	Neth: Wells	April 7
John Burgis	April 16	Eber Weaver	March 5 Ditto
Thomas Curloo	March 14	James Richard	march 5 Ditto
Jeremiah Cambell	19	David Altin	5 Ditto
Aaron Conkany	Feb 28 missing	Joshua Turner	15
Amos Ceser	march 28 Ditto	Reuben Fay	
Neth: Dunbar	Feb 28 Ditto	Will: Rogers	march 21 Ditto
Peter Ducy	march 22 Killed	Joseph Jones	march 21
William Fenni	17 missing	Elijah Lewis	March 8
Zebulon Field	18	Josiah Leichfield	21
Hez: Gorham	30	Dennis Morrison	March 21
William Gray	21	Joseph Mattarck	March 21
Ralph Haswell	march 21	John Neal	march 21
Ebenezer Hill	22	Simeon Nash	4
Thomas Hinds	march 11 Ditto	Alijah Knapp	3 Died June 13
John Holloway	Ditto		

FIGURE 11
List of men of Captain Samuel Thaxter's Massachusetts
company in the action at Fort William Henry. (© J. R. Maguire)

of truce in November 1759, Conkaney joined all those survivors who sought some compensation from the Massachusetts government, emphasizing that "now I have nothing [to] support me with and am not able to travil abought to Labour by Reason of my sore Leg."[43]

Some soldiers of the Fort William Henry garrison who were held by the Canadian government and had not been included in the fleet to Halifax in September 1757 were sent to Europe. *Le Rameau*, for instance, sailed from Canada to France soon thereafter with 118 prisoners, including some from the Fort William Henry capitulation, whom Vaudreuil admitted "consequently are free but they are not identified in the list."[44] Survivors reported that they were in French jails for at least ten months before being exchanged in England. For three of the six prisoners known to have made their way home to America, passage was promptly granted aboard Royal Navy vessels, and New Hampshire soldiers Josiah Bean, Surgeon John Lamson, and William Rackliff were back in America by the fall of 1758. Rackliff spent another four months walking and working his way from New York City to his home in Portsmouth, New Hampshire. For the other three, the route home was even longer. John Moor, of Richard Emery's New Hampshire company, also arrived back in New York in the fall of 1758, but was pressed aboard a man-of-war before he even came ashore. It was only after another year as a sailor to Louisbourg, Quebec, and Boston that he was discharged because of illness. Wells Coverly, of Thomas Cheever's Massachusetts company, also arrived back in New York in the autumn of 1758 "where directly on his Landing was Impressed into the King's Service among the Regulars and servd with them at the taking of Ticonderoga and Crown Point &c." He was allowed home on leave in January 1760, and he successfully petitioned the Massachusetts government for the standard grant of £8 given to prisoners who had been taken to Europe.[45]

As though the New Jersey Blues were ordained to experience the worst of everything, Sergeant William McCrackan of that regiment was the longest getting home from Europe. Sent from Quebec to La Rochelle in December 1757, he missed an exchange two months later because he was too ill. He was shifted to four French prisons during the next twenty months before his release. Pressed on board a man-of-war soon after arrival in Plymouth, England, McCrackan served for three months before being discharged in Dublin. Three and one-half years later, in August 1763, McCrackan paid his own passage to Philadelphia. Nearly another two years went by before the New Jersey legislature authorized his grant of £60.[46] Nonetheless, McCrackan was among the one-eighth of the "missing" who are known to have returned eventually; others were even more unfortunate (Table 2).

Disease, which Jonathan Carver saw as God's revenge on France's Indian allies for the killings, had been much less partisan. Rural Americans who had not been inoculated were vulnerable to smallpox, which thrived with armies and was one of several deadly diseases in urban prisons. A few American troops who had been at Fort William Henry, such as ranger captain Richard Rogers, whose body was reportedly dug up and scalped by unsuspecting Indians, had died of the disease before the siege began. During the fighting, smallpox and gunfire were lethal allies challenging English life and morale. At least one uncaptured New Hampshire soldier died of smallpox on his way home.[47] This epidemic, originating in Canada in 1755, had still been rampant enough early in 1757 to deter some Indian allies from joining the French expedition. At least twenty-seven parolees either survived an attack of the disease in Canada or showed symptoms on their passage from Quebec to Halifax.[48] Smallpox and other diseases probably killed most of the forty prisoners who are thought to have died in Canada and France, and likely killed some of the fifty-three last heard of while in Canadian or French custody (Table 2).

The maximum number of victims killed in the Indian attack at Fort William Henry remains impossible to count and difficult to estimate. To their relatives, friends, and comrades, all the 268 parolees, and perhaps 27 camp followers, who never returned were eventually regarded as killed in the "massacre" (Table 2). However, even a high estimate of those killed must deduct those who were known to have been prisoners in Quebec City or France (53) as well as those who died in both those places (40). Those actually killed on August 10, and those who happily or unhappily lived the rest of their lives in the villages and forests of New France's Indian allies, could not possibly have numbered more than 185 (175 soldiers and perhaps 10 civilians). All of them could have died in the "massacre" only if it is assumed that none were adopted by the Indians and that every soldier whose whereabouts after August 10 remains unknown is presumed to have been killed.[49]

The minimum number killed in the slaughter can be estimated from surviving accounts. Just after the surrender of the fort, at least four of the sick and wounded were killed, later described as "several" by witnesses Captains Arbuthnot and Ingersoll, and by Père Roubaud.[50] Roubard, who was answering anticipated accusations against the French in Europe, counted "hardly more than forty or fifty" killed in the entrenched camp the next day. These forty probably included the seventeen wounded from Colonel Frye's regiment, whose killing was described by their surgeon, Miles Whitworth.[51] To these forty-four should be added some twenty-five to account for the "Near Thirty Carcasses" seen along the road to Fort Edward by Monro's returning column. This total of sixty-nine killed entirely discounts the same witnesses' understandable supposition that "many more lay scattered about,"[52] and ignores casualties in the forest around the site and the parolee known to have been killed and eaten at Montreal five days later.

For most of the 2308 men who surrendered, and as many as 148 family and camp followers, the "massacre" was the fright of their lives. The only persons reported to have been wounded there were Ezekiel Stevens and two of the French escort. Although all the survivors had reason to believe that the casualties were much higher, 268 soldiers (11.6 percent) did not return. Those soldiers and civilians killed in the "massacre at Fort William Henry" numbered at least 69 (2.8 percent), but could not possibly have exceeded 185 (7.5 percent) people.

III

The fall of Fort William Henry sent tremors much farther than the northern American colonies and was felt long after the initial panic. What can now be recognized as the high-water mark of "Vaudreuil's offensive" and French fortunes in the war was, at the time, seen by the English as the worst year in a losing war. Minimal support for the English from a minority of the Six Nations now dwindled further and did not revive until early in 1759.[53] A correspondent of the *Scots Magazine* called the fall of Fort William Henry "a heavy loss to us: for if so considerable an army could come so near us, almost unobserved, when we had Fort William Henry, what may they not do, now that is demolished?"[54] The same magazine quoted a despondent New Yorker who noted sarcastically that "the more we are strengthened from G. Britain the more ground we lose against the French," and ended with the observation that "the French carry all before them, and what the next year will produce, God knows; I tremble to think."[55] In England, Horace Walpole saw the loss as another in a chain of "disgraces," and Lord Chesterfield wished that the year's events, "stained and blotted by our ignominy," could be entirely forgotten. William Pitt had just come to power, and blame could readily be shifted to the ousted faction led by the Duke of Cumberland, who had personally been forced to surrender an army to the French at Kloster Zeven early in September, weeks before London received news of the fall of Fort William Henry.[56]

Some of the terms of the capitulation at Fort William Henry were honored for a time. British regulars involved in the surrender were sent recruiting or posted well behind the lines of likely combat, the two ranger companies were disbanded, and the American provincial troops went home. Lord Loudoun complained privately to Montcalm and Vaudreuil that the "massacre" had violated the capitulation, and Loudoun made little effort to return Canadian, French, or Indian prisoners within the three months specified.[57] However, he put no men in danger of violating their parole and made no public pronouncements that might inhibit the return of prisoners from Canada. Vaudreuil apparently regarded Loudoun's failure to return French prisoners within the three months as a violation of the terms and considered himself absolved of Montcalm's promise to return the remaining English taken at Fort William Henry.[58]

Exactly nine months after the capitulation, all the paroled officers of the Thirty-fifth Regiment petitioned General Abercromby to be allowed to participate in the attack on Louisbourg. Abercromby announced to every unit of the British army in America and to Governor Vaudreuil that the capitulation was considered null and void because of the "murdering, pillaging and captivating [of] many of his Majesty's good subjects." Should any future English prisoners suffer because of their "pretended parole" at Fort William Henry, Abercromby threatened similar treatment for French prisoners.[59]

The Thirty-fifth Regiment joined the army, led by the newly arrived "Major General in America" Jeffrey Amherst, in what would be the successful British siege of Louisbourg. Amherst, who was outraged at the murdering and scalping of women and children, quickly displayed very strong prejudices against Indians that later helped provoke Pontiac's War. He sought to impose European definitions of war and of combatants more fully than had been the case to date. He formally ordered his own forces to respect noncombatants and urged Vaudreuil to do the same, threatening retaliation against prisoners if violations continued.[60] Louisbourg's inhabitants reportedly feared that the British army "would make reprisals for the inhuman infraction of the capitulation of Fort William Henry."[61] Amherst cited the Indian attack at Fort William Henry in denying French troops the honors of war at Louisbourg.[62]

The slow, methodical campaign that Amherst conducted on the Lake George–Lake Champlain frontier in 1759 was launched from the site of Fort William Henry on July 21 (Figure 12). Forced to retreat in the face of massive superiority in numbers, Chevalier de Bourlamaque acted on Governor Vaudreuil's orders by having Fort Carillon detonated on the night of July 26. Four days later, after stripping it of all that was useful for a new defensive position at the north end of Lake Champlain, Bourlamaque exploded Fort St. Frédéric, the fort that so many English had wanted to capture.[63]

FIGURE 12
Site of Fort William Henry.
Thomas Davies, *View of the Lines at Lake George, 1759.*
(Courtesy Fort Ticonderoga Museum)

Amherst sent two regular officers and a party of five Stockbridge Indians north, ostensibly to offer peace to the domiciled Indians of New France, but the whole party was taken captive by the Abenaki of St. François. Whether piqued by the Indians taking his officers, anxious to disrupt the Indian communities in the vicinity of Montreal, or sympathetic to the colonials' desire for revenge, Amherst approved a raid on St. François to be led by Robert Rogers. Amherst's instructions to Rogers recalled Fort William Henry:

> Remember the barbarities . . . committed by the enemy's Indian scoundrels on every occasion, where they had an opportunity. . . . Take your revenge, but don't forget that tho' those villains have dastardly and promiscuously murdered the women and children of all ages, it is my orders that no women or children are killed or hurt. . . .[64]

The predawn raid by 141 men and the resulting bloodshed, in which the village was torched and men, women and children were slaughtered, led to its own legends; estimates of the dead ranged from thirty to two hundred. The raiders recovered five English captives, including the two regular officers, but nothing was said of the five Stockbridge Indians. The raid demonstrated that the new British commander-in-chief accepted the view of Indian adversaries that Montcalm had suggested about Indian allies: they were to be excluded from the niceties of European military convention, for which they had no regard. Although Père Roubaud was among the few captured at St. François and released, five orphaned Abenaki youngsters were taken as captives, including Susannah Johnson's "little brother" Sabbatis, whom she visited on his way to captivity in New England.[65]

The counterattack of the Abenaki, in addition to a vigorous pursuit of the retreating rangers that killed as many as a third of them, was a small raid in June 1760. The target yet again was Susannah Johnson's village, Charlestown, New Hampshire. The entire family of her brother-in-law, Joseph Willard, was captured. Two young children died on the way, and the others were taken to Montreal a few days before it capitulated on September 8. Abenaki raiding, for honor and profit, had come to an end. The family was among those released soon thereafter. The Willards were able to bring back their niece, Susannah Johnson, namesake and last captive child of an English-speaking mother, whom she could talk to only in French.[66]

The fall of Montreal occasioned a symbolic remembrance of the incident at Fort William Henry. In the negotiations for the final surrender, General Amherst absolutely refused to grant the honors of war to some two thousand French regulars under Lévis. Once again, Amherst refused because of "a series of bad behaviour in the French during the present war in the country, in setting on the Indians to commit the most shocking cruelties." Lévis, who had actively attempted to limit the carnage at Fort William Henry, was furious enough to urge a suicidal defiance against the seventeen thousand English troops who surrounded the city. Vaudreuil, the Canadian sponsor of the mixture of regular and irregular war, would not hear of fighting for "the honors of war." An infuriated Lévis could only deny the symbols of victory to the British by having the French regimental colors burned ceremoniously and by breaking his own sword.[67] The French regulars had, once again, been dishonored by the "massacre" at Fort William Henry.

7

PERCEPTIONS

Within two weeks of the slaughter, a Boston newspaperman complained that the accounts were "so various that nothing of the Particulars can at present be depended upon."[1] Although the intervening centuries have seen the gradual publication of a surprising number of accounts by witnesses, their variety and inconsistencies have remained. Historians, attempting to understand how the incident occurred and how many victims there were, have been limited by the conflicting and incomplete evidence, yet particularly free to reveal their own assumptions. Interpretations of the "massacre" form an intriguing and disconcerting historiographical parade.

The story of the conquest and killings at Fort William Henry became part of the "usable past" from the appearance of the first newspaper account. Since then, both the remembering and the forgetting of that event have become part of the history of the British and French empires, and especially the history of the United States and of Canada. Although these perspectives developed in depressing isolation from each other, five general phases can be delineated. These can be punctuated by the appearance of books by witness Jonathan Carver (1778), novelist James Fenimore Cooper (1826), and historians Francis Parkman (1884) and H.-R. Casgrain (1891), who have been echoed more than challenged in the subsequent century.

The first printed versions of the incident were the contradictory news items that appeared in American colonial newspapers. The fullest and most inflammatory account, dated New York, August 19, was printed "by order," and helped inspire panic.[2] "Fugitives" who had reached New York City claimed to have witnessed French perfidy in letting the Indians loose. Many of the garrison and all the women and children were reported killed, and their bodies mutilated. This account ended with a rousing call to arms. Reprinted in British as well as in colonial newspapers, this horrifying account shared space with an entirely contrary perception of the incident, printed and reprinted without evident concern for the obvious discrepancies. Some officers, who had gained the protection of the French regular troops after the attack, supposedly reported: "They do not think we had above ten or twelve killed after the place was taken; but that the Indians had carried off several prisoners whom Montcalm engaged, upon his honour to return safe, as soon as he came up with them."[3] Perhaps the recruiting officers had noticed that the tales of terror were affecting their work. Here French honor and as few as ten killed were sharing a page with accounts of French duplicity and hundreds dead. In most newspapers, these first tangled reports were all that was printed about Fort William Henry.

The editor of the *Boston Gazette*, who had complained about the confusion of those first accounts, was able to publish a better authenticated story on September 5. The report, reprinted from the *New York Gazette* of August 29, was based exclusively on the evidence of "Gentlemen who were in the Siege from first to last, either in the Fort or Breast-Work, and from such as were put to Flight by the Indians." Although willing to give space to any further evidence, "we look upon this to be a Journal of the Siege, or, at least, next kin to it, and therefore may be esteemed the more authentick." One striking feature of this report was the first mention that, as the defeated garrison was about to leave the fort on August 9, "some Chiefs of the Indians went and accused the French General with having deceived them, in that he had promised them the Plunder of the English, which they found they were now deprived of by the Capitulation." In describing the attack on the column leaving the encampment the following morning, the article claimed that

the voracious Blood-Hounds fell to stripping and plundering them of all their Clothes, Arms and Baggage, killing and scalping every one that resisted, not even sparing the Wounded or Sick, and privately carrying off Prisoners all such as they could, notwithstanding all the Opposition of the French to the contrary.

Despite the designation as "blood hounds" in those first reports, the Indians were here depicted as intent on plunder that the capitulation had denied them, killing and scalping only those who resisted. The taking of prisoners as part of the booty was objected to by the French, but occurred nonetheless. There was no mention here of a slaughter of women and children.

This final version of the incident at Fort William Henry in the *New York Gazette* and *Boston Gazette* ended with a cautious and interim report on casualties: "Many of the English, seeing their Danger, took to their Heels and fled; and of this number upwards of 600 arrived soon after at Fort-Edward, giving out that they supposed all who did not escape as they did, were either massacred, or carried off by the Indians." The report, which used the term "massacred" but did not call the incident a massacre, noted that "300 and better" of the garrison gained help from the French, and readers were left to calculate for themselves that about half of the garrison was not yet accounted for. "As to the Prisoners, Mons. Montcalm promised to use his Utmost Endeavors to recover all that were carried off by the Indians, and to restore them." At this point, the French were not being accused of complicity or bad planning; the Indians were to blame, but had grievances. The American papers left the story there, with no reports of the 304 released prisoners returned by way of Halifax, and little further discussion of the incident.[4] Ironically, these newspapers also promoted the French version of this incident, both by emphasizing Indian ferocity and by printing the initial summons to surrender, the terms of capitulation, and Montcalm's explanatory letters to Webb and Loudoun.

The French version was entirely dominated by Montcalm, whose convenient explanation has been astoundingly successful for more than two centuries. He admitted privately to the French minister of war that there had been violations of the capitulation by the Indians, but "what would be a violation in Europe cannot be regarded as such in America."[5] If he had admitted publicly that the slaughter had been a French violation of the capitulation terms, he would have voided the parole agreement, aborted the exchange of prisoners, and dishonored a clear victory. Montcalm sent two letters to Fort Edward on August 14, one for General Loudoun and the other for General Webb, which Lieutenant Colonel Monro later dismissed by claiming that "almost this whole letter is false." Webb was told that the generous terms would not have been violated if the defeated had not given rum to the Indians, if the former garrison had kept better order as it was leaving the entrenched camp, and if the Abenaki of Panaouské had not had major grievances against the English. Montcalm sought an appreciation of the difficulty of working with Indians of thirty-three nations, who were exaggerated as numbering three thousand warriors. He credited his own efforts and those of his officers with preventing a slaughter and assured Webb that the return of the rescued had been arranged, the wounded had been taken to Montreal, and those still prisoners in Indian hands were to be gathered by Vaudreuil and sent to Halifax by way of Louisbourg. Montcalm advised that the French and Canadian prisoners should be returned by the same maritime route, since his apparently uncontrollable Indian allies (who had already left for Canada) made all communication by way of Fort Carillon unsafe. The letter to Lord Loudoun repeated most of the same points, but added that the defeated had been disorderly in their exit because they were terrified of the Indians.[6] The victims had been entirely blamed for their own misfortune.

In assembling information for these letters, Montcalm apparently had consulted Chevalier de Lévis, the officer commanding the right wing, including the Indians, and the first senior French officer on the scene. Lévis, who estimated that about fifty scalps and three hundred prisoners were taken, had recorded two major reasons in his own journal for the day of the carnage: the English gave rum to the Indians, who became drunk and uncontrollable; and the English failed to defend themselves.[7] The English, he thought, should be satisfied with the risks that French and Canadian troops and officers had taken on their behalf. Lévis may have written this account before Montcalm assembled the official version, but Lévis' defense of himself and his own men represented the essence of the whole case: the victims were responsible; the Indians were drunk and uncontrollable; the French and Canadians did everything they could to prevent a more extensive slaughter.

Since most of the Indians left immediately after the incident, Montcalm's impressions of their motives were to come only from two additional sources: the apologies offered by the Indians who turned their prisoners over to the French, and the Abenaki and Nipissing who remained with the French for a few days after the killings. In explaining themselves, the Indians could have found drunkenness attractive as an excuse. Indian perception of spirit forces included the view that one was not responsible for actions while drunk. Intoxication could also serve as a metaphor for uncontrollable impulses. Drunkenness was also a problem that European military commanders knew only too well. The Abenaki of Panaouské had another reason: they were still furious with the English for the murder of several of their sachems at a Massachusetts peace parley earlier that year.[8] Montcalm had all that he needed for a viable explanation that blamed the victims. Although Montcalm still expected the British to conform to the terms of the capitulation, it was significant that his reminder to the English about the return of French prisoners now made no mention of Indian prisoners.[9]

Montcalm's control of the explanation went much further than the letters, copies of which he sent to Vaudreuil and Bougainville. Bougainville had left Fort William Henry for Montreal the night before the killings. There, he not only forwarded Montcalm's letters to the French court, but also incorporated their information into his own letters to France.[10] In his own full and eventually influential journal, Bougainville recorded Montcalm's version of the event. When he rejoined Montcalm at the end of the month, Bougainville also returned to his duty of keeping Montcalm's journal. In reconstructing entries from August 10, Bougainville used the material from his own journal. It is also possible that the premonitions of a possible "massacre," mentioned in both journals for August 9, were added later.[11] Montcalm managed the story nearly completely in Canada, where there was no press. He also sought to control any information Vaudreuil sent to Paris. Montcalm created another even more falsified and self-promoting version of the incident, worded as a letter from Vaudreuil to the minister of marine, Peyrenc de Moras, an unsigned copy of which was somehow sent to the minister of war. Montcalm was not entirely successful in this ruse. Even before Bougainville sent Montcalm's letters to the court, Vaudreuil had penned his own letter to Moras in which he claimed that the incident might have been avoided if Montcalm had entrusted relations with the Indians to Vaudreuil's brother Rigaud, and to the missionaries, officers, and interpreters who understood the Indians. Vaudreuil underlined this by quoting an earlier letter he had received from Montcalm that denounced all these intermediaries as having "en général des esprits de républicains." But Vaudreuil was fighting a private political battle and not a public one. Montcalm easily won the publicity contest in Europe. His initial summons to Monro, the articles of capitulation, and the letters to Webb and Loudoun were all reprinted in France and in Britain, as they had been in English America. French diplomatic considerations alone were enough to make his explanations perfect; there were good reasons why French official accounts should agree, and they did.[12]

London heard the first, worst, and most confusing news of Fort William Henry from the reprinting of the New York newspapers by London papers on October 12 and 13.[13] Little was added to these accounts, except that the *London Evening Post* cautioned about the need for confirmation of all details and added an optimistic "some say" that British losses in the siege were one hundred, and French losses were fourteen to fifteen hundred. The later, better-authenticated colonial versions were not reprinted in England. The only documents made public in the course of these reprintings were Montcalm's initial summons to surrender, with its implication that further resistance would only invite Indian brutality, and the honorable articles of capitulation.[14] The *Scots Magazine* did reprint the jumble of colonial reports in its November 1757 issue, but also added a translation of a report from Rochelle, quoting extensively from Montcalm's explanatory letter to Loudoun.[15]

British publicists seemed so humiliated by losing yet another fort that they did not even seek to embarrass the French by dwelling on the violation of the terms. The loss of the fort, blamed squarely on General Webb, was a focus of attention in *An Enquiry into the Causes of our Ill Success in the Present War*[16] and in the *Scots Magazine*. Horace Walpole wrote to Horace Mann: "To add to the ill humour, our papers are filled with the new loss of Fort William Henry. . . . if we lose another dominion, I think I will have done writing to you, I cannot bear to chronicle so many disgraces."[17] The disgraces stopped under the new William Pitt ministry, Walpole continued to write, and the British made little political use of the incident at Fort William Henry.[18]

The first American captive to publish his version of the story was John Maylem, an ensign in the Massachusetts forces, who had been captured by Indians and taken to Montreal. Maylem's easily forgotten *Gallic Perfidy: A Poem* was dated March 10, 1758, and published in Boston four months later.[19] Maylem's pedestrian verse returned to his own initial perceptions, if not the archetypal captivity narratives. Men, women, and children were killed, and "The harmless Babe (torn from its Mother's Arms and dash'd, impetuous, on the Wave-worn Cliff!)." He mentions "naked flying Troops" fleeing through the woods, and French officers refusing to help. Taken north disguised as an Indian, Maylem saw Indians eating parts of a prisoner "on Montreal Plains."

There was no discussion of Maylem's stay in New France or his prompt return home via Halifax. He ended with an exhortation and vow to "chase the wily Savage from his secret Haunts." This wartime poem, ostensibly denouncing the French, contained little more than a general charge of betrayal. It was the Indians, portrayed as blindly savage despite Maylem's own survival in their hands, who were to pay for what had happened.

The first historian to examine the taking of Fort William Henry was the English schoolmaster and political writer John Entick, whose massive *General History of the Late War* appeared in 1763. Using reports from newspapers, the *Gentleman's Magazine*, and the *Scots Magazine*, Entick exaggerated the size of Montcalm's army and accused Webb of failure to act on information or to display any personal courage. Montcalm's summons, Webb's discouraging letter, and the terms of the capitulation were printed in full. Entick invented a single supreme "Indian chief," where his sources described several, who insisted that Montcalm keep his earlier promises. The French "in defiance of the faith of the capitulation and humanity, perfidiously and inhumanly gave way to the Indian demand." The majority of the garrison were "stripped, killed and skalpt." Entick reprints the "horrid barbarities" of the newspaper accounts, including the treatment of the Indians and the blacks, the disemboweling of women, and the smashing of children against trees and rocks. On the basis of the newspaper accounts, which indicated that nine hundred had returned, Entick concluded that "they murdered, at the capitulation, 1300 men, besides women, children and other attendants." The Indians were described as "savage blood hounds," and the French had agreed to the slaughter.[20]

Captain John Knox's massive *Historical Journal of the Campaigns in North America for the Years 1757, 1758, 1759 and 1760*, published in 1769, confined discussion of the fall of Fort William Henry to a long quote from a regular officer's letter written in New York City on August 13, 1757, in the midst of the panic. He expanded Montcalm's army to ninety-five hundred men and defended Webb as unable to reinforce Monro because of provincial tardiness. Capitulation came just after a "mysteriously forlorn" Monro received both Montcalm's summons (actually August 3) and Webb's intercepted letter, which Montcalm forwarded immediately on receipt (actually received on August 5 and not forwarded until August 7). The English casualties in the siege were exaggerated to three hundred and the French casualties even more, to twelve hundred. According to Knox, Webb was not culpable nor were the French, but the Indians, "who before had been flattered with great hopes of plunder and scalps," were disappointed, attacked the column "with barbarous rage," and "basely butchered several hundred."

The History of the Late War in North America (1772) included an account of the fall of Fort William Henry that challenged Entick in several respects. The author, Thomas Mante, had been an engineer with the British Army at Havana in 1762, and a major with John Bradstreet's expedition against Pontiac two years later. A translator of French military manuals, Mante knew both sides of the story when he wrote what amounted to a gallant defense of Montcalm, "a noble enemy and an excellent soldier."[21] Mante's account of the siege and surrender suggested knowledge of the colonial newspaper accounts as well as the official French version, though his vilification of General Webb derived from the British army opinion, which denounced but never court-martialed the cautious commander of Fort Edward.[22] Like the author of the "journal" published by the *New York Gazette* of August 29, 1757, Mante wrote that the Indian chiefs had insisted on Montcalm's earlier promise of plunder and, when he refused, they proceeded "to execute the agreement themselves. Accordingly, as soon as the garrison had surrendered, they began an assault upon the men, killing and scalping about ten or a dozen of them." Mante accepted that Monro and many others found protection with the French and that about six hundred fled to Fort Edward on their own. French enslavement of the English Indians and the blacks struck Mante as no more unusual than French confiscation of the artillery and stores.[23] His account fits the "most restrained" version of the incident as it was remembered somewhere in the regular British army.

Mante vehemently denied charges that Montcalm had consented to the outbreak of violence, which Mante nowhere called a massacre, and rejected the claim that "a partisan who led the French savages, gave the death hallow, when the English marched out of the Fort, to gratify the Indians in their lust for blood and plunder." Such accusations were current in Britain, and Mante answered them more vehemently than anyone else. Montcalm not only had offered himself "and bade them kill their father" rather than the English he protected, but, Mante claimed, had urged the parolees to fire on the Indians in defense of themselves; "but the English were seized with such an unaccountable stupor, that they submitted to the tomahawk without resistance." He stated that the French officers were wounded while defending the English and also guarded them until "the fury of their savage allies had subsided." Mante scolded the credulous, presumably including Entick, for accepting the wild exaggerations that are usual in "incidents of this kind." Nor did Mante accept that Montcalm should have provided more protection for the defeated. He argued that the English were armed, had ammunition, outnumbered the Indians, and had been invited to defend themselves. Montcalm could not have gone further without failing in his political duty, which included keeping the support of the Indians, who held "the balance of power in North America." Montcalm's most enthusiastic supporters could not have worked harder to remove this "undeserved blot" on Montcalm's reputation than did this English soldier.[24]

The complete 1790 edition of the British novelist Tobias Smollett's *History of England from the Revolution to the Death of George II* not only was published, but also was partly written long after its principal author died in 1771. Although Mante's volume appeared a year after Smollett's death, the latter's fifth volume included a discussion of the taking of Fort William Henry that repeatedly plagiarized and paraphrased Mante.[25] The Smollett history was dedicated to making William Pitt the hero of the war. The loss of Fort William Henry had marked the end of the third disastrous year for an army that had prodigious advantages over its enemy, yet "we abandoned our allies, exposed our people, suffered them to be cruelly massacred in the sight of our troops, and relinquished a large and valuable tract of country, to the eternal reproach and disgrace of the British name." In reaching such a conclusion, the compilers of Smollett's history did not want Mante's minimized view of the incident. While the issue of Montcalm's responsibility "we cannot pretend to determine," the Indian attack was described in detail. As the British troops marched out of their camp, the Indians

> despoiled them of their few remaining effects, dragged the Indians in the English service out of their ranks, and assassinated them with circumstances of unheard-of barbarity. Some British soldiers, with their wives and children, are said to have been savagely murdered by those brutal Indians, whose ferocity the French commander could not effectively restrain.[26]

Savagery of the Indians was explanation enough, and the theme of broken French promises to the Indians disappeared. Casualties were not estimated, but heresay about a more extensive slaughter was reintroduced.[27]

The most influential "eyewitness" account of the killings at Fort William Henry was published in London in 1778, amid the American

Revolutionary War, which had just become yet another Anglo-French war. Jonathan Carver's very popular *Travels through the Interior Parts of North America in the Years 1766, 1767 and 1768* included a long digression on the "massacre," offered to illustrate the fierceness of the Indians in war.[28] Like John Maylem, Jonathan Carver had been with the Massachusetts provincials at the siege.[29] Unlike Maylem, Carver had escaped from Indian captors at the scene and wandered in the woods for three days before arriving at Fort Edward. Carver has since been proven an unreliable witness in numerous respects and not the real author of much that appeared in his book. However, his recollection of this incident, probably committed to paper more than a decade after the event, sounded much like the versions given by others who fled through the woods to Fort Edward and arrived ahead of him. Carver's version was colored by the passage of time. His exaggerated view of the size of the French army and the number of victims was understandable for a fugitive who did not learn or remember much of the subsequent news, but could not forget his own harrowing experience.

Carver's general account of the siege was very brief but offered intriguing details. He used Knox's garbled version of negotiations between Montcalm and Monro, who "hung his head in silence" on reading the discouraging Webb letter.[30] Carver recalled that, as the defeated garrison gathered to leave, Indians began to plunder and the men were powerless to prevent it, having arms but no ammunition. Those sick and wounded who were unable to crawl into the ranks were killed, and the column set out without the promised French guard. The front ranks were soon driven back, and the whole group was surrounded by Indians who began stripping everyone and tomahawking those who resisted.

Carver's own experiences in the incident deserve closer scrutiny. He was held by three or four Indians, threatened by others, and "disrobed" to his shirt and breeches, presumably without resisting since he was not tomahawked. Carver then ran to "a French sentinel" posted nearby to claim his protection, and was refused. It is quite likely that neither Carver nor the French guard understood the other's language. Carver then claimed to have made his way through so many Indians that they could not strike at him without endangering one another. He was slightly wounded twice by spears but lost only his shirt at this time. The spears suggest that he was among the Indians of the *pays d'en haut*, who could be expected to be the most ferocious. Once Carver rejoined his fellows, the war whoop was heard, and "men, women, and children were dispatched in the most wanton and cruel manner, and immediately scalped" by Indians who apparently took time to drink the warm blood of victims while others ran away.[31] Carver was one of about twenty provincials who tried to break through the surrounding Indians, but he was caught again by "two very stout chiefs, of the most savage tribes" and pulled through the crowd. Carver, amazed that they did not kill him, could not admit the obvious—that he was being taken prisoner. One of his captors was distracted by a fugitive in scarlet velvet breeches, and, as that man tried to escape, the other chief let go of Carver to aid his friend. Carver fled but saw the soldier struck in the back with a tomahawk. Carver also mentioned a twelve-year-old boy whom he saw hauled away by Indians. He heard the boy's shrieks and presumed, understandably, that the lad had been butchered. Amid all this activity, which took him from the back of the column, through captivity, to the front of the column, Carver saw the actual killing of only one man, who tried to escape from his captors, and assumed the death of one other. Anything resembling Indian blood lust should have caused his death on several occasions. Carver's antics in the face of murderers suggest that if murder was their intent, they were very inept.

After again racing through a maze of Indian warriors, Carver finally reached the woods and safety. There he recovered his breath and struggled for "some hours" to climb a hill from which he "could discern that the bloody storm still raged with unabated fury." This observation is the context for Carver's famous statement: "It was computed that fifteen hundred persons were killed or made prisoners by these savages during this fatal day."[32] This computation was certainly not derived from any estimate of how much killing sixteen hundred warriors could inflict on more than twenty-three hundred defenseless people in "some hours."

Even if Carver had a superb memory and few cultural filters to cloud perception, which is doubtful,[33] he had two conflicting purposes in his recollection. On the one hand, he had to exonerate himself from any suspicion that he had fled in cowardice, leaving others to their fate. Carver returned to his fellow soldiers twice during the trouble, was stripped by some Indians and captured by others, and ran through groups of enraged Indians at least three (and perhaps five) times within a matter of minutes. On the other hand, he wanted to demonstrate the savage ferocity of the Indians, though this was not convincingly displayed in much of his story. Carver's claim of a wanton "slaughter" was supported only by a general comment about murdering, which "it is not in the power of words to give any tolerable idea of" (a sentiment that had been shared by John Maylem); the mention of Indians drinking blood just as the slaughter began; and the comment that the killing was still going on "some hours" after it began.

Carver's view was shared by other terrified men after they had staggered into Fort Edward and gained a sense of how many of their fellows had failed to do the same. Carver, like Smollett, sought to demonstrate a blind Indian fury; Indian grievances that had been mentioned in the earlier English newspaper accounts, and in Entick, Knox, and Mante, had disappeared.

Carver regarded Indian savagery as uncontrollable, but still saw French complicity that went beyond the uncaring sentinel who called him an "English dog." Amid the slaughter, Carver claimed, the French "tacitly permitted" the violence, for he "could plainly perceive the French officers walking about at some distance, discoursing together with apparent unconcern." He went on to hope that the entire incident "proceeded rather from the savage disposition of the Indians, which I acknowledge it is sometimes almost impossible to controul," than from any premeditation by Montcalm. However, Carver was confident that the French troops "had it in their power to prevent the massacre from becoming so general."[34]

Carver had another unique way of evaluating guilt. "I mean not to point out the following circumstances as the immediate judgment of heaven," he wrote, as he began to do the opposite. He claimed that very few Indians lived to return home because smallpox contracted from the Europeans "made an equal havoc to what they themselves had done." He added that Montcalm's death and the fall of New France were also "the vengeance of heaven."[35]

II

The publication and popularity of Jonathan Carver's reminiscences seem to have affected the accounts of the slaughter in two ways. Although Carver stayed in Britain throughout the American Revolutionary War, his version was to become the American version. He gave credence to the initial exaggerations at Fort Edward and shared John Maylem's notions about unprovoked Indian savagery, some French complicity, and a very extensive slaughter. Carver's book was also good British wartime propaganda in 1778, and it preceded, if it did not directly prompt, the publication of two French accounts of the incident and provoked the writing of a third, parts of which were published much later.[36] Before tracing the more dominant American view, it is helpful to look at the first unofficial French accounts to be published.

The most vividly detailed account of the incident, apparently penned little more than two months after the event, was printed in Paris in 1781 as part of the Jesuit *Lettres edifiantes et curieuses écrites des missions étrangers*.[37] By the time of publication, Père Pierre-Joseph Antoine Roubaud had long since ceased to serve his country or his church. The letter embarrassed its author, who had become an informant and a forger in the service of the British and was claiming compensation for services to the English at Fort William Henry, which this letter did not sustain.[38] With Britain and France again at war, the publication of this letter was also a timely defense of French conduct against the attack of Jonathan Carver.

Despite the propaganda function of this publication and the scandals surrounding its author, the letter was generally consistent with known facts, and it was written quite promptly and independently.[39] This Jesuit missionary, who accompanied his Abenaki warriors on the campaign, had learned their language well enough to preach in it and was present at the scene of the "massacre." He was perceptive, articulate, and well informed, and his letter suggests sympathy for his Abenaki and for the captured English, as well as concern for the honor of France. Digressions to describe the funeral of a Nipissing sachem or the nature of rattlesnakes indicate that the letter was intended for publication. Certainly much of his description of Indian customs was not of particular concern to Roubaud's superior at Quebec, the presumed original recipient of the letter.[40]

Roubaud's account of the entire Fort William Henry campaign was crafted to prepare the reader for the gruesome climax. He was curious about an intertribal war feast attended by his Abenaki, before the forces left St. Jean, and compared this "comic farce" with the reverent religious observances of his own neophytes.[41] When captives of the Parker expedition were brought into camp, Roubaud reported the frenzy of those waiting to club the prisoners. The Jesuit knew that his own protests would be drowned by the noise, by the variety of languages, and "plus encore la férocité des coeurs."[42] Later Roubaud discovered a group of Ottawa eating a prisoner and was horrified, and also helpless to negotiate for another who was still alive.[43] Roubaud was convinced that the Indians from the west were furious brutes and that, as the campaign progressed, they were influencing the domiciled tribes. Despite his admiration for the eloquence of their orators, the initial earnestness and propriety of his own converts, and the adeptness of Indians who quickly learned military techniques of siege warfare, Roubaud felt he was fighting liquor, idolatry, and a commendable but troubling independence that was natural to the Indians. He saw the Indians of the *pays d'en haut* as victims of their untamed passions, in need of regular religion which their wandering lives made impossible.[44] The carnage was an outburst of ferocity and independence that the French were powerless to prevent or end.

Roubaud's account was intended to dispel charges of French duplicity, miscalculation, or insensitivity, charges that he assumed were echoing throughout Europe.[45] He had arrived as the Indians began taking prisoners, and the desperate were running in all directions. Lévis was there by then, energetically and fearlessly helping the English and inspiring French and Canadian soldiers to follow his example. One French officer was severely wounded, and another injured by a spear, but most of the French army was too far away to be of any help. Montcalm arrived as soon as he heard of trouble and intervened energetically, pleading, promising, threatening, and physically forcing the release of prisoners. According to Roubaud's account, which did not include a bare-chested Montcalm offering himself instead of his enemies, Montcalm had not stopped the killing. It had already stopped, though the commander inadvertently provoked the slaughter of several prisoners while attempting to free others.

Roubaud's fascinating letter contributes a great deal to the understanding of what he called "le massacre," if his perspective is kept in mind. His perception of Indian motives was revealing, though biased, and his defense of the French and himself was more detailed than any other account. The deaths of some wounded English, within the casements of the fort on August 9, were reported more fully than anywhere else, and he provided valuable information concerning the killing on the morning of August 10 (though he gave no graphic detail at all of those he presumably saw slain in response to Montcalm's rescue of Young's nephew). Roubaud also recorded that it was only in the burning of the fort that the French discovered many more English bodies in the casements and secret underground passages.[46] These burned bodies, which may have included those who died of disease as well as of wounds in the course of the siege, provided the ghastly scene that Israel Putnam saw some days later, and that he later claimed had been created by Indian slaughter.[47] Roubaud's letter was used as a convincing reply to Jonathan Carver.

The same year that Roubaud's letter was printed saw the post-humous publication of the three-volume *Mémoires sur la dernière guerre de l'Amérique septentrionale* by Captain Pierre Pouchot of the Béarn regiment. Although he was not present at Fort William Henry and wrote his work in self-defense in 1769,[48] there were several interesting features in his brief account of the killing. An excellent military engineer, Pouchot had been commandant of Fort Niagara in the summer of 1757 and was particularly proud of his success at Indian diplomacy.[49] Some of the peculiarities of Pouchot's version of the slaughter came from the reports of the far-west Indians whom Pouchot thought highly of. According to Pouchot, the slaughter occurred after the French escort left the column well on its way to Fort Edward. Harassment began as Indian demands for equipment, which may have been encouraged by the French interpreters.[50] Those English who resisted were killed, and twelve hundred to fifteen hundred were taken prisoner but released through Montcalm's efforts. Like other French chroniclers, Pouchot blamed the English for initially giving in to Indian demands, though he admitted that the English "might readily believe" that the French would attack if the parolees had fought the Indians. He blamed this incident on Canadians inspired by greed, not on Indians angered by French betrayal. *Pays d'en haut* warriors helped Pouchot come to the judgment that much more would have been accomplished on the New York frontier if Montcalm had valued the far-west Indians more highly.

Only one direct response to Jonathan Carver was written by anyone with the French forces at Fort William Henry, and it was never published in its entirety. Captain Jean-Nicholas Desandrouins had been the engineer in charge of preparing the trenches of the besiegers and had arrived at the scene of the carnage a little later than Père Roubaud. On his death in 1792, Desandrouins left a fifteen-page manuscript entitled "Notes sur le voyage de M. Jonathan Carver dans l'Amerique Septentrionale, au sujet du massacre des Anglois, par les Sauvages, après la capitulation du fort William-Henry, en 1757."[51] Like Roubaud, Desandrouins divided his subject into a general account, which was gathered from others, and a particular account of his own activities once he arrived at the scene. Desandrouins' main concern was to clear the French of Carver's charge of conniving at or tolerating what he did not hesitate to admit was a "massacre."

In his overview of the incident, Desandrouins included the plan to evacuate the English garrison late on August 9, canceled because of fear of the Indians, which provoked a meeting of French officers, interpreters, and missionaries.[52] As the column was leaving the next morning, a few Indians, perhaps fifty, entered the entrenched camp more out of curiosity than cupidity. Stragglers threatened by these warriors gave up their packs readily and hurried to join the column.[53] More warriors entered the entrenchment to take the remaining goods, and blacks and perhaps some of the camp followers were carried off in the confusion. Desandrouins' most thoughtful contribution to the understanding of the Indian attack was his description of what happened next, to which he was probably not an eyewitness. The Indians who acquired booty or a prisoner hurried to the nearby Indian camp in triumph, prompting those of other tribes to hurry out for something to represent their contribution to the victory. Some of them gave the war whoop as they arrived to expand the violence. Desandrouins shifted attention to the Indian encampment where warriors who were initially content with their share of the goods now went in search of more prisoners, scalps, or clothing. At this point, Desandrouins mentioned that warriors attacked the hospital and killed all the wounded for their scalps. The French did all they could to save the English. Montcalm, Lévis, and Bourlamaque came running and ordered the use of force where necessary. Interpreters, officers, missionaries, and Canadians all did their best, though no one could be heard above the din. Several prisoners were killed because warriors did not want to be forced to release them, and a great many were carried off to canoes. Desandrouins had the incident end when Montcalm offered himself and the Indians realized, too late, that he was angry. The French recovered about three hundred of the English, and more than four hundred were whisked away by the Indians, whose return route took them through Montreal. Vaudreuil did not have the manpower to force the release of these prisoners, but bought some of them with liquor.[54]

Desandrouins, even more than Pouchot, offered a very rational explanation of the Indian's behavior in the killing despite their violation of his sense of decency.[55] He concluded with the observation that he knew of no prisoners who returned to their own country after being taken beyond Montreal by their Indian captors. While Desandrouins was outraged that the ungrateful English had forgotten both French efforts and revulsion at what happened, he did not directly dispute Carver's figures on the number of victims.[56] While accounting for some seven hundred of the garrison, Desandrouins said nothing of those who, like Carver, had escaped on their own to Fort Edward. Desandrouins was passing some of the blame to the English, as Montcalm had done, and disputing Carver's charges of French complicity; he was not challenging Carver's claims about the scale of the disaster.[57]

Desandrouins participated in the reimposition of civility on an ugly incident. Without any knowledge of Indian languages, he reported the discontents of the warriors, as well as the envies and ambitions that fueled the spread of the attack. He saw no one die[58] and reported no scene of dead bodies like that Roubaud saw inside the entrenched camp. Yet his challenge to Carver was to exonerate the French in the atrocity by suggesting how the Indians came to do it, and how English behavior aggravated matters. Desandrouins and Pouchot had not described noble savages or cheated allies; they described Indians who were motivated like any other people. This perspective, also evident in some early English accounts, was lost, for Montcalm's and Roubaud's views meshed better with the purposes of the nineteenth century.

Jonathan Carver's account of the slaughter became the basis for a more truly American heroic account with the appearance of David Humphreys' *Essay on the Life of Israel Putnam* in 1788. Putnam was not at the siege, but claimed he would have been if Colonel Webb had not reversed an order that supposedly sent hordes of colonial militia, including Putnam's rangers, several miles down the road from Fort Edward to Fort William Henry. Humphreys also claimed that Montcalm later told Putnam that such a colonial force was spotted, the siege suspended, and a French retreat prepared.[59] This puffery accompanied Putnam's graphic recollection of the burning scene at Fort William Henry after the French withdrawal. Putnam recalled that he had seen

> innumerable fragments of human skulls and bones, and, in some instances carcasses half-consumed. Dead bodies, weltering in blood were everywhere to be seen, violated with all the wanton mutilations of savage ingenuity. More than one hundred women, some with their brains still oozing from the battered heads, others with their whole hair wrenched collectively with the skin from the bloody skulls, and many (with their throats cut) most inhumanly stabbed and butchered; lay stripped entirely naked, with their bowels torn out, and afforded a spectacle too horrible for description.[60]

Putnam definitely had scouted the site of the fort, but not until August 21 or 22.[61] Looking back thirty years later, he recalled more "weltering" and "oozing" than seems likely eleven days after the Indians had left. Although Putnam could not distinguish among butchery, mutilation of the dead by men or by animals, and fire damage to bodies that

Roubaud claimed were discovered only after the fort had been burned, Putnam's description supported Carver's "slaughter."[62] Putnam's version was even better suited for the new American republic. The story was peopled by British incompetents, Americans who were able and ready to prevent the disaster but were frustrated by British stupidity, savages who could not be restrained, and Frenchmen who subsequently became allies in helping America win independence and were not to be blamed for this "spectacle too horrible for description."[63]

The most immediate and authoritative American eyewitness account of the siege and of the Indian attack was that of Joseph Frye, colonel of the Massachusetts forces at Fort William Henry. His journal was presented to Governor Pownall of Massachusetts on September 4, 1757. When finally published in 1819, it revealed almost everything that would subsequently become known of that event from the perspective of a Massachusetts soldier. Frye's journal differed noticeably from Carver's in withholding all information about the author's own activities on August 10. Apparently, Frye's experience had been similar to Carver's; he was missing for two days and presumed lost, and then arrived at Fort Edward clothed only in his shirt.[64] Frye offered none of the self-justifications of Carver, though his was a report to officials from the perspective of the officer in charge of a regiment that was severely abused in the incident.

Frye was in the entrenched camp after the capitulation was signed and was wary of the Indians. He emphasized, as though he were retorting to Montcalm's analysis, that the English supply of liquor had all been destroyed. Lieutenant Colonel Monro was credited with the idea of leaving on the night of August 9, but changed his mind once it was learned that a large party of Indians seemed poised to intercept the English garrison on the road.[65] Monro eventually agreed to the French officers' misguided suggestion that giving the baggage to the Indians would improve matters. Frye joined the many who claimed that this provoked the Indians to strip officers of everything but their shirts, and some lost those as well. Frye was the only one to state that one of the Indians in the provincial regiment was subsequently burned alive by his captors. The English column had been ordered to halt and did so in confusion; then those in the front surged forward again when they learned that the rear had been attacked,

> and thus the confusion continued and increased, until we came to the advanced guard of the French, the savages still carrying away officers, privates, women, and children, some of which latter they killed and

scalped in the road. This horrid scene of blood and slaughter, obliged our officers to apply to the officers of the French guard for protection, which they refused, and told them they must take to the woods and shift for themselves, which many did, and in all probability many perished in the woods, many got into fort Edward that day, and others daily continued coming in, but vastly fatigued with their former hardships, added to this last, which threw several of them into deliriums.[66]

Refusal of the French advance guard to leave their post and enter into a melee with vastly greater numbers of Indians was here presented simply, without Carver's malice. Frye went on to report, what he heard from others, that Monro and a number of officers and men were returned to the safety of the French camp, and that some prisoners were released on orders of Montcalm. At the time he submitted his journal, Frye had not seen any muster sheets for his own regiment, and he ventured no guess as to casualties. For Frye, the Indians were savages in a bad temper, and the French, though not condoning the slaughter, failed to enforce the terms of the capitulation.

Publication of Joseph Frye's factual and promptly written journal had little effect on the dominant American view of what was becoming a myth derived from Carver and Putnam. Frye's journal was used by Epaphras Hoyt in his 1824 *Antiquarian Researches*, a history of Indian wars in the Connecticut River region. Hoyt followed Frye's account very closely, but added embellishments from the most lurid newspaper account, Carver's *Travels*, and Humphreys' *Putnam*. Hoyt tried to infuse increasingly popular "Indian fighter" elements into the story by adding untraceable tales of courageous escapes by Frye and several of his officers, as well as recounting Carver's marathon. In estimating the number of victims, Hoyt dismissed Carver as exaggerating, acknowledged historian Jeremy Belknap as discussing New Hampshiremen who had been hit particularly hard, and somehow concluded that "it is probably that the whole number massacred and carried off by the savages was less than three hundred." Hoyt added an ambiguous caution: "And for the honor of His *Most Christian* Majesty's troops, it is hoped that even this exceeds the real number of the sufferers."[67] Neither Frye nor Hoyt had much immediate impact on the legend that had been built by Carver and Humphreys, was being reinforced by Timothy Dwight, and then cemented in legend by James Fenimore Cooper.

Timothy Dwight was a Congregational minister, nationalist poet, and president of Yale for twenty-two years before his death in 1817.[68] He had not had an opportunity to read Frye's journal when preparing his reflections on the killings as part of his famous *Travels in New England and New York*, which appeared posthumously in 1821 and 1822. He had found the grass-covered remains of the beachfront fort well placed in terms of immediate access, but derided its position as readily commanded by the hill on which Fort George was later built.[69] For his history of the "massacre," Dwight relied on Jonathan Carver and the initial newspaper reports from New York City.[70] Having said that it was impossible to know how many were killed, Dwight cited Carver's figure of fifteen hundred and pointed out that the New Hampshire regiment "lost" eighty out of two hundred. He was not the last to distort Belknap's newspaper-based figures for those killed and captured from that regiment.[71] Dwight did not "particularize the enormities" of what happened, but he warmed to the task of denouncing those on both sides of the Atlantic who had tried to defend Montcalm. Dwight saw Montcalm as knowingly repeating the deceit of Oswego: "That the marquis was brave, no well-informed man can doubt. His faithlessness and inhumanity are equally indubitable." The guard was nonexistent or inadequate; the Indians were "tigers in human shape" or "wretches."[72]

Although Dwight claimed that "from that day to the present," the tragedy at Fort William Henry "has been familiarly known by the emphatical appellation of the massacre at Fort William Henry," he was the first to print the phrase. Early newspaper accounts and Smollett had mentioned victims being "massacred," and both Carver and Roubaud used the term "massacre." Samuel Niles wrote of "this barbarous massacre" soon after the event and Desandrouins' paper was "au sujet du massacre des Anglois," but neither of these narratives had been published. Dwight's catchphrase, "the massacre at Fort William Henry," soon popularized by James Fenimore Cooper, emphasized the European perception of this event as an extensive, nonmilitary slaughter of those who had just become civilians. Compared with the well-known Deerfield or Lachine massacres and the well-used "Boston Massacre" of 1770, there was no doubt that the scale of killings at Fort William Henry was immense. Henceforth the incident bore that evocative name.

Dwight also furthered the Americanization of the story by adding his own version of Putnam's account of a frustrated rescue by a New York militia. Dwight heard from a Captain Eli Noble, who was at Fort Edward, that Sir William Johnson and the militia (who had, almost to a man, volunteered for the assignment) had set out for the relief of Fort William Henry when the incompetent Webb countermanded his own orders. Although Monro was allowed his bravery, Webb and Loudoun were denounced: "Two more absolutely inefficient men than the Earl of Loudoun and General Webb have rarely been employed in important military command in the same country during the same campaign."[73] Dwight had also made the siege itself into a contest pitting three thousand men, mainly regulars, against eight thousand, including Indians. In his view, this was a British military defeat, not an American one.

The "massacre at Fort William Henry" was rescued from the historians and fixed in American legend by *The Last of the Mohicans: A Narrative in 1757.* James Fenimore Cooper's classic novel showed no evidence that he had used the initial reports of the incident or the English or French histories and memoirs printed before he began writing the book in 1824. One can only imagine what Cooper might have done if he had Père Roubaud's letter to contrast with Jonathan Carver's *Travels.* Cooper made some use of Humphreys and Dwight, but owed more to Carver.[74]

In some significant respects, the novelist was more accurate than his selected and biased sources. Cooper's portrayal of Indians was stereotypical, though his sense of their motives represented considerable sensitivity in the face of his historical sources. The noble Uncas and the demonic Magua hold a foreground that cannot entirely obscure the two thousand nameless "raging savages" who responded to Magua's war whoop to perpetrate the massacre.[75] Yet Cooper did wrestle with cultural relativities through Hawkeye and occasionally through Chingachgook.[76] Indian discontent with the paleface peace, last noted in print by Mante, whom Cooper did not use, was revealed through Magua's imaginary meeting with Montcalm, at which the Huron complained, "Not a warrior has a scalp."[77] Cooper saw the trouble as starting when a greedy and disobedient provincial attempted to make off with goods that others had abandoned as they left.[78] A tussle over these legitimate prizes was again an understated explanation that was truer than Carver's.

Cooper's portrait of French culpability also showed more sensitivity than Carver's denunciations, though Carver and Dwight were Cooper's sources. Montcalm's reflection on the difficulties of limiting "my red friends" to the usages of war was inserted in a supposed re-creation of personal negotiations, making it at once a ploy and a premonition, as was true in Montcalm's actual summons to surrender at the beginning of the siege.[79] Montcalm mistrusted the likes of Magua and worried about a repeat of the violations of Oswego, but ultimately "felt that his influence over the warlike tribes he had gathered was to be maintained by concessions rather than by power."[80] This may not have been intended as a parody of the argument of those defenders of the French who claimed that the English prisoners brought on the slaughter by giving in to minor demands. Cooper's heroine-captives, like Carver, climbed a mountain and then looked down to see the slaughter, continuing "while the armed columns of the Christian King stood fast, in an apathy which has never been explained, and which has left an immovable blot on the otherwise fair escutcheon"[81] of Montcalm. Cooper could not bring himself to the same shrill denunciations as Dwight, but saw the French commander as possessed of a "cruel apathy" and "deficient in moral courage."[82] Since Cooper's sources made no mention of the efforts of the French or Canadians to save the English, and made little mention of the Indians taking prisoners rather than slaughtering them, Cooper's judgment was not harsh. Although Cooper was unaware of how quickly the killing changed to a scramble for prisoners, Magua's capture of Cora and Alice was closer to reality than were the accounts of Carver, Humphreys, and Dwight. The archetypal captivity narrative again reaffirmed its long-established place in American literature and seemed closer to the truth than the simple savage butchery that Carver had wanted to convey.

Cooper's literary purposes did not require him to make any estimate of the number of victims of the "massacre." He portrayed carnage that went on for hours, until finally "cupidity got mastery of revenge. Then, indeed, the shrieks of the wounded, and the yells of their murderers, grew less frequent, until finally the cries of horror were lost to their ear, or were drowned in the loud, long and piercing whoops of the triumphal savages."[83] Carver had led Cooper to this frightening finish. The 1831 edition of the novel included in a footnote: "The accounts of the number who fell in this unhappy affair, vary between five and fifteen hundred."[84] While these numbers did not represent the range of estimates then available in print, Cooper was again bringing his fabrication a little closer to reality than were the frozen memories of his eyewitness, Jonathan Carver.

III

From Cooper's time, the "massacre at Fort William Henry" came to have two discernible roles in the emerging history of the United States, one in the context of Indian policy and the other in the service of Whig nationalism. The portrait of fundamental Indian savagery supported both the Jacksonian forced migration of Indians to the west of the Mississippi in the 1830s, and the wars of extermination against the Indians of the plains in the generation after 1860. The "Black legend" was popularized by Henry Trumbull's *History of the Discovery of America*, reprinted eighteen times between 1802 and 1840 before being revised as *History of the Indian Wars* and reprinted at least seven more times between 1841 and 1854. Trumbull represented an assertion of New England's participation in Indian wars in the face of the growing popularity of tales originating west of the Appalachians. It was also a tract to discourage the increasing New England emigration westward. In later editions, Trumbull pirated Epaphras Hoyt's entire eleven-paragraph account of Fort William Henry to these purposes, omitting only Hoyt's qualifying hope that the casualties were fewer than he had estimated.[85] Editions of Trumbull shared the popular market with Samuel G. Drake's numerous editions of captivity narratives, Indian biographies, and accounts of earlier Indian wars.[86] John Frost, under the pseudonym William V. Moore, wrote the popular *Indian Wars of the United States from the Discovery to the Present Time*, which was published in Philadelphia in 1840 and reprinted twenty-three times in the next nineteen years. His brief sketch of the fall of Fort William Henry portrayed Webb as failing to do his duty, and Montcalm's "daring spirit" as inspiring troops of all colors in the siege, but he was in "eternal disgrace" for the slaughter that followed. "At least fifteen hundred persons were thus slaughtered or carried into captivity."[87]

A more scholarly approach, already evident in some state histories, was also affecting the broader national studies of the young United States. From 1824 to 1836, James Grahame was researching and writing his four-volume *History of the United States of North America, from the Plantation of the British Colonies till their Assumption of National Independence*. This scholarly Scottish lawyer, enamored with America, developed an excellent synthesis of printed sources, including the best state histories. State histories usually had little room, however, for a story of a disaster that struck New Englanders in what had later become New York. Grahame's brief discussion of the taking of Fort William Henry relied on Jeremy Belknap's study of New Hampshire, George Minot's history of Massachusetts, and Benjamin Trumbull's study of Connecticut,[88] as well as Carver and Dwight. Loudoun was pilloried for bad judgment and bad manners, and Webb was presented as either indolent or timid. Grahame mentioned Indian resentment, that Montcalm preferred his enemies to his allies, and claimed the Indians were determined to force Montcalm to betray the English rather than themselves. Grahame tried to be both philosophical and sympathetic about the discrepancies and exaggerations of surviving accounts: "surely, it is absurd to expect scenes of atrocious cruelty and injustice should be dispassionately described either by the victims or their friends." He accepted Carver's count of the victims and, like Dwight, saw them as supported by Belknap's findings: "Of the garrison of Fort William Henry scarcely a half were enabled to gain the shelter of Fort Edward in a straggling and wretched condition." As with Dwight and Carver, the inadequacy of the French escort and a similar incident at Oswego had sullied "the character of Montcalm with an imputation of treachery and dishonour, which, as it has never yet been satisfactorily repelled, seems likely to prove as lasting as his name."[89]

In 1844, the careful study of early American history was greatly advanced by the return of John Romeyn Brodhead from Europe with eighty volumes of copied documents from European archives relating to the history of New York. Even before the appearance of his four-volume *Documentary History of the State of New York* in 1850 and 1851, or the massive fifteen-volume *Documents Relative to the Colonial History of the State of New York*, published between 1853 and 1887, his transcripts were available to some historians, including George Bancroft.

George Bancroft wrote what quickly became the standard and very popular ten-volume *History of the United States*. This sweeping story of the victory of democracy found room for a chapter on 1757, first published in 1852. The Fort William Henry campaign had been another failure of the aristocratic British government that could "paralyze the immense energies of the British empire."[90] Loudoun's strategy was absurd, and Webb was a coward. Bancroft accepted Montcalm's explanation of English liquor and earlier English treachery against the Abenaki as causing the killing, but omitted the supposed unwillingness of the British and Americans to defend themselves. Lévis and the French officers intervened, and Montcalm offered himself in place of the English. "Twenty, perhaps even thirty, persons were massacred, while very many were made prisoners."[91]

In his casualty figures and explanations, Bancroft was led by available French sources toward conclusions that supported Franco-American amity. The accounts of both Montcalm and Roubaud were central, and Bancroft used them more than his footnoting indicates to modern readers. More significantly, he used Brodhead's still-unpublished copies of numerous French manuscripts, including a long descriptive letter by Bougainville, dated August 19, 1757. Although Bancroft subjected all of this excellent material to a blinding concern for the later Revolution, his work represented a significant advance in the use of manuscript sources. He made revisions in subsequent editions in response to criticisms, but there were no changes in his version of the "massacre."[92] He followed Montcalm in exonerating the French, blaming the British, and reducing the casualties sufficiently to minimize what he nonetheless called "the massacre."

In the three decades between the publication of Bancroft's version and that of Francis Parkman, comparatively little new material was printed concerning the incident. New England folk memories were stirred by two publications in 1861. M. A. Stickney, whose grandfather and great-grandfather had been at the fall of Fort William Henry, published a short article on "the massacre."[93] Reminiscences of the number in Montcalm's force "supposed, by those in the fort at the time, to be near 15,000 men" were cut by Stickney to under thirteen thousand, "but in the account of the numbers engaged, and in many other respects, writers do not agree." Stickney's ancestors and their friends had particularly remembered the French howitzer shells "filled with deadly missiles" that exploded in the fort during the daytime; their lighted fuses made them easier to avoid at night. Recollections of Webb were particularly bitter. Stickney repeated Israel Putnam's myth of William Johnson leading provincial volunteers three miles up the road from Fort Edward to relieve the besieged fort, causing Montcalm to prepare to retreat until Johnson was recalled by Webb. The patriotic story had improved even further with retelling. Johnson had attempted to run Webb through with his sword and, when prevented, broke it in disgust. Webb's letter, advising Monro to make terms, came to Montcalm "as it is supposed" Webb had intended. Carver's version of the final negotiations and the slaughter was repeated, including the casualty figures and Belknap's supporting numbers from the New Hampshire regiment.[94] Putnam's other myth, of over a hundred mangled bodies of women and children seen in the burned fort, was also still believed.

The other Massachusetts account, written during the Seven Years' War and finally published in 1861 (the year the Cheyenne–Arapaho War began), was the last installment of Reverend Samuel Niles's "Summary Historical Narrative of the Wars in New England with the French and Indians in the Several Parts of the Country."[95] This predecessor of Epaphras Hoyt, Henry Trumbull, and John Frost exaggerated the size of both armies and incorporated the more lurid newspaper descriptions. His most original fantasy was that Montcalm was a Scottish Jacobite, who fled to France after the failure of the '45, "and now had given vent to his rage against the English, and the Protestant religion, mostly professed among them." Writing of "this barbarous massacre" from Massachusetts even before Carver's *Travels* appeared, Niles estimated that the slaughtered "at the lowest computation were two hundred and fifty persons."[96]

Francis Parkman brought together the popular and the scholarly accounts masterfully in his classic *Montcalm and Wolfe*.[97] In reviewing Cooper's *Last of the Mohicans* some thirty-two years earlier, he had quibbled about improbabilities in the plot but objected primarily to the idealized Indian portrayed by Uncas. "Magua, the villain of the story, is a less untruthful portrait."[98] In preparing his own account, Parkman gathered an impressive array of manuscripts with the help of his friends Pierre Margry[99] in Paris and Abbé Henri-Raymond Casgrain in Quebec. Parkman was able to see the soon-to-be-published journals of Lévis and Anne-Joseph-Hippolyte de Maures, Comte de Malartic, the correspondence of Bigot, Montcalm, and Vaudreuil, as well as that part of Bougainville's journal covering the Fort William Henry campaign.[100] In the British Public Record Office, Parkman found new letters by Frye, Monro, and Webb, as well as the Miles Whitworth affidavit about the killing of the Massachusetts wounded.

Parkman combined large sections from Bougainville and Roubaud with his own knowledge of the geography to create a graphic description of the siege.[101] The defenders, at twenty-two hundred, are fewer than Parkman's sources claimed; and the French mortars and howitzers, at fifteen, were more than triple the reports in his sources. The substantial earthen structure of the fort itself was not described specifically, and Parkman nearly tripled the English casualties counted by his French witnesses.[102] He recognized that Webb had only sixteen hundred men at Fort Edward and gently criticized him for being tardy in seeking provincial reinforcement, but Parkman nonetheless expected him to have attacked. It is interesting that Parkman's efforts to enhance the heroic did not include acceptance of Israel Putnam's story of provincials launching such an expedition.

In assigning responsibility for the "massacre," Parkman admitted that Montcalm "might well have done more," but protected the reputation of his tragic hero. He echoed Montcalm's three excuses for blaming the English. Parkman entirely invented the image of Indians demanding rum as the column left, "and some of the soldiers, afraid to refuse, gave it to them from their canteens, thus adding fuel to the flame."[103] The Abenaki were blamed for starting the killing, though nothing was mentioned of the Abenaki grievances that Montcalm had highlighted. Parkman did not agree with Montcalm's claim that the English failed to defend themselves, but said that "something like a panic seized them: for they distrusted not the Indians only, but the Canadians."[104] Some of the Canadians were also accused with a sly "It is said that some of the interpreters secretly fomented the disorder" based on Pouchot's comment.[105] In general, Parkman exonerated the French, the English, and most Canadians in order to denounce the Indians.

Parkman's massacre was by Indians whose savagery he saw primarily as neither provoked nor alcohol-induced. Roubaud's account of fighting between allied warriors became, with Parkman's invention, "sometimes, when mad with brandy, they grappled and tore each other with their teeth like wolves."[106] At the Indian conference held during the surrender negotiations, the chiefs "approved everything and promised everything."[107] Parkman's creativity was all too obvious when he went well beyond Frye's journal of August 9. The English had destroyed the rum barrels in their encampment,

> but the Indians were drunk already with homicidal rage, and the glitter of their vicious eyes told of the devil within. They roamed among the tents, intrusive, insolent, their visages besmirched with war-paint; grinning like fiends as they handled, in anticipation of the knife, the long hair of cowering women, of whom, as well as of children, there were many in the camp, all crazed with fright.[108]

This was no search for legitimate loot by those who felt cheated, but a fiendish preview worthy of Cooper's Magua, and just as imagined.

In counting the victims, Parkman employed some sleight of hand to bring together New England legend and the minimal French embarrassment accepted by Roubaud and Lévis. Admitting that it was impossible to count those killed, Parkman mentioned Roubaud's forty to fifty and Lévis' fifty, to which he added the sick and wounded killed in the fort and in the camp. Parkman went out of his way to "correct" Jeremy Belknap after somehow joining those who misread the latter's statement that, of the New Hampshiremen in the siege, "out of two hundred, eighty were killed and taken."[109] Parkman claimed that "it is certain that six or seven hundred persons were carried off, stripped, and otherwise maltreated," recovering certitude from someplace other than his sources. Four hundred were recovered by Montcalm, and the

Indian captors headed for Montreal with plunder and "some two hundred prisoners, who, it is said, could not be got out of their hands."[110] By going back to the "it is said" of the initial newspaper propaganda, and by saying nothing whatever about the return of any prisoners from Canada by way of Halifax, Parkman had reconciled the French and American numbers. In all, about seventy had been killed and two hundred were left in Indian hands. It was probably coincidental that he ended his chapter with wolves, his earlier metaphor for the Indians: "The din of ten thousand combatants, the rage, the terror, the agony, were gone; and no living thing was left but the wolves that gathered from the mountains to feast upon the dead."[111]

IV

Despite Parkman's visits, correspondents, and public recognition in the province of Quebec, he had very little sympathy or understanding for their perspectives on the Seven Years' War.[112] François-Xavier Garneau, in his four-volume *Histoire du Canada* of 1845 to 1852, had displayed nationalist, liberal-democratic and anti-clerical concerns. He credited the Canadian Vaudreuil with all the initiative, while the French Montcalm was fatalistic and apathetic. The conquest of Canada was due to abandonment by the unreformed French government, defeated inevitably by a more representative British government.[113] A Canadian counterpart to Bancroft, without the latter's printed notes on sources, Garneau can be regarded as the first French-Canadian historian.

Success at Fort William Henry was a little awkward for Garneau, as it was to be for some later French-Canadian historians trying to blame the French for the English conquest. The garrison fell because Webb misjudged the size of the attacking force. Garneau appreciated that the Indians had again been deprived of plunder and mentioned the Abenaki and the English liquor, but regarded barbarism as the main cause of the "still regrettable incident." Although he had sympathy for Indian religious ideas, which supported his anti-clerical views, Garneau saw Indian barbarism as justifying his own faith in civilization. The use of French force seemed to have ended the slaughter for Garneau, who claimed that members of the French escort were killed as well as wounded. Without estimating the English killed, Garneau accounted for the return of thirteen hundred of the twenty-five hundred he thought had survived the siege. Garneau was the first historian to mention that two hundred prisoners were ransomed by Vaudreuil at Montreal.[114]

Franco-Canadian tensions, so central to most French-Canadian versions of the war from Garneau to Guy Frégault, had little place in French accounts. The French historian Louis-Etienne Dussieux published a military history, *Le Canada sous la domination française d'apres les archives de la marine et de la guerre*, in 1855. Drawing on familiar and new French military sources, Dussieux portrayed the attack on Fort William Henry as a joint plan by the governor and the general to fulfill a defensive purpose. Rigaud's winter attack was changed to a spoiling raid because it had not been able to surprise the garrison. Dussieux gave no detail of the August siege, but offered a correction to Cooper's version of the massacre. The English, in their hurry to leave on the morning of August 10, did not wait for their escort, an explanation that even Montcalm had not claimed. Dussieux portrayed the English giving rum to the Indians and then being too terrified to defend themselves. He numbered the dead at a score and praised both French efforts to protect the English and Vaudreuil's expensive ransom. Dussieux was the first to use and reprint the Vaudreuil letter of September 1757, which he did not know was actually a draft by Montcalm.[115] A long footnote answered Cooper, using Malartic's manuscript journal and comparisons with the Raisin River massacre of 1813 to defend the honor of the French military.[116]

The direct Canadian challenge to Garneau came from Abbé J.-B.-A. Ferland, whose two-volume *Cours d'histoire du Canada* appeared between 1861 and 1865. In this ultramontane Catholic account, French and Canadian forces were seen in harmony, fighting and suffering together, though the victory at Fort William Henry was due to divine providence. Roubaud was not mentioned by name, but provided most of the unacknowledged detail concerning the siege and the butchery. The Indians received no understanding from Abbé Ferland; "the massacre" was caused, as Roubaud had claimed, by "insatiable ferocity" as well as by "excessive independence" among the Indians and by their hatred for the English. Ferland quoted Montcalm's letter to Loudoun to explain the reasons for the killings, but preferred Roubaud's estimate of the number killed.[117] Neither Garneau nor Ferland exerted himself to defend Montcalm against charges of complicity raised by Niles, Carver, Dwight, Cooper, and Grahame. For Garneau, who was familiar with American historians, Bancroft had already answered those charges adequately.

Sensitivity to the American accusations was still considerable when American presidential-hopeful General George Brinton McClellan made a speech from the balcony of the Fort William Henry Hotel in 1864. His reference to Cooper's description of Montcalm's "cruel apathy" was widely reported in the American press, provoking the only Canadian publication concentrating specifically on the massacre. James MacPherson Le Moine's *Mémoire de Montcalm vengée ou le massacre au Fort George. Documents historiques* defended Montcalm's generosity and chivalry and referred McClellan to Bancroft. Most of the long pamphlet was a reprint of Carver and Roubaud. Le Moine concluded by pointing out the complete power that an Indian captor had over his victim and by confidently inviting readers to choose between the two witnesses.[118]

The classic French-Canadian version of the Seven Years' War, imitating yet counteracting Parkman, was the work of the romantic nationalist Abbé H.-R. Casgrain. His twelve-volume edition of *Collection des manuscrits du Marechal de Lévis* (1889–95) consisted of most of the relevant French military journals and much of the pertinent correspondence. His bias against France, that "frivolous, decadent, immoral and impious"[119] power which allowed Canada to fall, became evident with his *Guerre du Canada 1756–1760. Montcalm et Lévis* (1891). Casgrain, then sixty, was recalling the invasion fears of the 1860s and urging his people to recover the vigor of an earlier time. For him, the fall of New France was a blessing, saving Canada from the anti-religious fanaticism of the French Revolution.

In discussing Fort William Henry, Casgrain used Parkman's technique of stringing together quotations from his sources. Rigaud's winter raid became Vaudreuil's surprise attack, which inflicted great losses and accomplished all that could have been expected.[120] Canadians Langlade and de Corbière were, for Casgrain, firmly in command in the great victory over Parker at Sabbath Day Point, "one of the most horrible tragedies one can mention in American annals." Casgrain saw this as a greater English disaster than the "massacre" at Fort William Henry, without appreciating that the Indians regarded both as comparable acts of war.[121] The sensitive comments by Desandrouins, parts of which had been printed in a biography that appeared in 1887,[122] gave Casgrain some detail, which he used, and some understanding of the Indians, which he did not use. For Casgrain, the English had helped provoke their difficulties, and Roubaud and Lévis were correct in noting that about fifty of them were killed. Bougainville, whose journal Casgrain deliberately suppressed, had accused the

Canadian interpreters of encouraging Indian pillaging of the English, and Parkman had promulgated it. Casgrain made a special effort to clear the Canadians of this charge, claiming that Bougainville himself had not been able to save the wounded in the fort on August 9.[123]

Surprisingly like Parkman, Casgrain said nothing whatever of Vaudreuil's ransom of prisoners, though he echoed Desandrouins in noting that Vaudreuil did not have enough troops at Montreal to compel the Indians to give up their prisoners. The Indians, and not the French, were primarily responsible for the incident, and Casgrain joined Carver in regarding the smallpox, that they subsequently suffered as divine retribution. His chapter ended, in direct imitation of Parkman's romantic finale, on the site which had become silent, except for the sinister cries of night birds and wild beasts, drawn by the smell of the dead.[124]

Amid those seeking to diminish Montcalm's responsibility in the "massacre at Fort William Henry," one dissenting voice came from a self-taught English-Canadian historian, William Kingsford. In his ten-volume history (1887–98), celebrating the wonders of responsible government, he turned his Whiggery to support the British in the 1757 campaign. Kingsford found Webb sensibly prudent and judged unfairly by those who saw only "the earnestness of Monroe's appeal to him."[125] Although he supported Montcalm in his disputes with Vaudreuil, Kingsford found him culpable in the incident. From the initial summons to the surrender terms, Montcalm was ignoring his own previous negotiations with the Indians and his experience at Oswego. Kingsford dismissed rum, English cowardice, and Abenaki revenge as excuses. The Canadians had known from past experience that it was necessary to gratify Indian "instincts for blood, plunder, and prisoners." About fifty people died because Montcalm failed to prevent the disaster.[126] Kingsford's attack would eventually be countered, but not by ardent French-Canadian nationalist historians.

Although French historians have had little reason to lavish much attention on the Seven Years' War in North America, Dussieux's work was followed by one of the most enduring studies of the subject, Richard Waddington's *Guerre de septs ans*. Drawing more fully on American, Canadian, British, and French documents and historians than any previous writer, Waddington achieved what was long considered a convincing general synthesis. In discussing the Fort William Henry campaign, the unruly and ferocious Indian allies were described, and Montcalm was quoted at length concerning the attack on Colonel Parker's expedition. The well-directed siege was applauded, but the "horrible massacre" blotted the reputation of Montcalm and his army. Despite numerous intimations of trouble, the French escort provided was much too small, and the tired Canadian officers who had influence with the Indians had left, presumably after their night's vigil. Waddington appreciated Desandrouins' sense that rivalries and greed accelerated the violence, and the historian accepted Parkman's story of the rum from the canteens. The outburst of Indian fury was followed by rescue, involving Montcalm, officers, interpreters, missionaries, and Vaudreuil in Montreal. Waddington adopted the Lévis and Roubaud estimates of fifty casualties, adding that others died in the woods and on the return to Montreal. While he cited Mante, who had accepted Montcalm's attempt to blame the English for their own difficulties, Waddington recognized this self-serving tactic. He also supported these few critics who claimed that Montcalm should have proceeded to Fort Edward.[127]

Attacks on Montcalm's general reputation had been a common feature of French-Canadian history, and Niles, Carver, Dwight, Cooper, Grahame, and Kingsford had also attacked the martyred marquis for his conduct at Fort William Henry. Felix Martin, the Jesuit historian of the Canadian missions, wrote a biography of Montcalm that beatified a tragic hero. After recounting the killing of some prisoners in Fort William Henry on August 9, Martin was entirely satisfied with Montcalm's arrangements to fulfill the surrender terms. English officers had given drink to the Indians, "provoking their rage and wakening their worst instincts," allowing a night of drunken excess. Abenaki grievances were recalled, and the escort and the French officers, led by Montcalm, had done everything possible.[128] Denouncing Cooper for following biased English sources, Martin countered by using only the supposedly unbiased French ones, beginning with Montcalm. Defending Montcalm was largely a matter of repeating Montcalm, evidence of the care with which the marquis had assembled his own defense.[129]

The most convincing defense of Montcalm was the work of Thomas Chapais, professor of history at Laval. His first life of Montcalm, appearing in 1901, included a creditable sketch of the siege of Fort William Henry, with the significant absence of any reference to Marin's raid or the battle of Sabbath Day Point. He then approached "one of the most tragic episodes in the stirring annals of these times" in the hope that "truth and justice" had finally overcome "the angry feelings and passionate misrepresentations." The Indians were given English liquor, "pouring oil on the unholy fire already kindled in the savage beast."[130] Accepting Lévis and Roubaud, Chapais attacked Cooper as "reckless" about the scale of the "massacre" and quoted Bancroft at length to refute him. A decade later, Chapais' impressive monograph, *Le Marquis de Montcalm (1712–1759)*, offered a more thoroughly researched defense. Chapais used Roubaud more extensively here to portray the raucous Indian allies, but put the Canadians firmly in charge of these "amphibious monsters" during their victory at Sabbath Day Point. Montcalm was masterful throughout the siege and surrender at Fort William Henry. Desandrouins was used, but not to add any rational motives to the Indians' "ferocious instincts" exacerbated by rum.[131] Chapais had sympathy for Frye and Carver and argued that the Canadians arrived late that morning and some may have encouraged the Indians, but he firmly defended the French. Montcalm's personal interventions on behalf of prisoners were emphasized, and Chapais confidently concluded that he had examined all the evidence and refuted the calumnies of Carver and Cooper. The slaughter had resulted from Indian ferocity aggravated by English rum and panic, which Montcalm could not have foreseen. Understandably misled by what Dussieux had published as an authentic Vaudreuil letter, Chapais carefully assembled statistics that counted fifty dead, a wonderful eighteen hundred returned by Montcalm on August 10 and 14, with two hundred more escaping through the woods, and another two hundred in the hands of the Indians to be redeemed by Vaudreuil.[132] Montcalm had been convincingly exonerated on all counts.

By 1900, other French-Canadian historians had come to describe the essential features of the Fort William Henry campaign much as had Parkman, and also joined him in assigning this awkward French victory only minor significance. The siege was unwanted evidence of effective cooperation between the French and the Canadian leaders, soldiers, and methods of war. Like Vaudreuil's dispatches, Canadian historians attributed every Indian success to the Canadians who "led" them. However, the Canadians apparently had no control over and no connection with the Indians during the brief and minimal slaughter that Montcalm and Roubaud were called on to describe. The whole campaign was a mild embarrassment to those Canadian historians who argued that Montcalm was inflexible and passive, and that France abandoned Canada. Abbé Lionel Groulx, who continued the nationalist tradition, quickly passed over the incident as one of the few sunny days in the gathering gloom for New France.[133]

V

If "Remember Fort William Henry" had once been a battle cry, the twentieth century has largely forgotten it. This is true of the siege and the "massacre" that Kingsford had called "one of the best remembered [scenes] in the history of the continent."[134] Parkman and Casgrain, for all their scholarly and personal differences, had told the story in ways that were fairly complementary. Consensus had been reached on the causes of the incident: the natural ferocity of the Indians, aggravated by their hatred for the English and their susceptibility to English rum, explained what American and Canadian historians agreed was a minor incident detracting from a minor French victory. American historians might emphasize British incompetence and French-Canadian nationalists might be unfavorably inclined to Montcalm, but these concessions to patriotism upset only the dwindling number of Montcalm's defenders. As antagonism between Britain and France yielded to more cooperative military concerns in the twentieth century, the Seven Years' War and the "massacre" became even more distant for historians of those nations.[135]

Although British imperial historians have, understandably, shown more enthusiasm for the Seven Years' War in North America than have French historians, Fort William Henry has not been very usable from their perspective. The Royal Navy was necessarily absent, and this textbook defeat in a wilderness siege of a mixture of British and American forces was much less interesting than the failure of Braddock.[136] The "imperial school" of early American history included two historians who made some use of the greatest new source, the Loudoun Papers in the Huntington Library, in reviewing the Fort William Henry campaign. Stanley M. Pargellis' *Lord Loudoun in North America* (1933) included a defense of Loudoun's general plan for 1757, a denunciation of Webb, and a misleading suggestion that the Loudoun Papers offered little that was new about the incident.[137] Lawrence Henry Gipson's monumental work included an unexceptional account of the campaign in which English colonists were accused of a reluctance to fight, Webb was pilloried, and Montcalm was chided for faulty planning of the escort, though praised for personal courage. Without any explanation, Gipson stated that the victims numbered "probably not less than two hundred and may have greatly exceeded that number."[138] Subsequent American military historians have, without returning to the surviving sources, offered estimates that range from Bancroft's twenty to Gipson's two hundred victims.[139]

One scholarly modern monograph, Guy Frégault's *Guerre de la conquête*, returned to many of the original sources to reinforce earlier French-Canadian nationalist concerns. Vaudreuil was the Canadian hero of the "Victorious Resistance" of 1755 to 1757. Rigaud's raid was an entirely successful preliminary isolation of the target. Montcalm was so pessimistic and defensive that Frégault called General Webb "un autre Montcalm."[140] Without any discussion of the successful siege of Fort William Henry, Frégault focused on Vaudreuil's disobeyed orders for Montcalm to proceed to Fort Edward. The terror in the English colonies and the pessimistic predictions of their military leaders were used to support Vaudreuil's claims that Montcalm should have continued the campaign. After making Vaudreuil's guerrilla warfare a central theme of his book, Frégault entirely sidestepped the "épisode," which was a predictable result of Vaudreuil's applauded method. Only by ignoring the significant Indian victory over the Parker expedition and the Indians' "mutiny and desertion" of August 10 could Frégault argue that Montcalm should have proceeded to Fort Edward. Once again, the nationalist argument found little room or need for discussion of the campaign at Fort William Henry. Subsequent Canadian studies have returned rather too easily to Montcalm, in blaming only the English and the Indians, and have discovered a surprisingly consistent casualty estimate of twenty-nine, well below "massacre" proportions.[141]

Historians anxious to promote a better understanding of Indians have generally preferred to study clearer instances of injustice to Indians, rather than answer historical slurs in such a well-documented context that included Indians making their own history, but also eating prisoners. Even writers sympathetic to the Indians have assumed that there was a universal and self-evident distinction between a "battle," like the ambush at Sabbath Day Point, and a "massacre," like Fort William Henry. It has also been assumed that this European distinction should have controlled the actions of everyone.[142]

The incident at Fort William Henry has had many uses. Initially it was to rally vengeful British and American colonial soldiers and to inflate the reputation of William Pitt in comparison with his predecessors. Amherst used the "massacre" to deny the honors of war to the defeated French at Louisbourg and Montreal, and as an excuse for his own firm exclusion of Indians from the "civilized" conventions of war. During the American Revolutionary War, Jonathan Carver's "massacre" was used by the British to denounce the French and by Americans to damn the British. "The massacre at Fort William

Henry" was coined in time to help justify the removal and elimination of American Indians. In the century since the last Indian wars marked the closing of the American frontier, this incident has become part of the "unusable past" and has been left to those enamored with the imagination of James Fenimore Cooper or Francis Parkman. Canadian historians have had even less use for the subject. English-Canadian historians and their audience have not been nearly as anxious as Kingsford to dwell on their own or their country's historical schizophrenia. French-Canadian nationalists have little use for Montcalm's military success, in what soon became the New York wilderness, or for a massacre by Vaudreuil's disgruntled allies that Canadians did not conspicuously resist.

There has been one dominant consistency in historical accounts of the "massacre at Fort William Henry"; it has been portrayed as an attack of irrational Indian ferocity, implying that it might be overcome like other wild hazards of nature. This nineteenth-century view ignored the betrayal of the Indians evident in early English accounts in newspapers, Entick, Mante, and Grahame. This oversight has continued, ignoring the Indian motives suggested by Pouchot, Desandrouins, and Malartic, who could not admit the French betrayal of the English or the Indians, but at least sought explanations for Indian actions. Despite their obvious motives, Montcalm, Bougainville, and Roubaud have been the preferred witnesses, not only for what they saw, but also for their explanations of the actions of the Indians of the *pays d'en haut*. Historians have not recognized the victory over Colonel Parker as belonging to the Indians or given it the strategic importance it deserves. Negotiations to send the resulting prisoners to Montreal have been overlooked, as have the Indian military conventions that they reveal.

While Europeans and some of their colonists accepted new and curiously humane conventions that made killing some soldiers a great victory and killing others a "massacre" of innocents, the Indians maintained clearer definitions between themselves and their enemies. Most of the English and French were understandably horrified by the violation of their conventions, but it is helpful to place the incident in the context of a very strained military alliance. Loot, scalps, and prisoners were the essential symbols of martial success for the Indians and had been promised repeatedly. The collusion between their French allies and their English enemies became increasingly evident in the French negotiations to take the Indians' prisoners after the battle at Sabbath Day Point, in the generously negotiated capitulation, in the

French control of booty in the fallen fort, in the protection of enemy goods and persons in the entrenched camp, and in the attempt to evacuate the English at night. These were all betrayals that helped provoke the Indians to fulfill their own martial purposes on the morning of August 10, 1757. Although French indignation at the Indian attack was measured, French confiscation of prisoners only added to a series of disappointments, which convinced the Indians from the *pays d'en haut* and many of the "mission" Indians that their participation in the war was now over.

APPENDIX:
MISSING NEW ENGLAND
PAROLEES

MASSACHUSETTS

Surviving muster rolls and petitions are in the Massachusetts Archives (Mass. Archives) and the Massachusetts Historical Society, Boston (MHS), and in the American Antiquarian Society, Worcester (AAS), Massachusetts. An additional list, of part of Captain Samuel Thaxter's company in the siege, is in the private collection of J. Robert Maguire (Maguire) of Shoreham, Vermont (Figure 11). The Loudoun Papers (LO) in the Huntington Library (HL) contain five lists of parolees returned to Halifax and Boston [LO 4758, 4778, 4994, 6678, 6795] and a list of sick and wounded prisoners in hospital at Montreal [LO 3893]. Governor Thomas Pownall's list of missing soldiers from the capitulation preserved in the Public Record Office, London (PRO), is not entirely reliable, nor is the report of deaths in French prisons printed in the *Boston Gazette* (*Bos. Gaz.*) on October 9, 1758. Emma Lewis Coleman, *New England Captives Carried to Canada between 1677 and 1760 during the French and Indian Wars*, 2 vols. (Portland, Me., 1925–26), is very valuable, though a few corrections and many additions are included below.

Alger, John   To Canada. RETURNED by Halifax in 1757 [HL, LO 6678]
Allen, Charles   To Canada, still missing 1758 [PRO Adm. 1/3818; Coleman 2:344]
Archbow, Jonathan   To Canada. RETURNED by Halifax in 1757 [HL, LO 4778]
Astin, David, of Samuel Thaxter's co.   Missing [Maguire]

Atwood, Amos, of Salem   To Canada [Coleman 2:345]

Bailey, Jonathan, of Rowley, Israel Davis co.   RETURNED to No. 4 fort Nov. 22, 1759. Taken by Indians, escaped to Quebec, until Nov. 10, 1759. Smallpox [Mass. Archives, 78, pp. 718 & 659; Coleman, 2:346]

Bartlett, Joseph, of Methune   Missing [MHS Saltonstall 1757]

Baxter, James   To Canada. RETURNED by Halifax in 1757 [HL, LO 6678]

Begard, John   To Canada. RETURNED by Halifax in 1757 [HL, LO 6678]

Bekers, John   To Canada. RETURNED by Halifax in 1757 [HL, LO 6678]

Blake, Abel, of Milton   To Canada [Mass. Archives, 95, pp. 506–7; Coleman, 2:337]

Blood, Joseph   To Canada. RETURNED by Halifax in 1757 [HL, LO 6678]

Bosworth, Elisha   To Canada, still missing 1758 [Coleman 2:346; PRO Adm. 1/3818]

Bowen, James, of Marblehead   Missing [MHS Saltonstall 1757]

Boyd, Martin   Missing. [PRO Adm. 1/3818]

Bradbury, Moses   "In Canada if alive," still missing 1758 [Coleman 2:346; PRO Adm. 1/3818]

Bradford, Lieutenant Joel, of Taunton   DIED in Canada [Coleman 2:337]

Bradley, Moses, of Endicott's   To Canada [Coleman 2:337]

Brewer, Peter   To Canada. RETURNED by Halifax in 1757 [HL, LO 6678]

Bristol, James, mulatto   Still missing 1758 [Coleman 2:346; PRO Adm. 1/3818]

Brown, Gideon, of Rehoboth (or Taunton?) servant of Mr. Turner   To Canada, still missing 1758 [Coleman 2:346; PRO Adm. 1/3818]

Bryant, William, of Taunton, in Arbuthnot's co.   RETURNED via Halifax Nov. 7, 1757 [HL, LO 4758; Mass. Archives, 95, pp. 506–7]

Bullman, John, of Boston, mariner, in Ingersoll co.   Stripped of all he had at Fort William Henry, RETURNED same year [Mass. Archives, 80, p. 27; Coleman 2:346]

Bush, John   To Canada, died in passage to France [PRO Adm. 1/3818; *Bos. Gaz.* Oct. 9, 1758]

Bush, Zebadiah   Missing 1758 [PRO Adm. 1/3818]

Butterfield, Elijah   To Canada [Coleman 2:347]

Caesar, negro of Jacob Bigelow   Held in Canada. RETURNED Oct. 1760. £8 to his master [Mass. Archives, 80, p. 83; Coleman 2:347]

Calef, James, of Haverhill, of Saltonstall's co.   Carried away by Indians [MHS Saltonstall 1757; Coleman 2:347]

Calef, Samuel, of Haverhill   In jail at Quebec [MHS Saltonstall 1757; Coleman 2:347]

Ceser, Amos, of Samuel Thaxter's co.   [Maguire]

Chaffs, Thomas, of Bayley's co.   RETURNED by Halifax in 1757 [HL, LO 4758]

Church, Joseph   Missing 1758 [PRO Adm. 1/3818]

Clough, Nathaniel   Missing 1758 [PRO Adm. 1/3818]

Cloutman, Benjamin, of Marblehead   Left sick at Rochel, France [*Bos. Gaz.* Oct. 9, 1758]

Coffy, James   To Canada. RETURNED by Halifax in 1757 [HL, LO 6678]

Coneby, John   To Canada. RETURNED by Halifax in 1757 [HL, LO 4758, 6678]

Conelly, William   To Quebec & Plymouth, England Nov. 2, 1758 [N.J. State Archives, Colonial Wars, Box 3, no. 214]

Conkaney, Aaron, of Bridgewater, Samuel Thaxter's co.   Taken from Fort William Henry to St. François for 14 months. Sold to French for 150 livres and put to hard service. May 1759 to prison. Nov. 2, 1759 RETURNED to Crown Point under flag of truce. Home Dec. 11, 1759. [Mass. Archives, 78, pp. 77, 751; Coleman 2:347; Maguire]

Coppy, John   To Canada. RETURNED by Halifax in 1757 [HL, LO 6678]

Cory, William, of Cheever's co.   To Canada [Mass. Archives, 96, p. 53; Coleman 2:337]

Coverly, Wells, of Boston, in Thomas Cheever co.   RETURNED by New York in 1758. Cruelly treated by Indians to Canada, and old France. In filthy jail 12–13 months. To England and then to New York. There impressed into King's service with the regulars. Has been at Lake George and Ticonderoga, and now has a leave, not being discharged. [Mass. Archives, 78, p. 763; 96, p. 53; *Bos. Gaz.* Oct. 9, 1758; Coleman 2:348]

Courtney, John   To Canada. RETURNED by Halifax in 1757 [HL, LO 6678]

Cuggo, Canada, negro   Missing 1758 [Coleman 2:349; PRO Adm. 1/3818]

Davenson [Davidson], Peter   Missing [Mass. Archives, 96, p. 53]

Davis, Nathaniel, of Berwick   To Canada, home via Halifax 1757 [HL, LO 4758; Mass. Archives, 78, p. 268; Coleman 2:349]

Day, Lieutenant David   RETURNED via Halifax 1757 [HL, LO 4758, 4944]

Dawson, John of Tapley's co.   To Canada. RETURNED by Halifax in 1757 [HL, LO 4758; Coleman 2:349]

Dean, John   To Canada. RETURNED by Halifax in 1757 (HL, LO 6678]

Dennis, William, of Samuel Thaxter's co.   To Canada. RETURNED by Halifax in 1757 [Maguire; HL, LO 6678, 4778]

Downing, Jonathan, of Endicott's co.   RETURNED by Halifax in 1757 [HL, LO 4758]

Drake, Abraham   To Canada. RETURNED by Halifax in 1757 [HL, LO 6678]

Dunbar, Nathaniel, of Elisha, in Samuel Thaxter's co.   Still missing 1758 [Maguire, Coleman 2:349; PRO Adm. 1/3818]

Duey [Dewey?], Peter   KILLED at Fort William Henry [Maguire]

Dunfee, Thomas, of Waldo's co.   RETURNED by Halifax in 1757 [HL, LO 4758]

Fair, Elijah, of Arbuthnot's   To Canada [Mass. Archives, 95, pp. 506–7; Coleman 2:337]

Farrand, Thomas, Jr.   DIED in France [Coleman 2:349; *Bos. Gaz.* Oct. 9, 1758]

Finney, Francis   To Canada. RETURNED 1759 [Coleman 2:349; PRO Adm. 1/
3818; AAS *Transactions*, 11:155]

Flagg, Enoch   To Canada [Coleman 2:349]

Flower, John   To Canada. RETURNED by Halifax in 1757 [HL, LO 6678]

Flynn, John, of Milton   Missing [Mass. Archives, 95, pp. 506-7]

Folley, Richard, of Ball's co.   RETURNED by Halifax in 1757 [HL, LO 4758]

Fookett, James   Still missing 1758 [PRO Adm. 1/3818]

Forbes, William, of Arbuthnot's   In Canada [Coleman 2:338]

Fosters, Zebediah, of Roxford, sergeant in Saltonstall's   RETURNED via
Halifax 1757 [MHS Saltonstall 1757; HL, LO 4778]

Franklin, Ichabod   To Canada. RETURNED by Halifax in 1757 [HL, LO 4778,
6678]

Freeman, George   Sick in France [PRO Adm. 1/3818; *Bos. Gaz.* Oct. 9, 1758]

Furbish (Furbush), William, of Berwick, of Endicott co.   Taken to Montreal,
then to Quebec, had smallpox, to France, then England, and RETURNED
1758 [Mass. Archives, 78, p. 120; Coleman 2.350; PRO Adm. 1/3818]

Furbish, William, Jr.   Missing 1758 [PRO Adm. 1/3818]

Furgo, Peter, of Marblehead, servant of Elias Cursely, in Saltonstall's
co.   Missing [MHS Saltonstall 1757]

Gardner, James   To Canada. RETURNED by Halifax in 1757 [HL, LO 6678]

George, Jonathan, of Rehoboth, Indian servant of Aaron Wheeler   Still
missing in 1758 [Mass. Archives, 95, pp. 506-7; PRO Adm. 1/3818;
Coleman 2:350]

Gilman, Antipas, of Exeter   RETURNED by Halifax in 1757 [Coleman 2:350;
HL, LO 3893, 4758]

Gilson, Zechariah, of Hatfield   "By the hands of a Savage bloodthirsty &
barbarously cruel Enemy" stripped, abused, to Montreal, redeemed by
French, to Halifax (smallpox there), and RETURNED in 1758. Granted £5
[Mass. Archives, 78, p. 216]

Goodnow [Goodnay?], Benjamin, of Hardwick, in John Burk co.   To Montreal & Caughnawaga to August 1759. Escaped to General Amherst,
RETURNED. Granted £10 [Mass. Archives, 79, p. 311]

Gough, Nathaniel   Still missing 1758 [Coleman 2:350; PRO Adm. 1/3818]

Green, Francis   Still missing 1758 [PRO Adm. 1/3818]

Greenleaf, Joseph, ensign, of Newbury   To Canada, RETURNED by Halifax in
1757 [Mass. Archives, 79, p. 53; HL, LO 4758, 6795; Coleman 2:351]

Greenleaf, Thomas, of Newbury, apprentice, in Israel Davis co.   To
St. François, Montreal. RETURNED by Halifax, & Boston, 1757 [HL, LO
4758; Coleman 2:351]

Grezo, George   To Canada. RETURNED by Halifax in 1757 [HL, LO 6678]

Grinmon, Edward, Sr. of Swanzey   KILLED in massacre [Coleman 2:351]

Grinmon, Edward, Jr. of Swanzey   To Quebec. RETURNED Nov. 7, 1757 via
Halifax, where he had smallpox [Mass. Archives, 95, pp. 506-7; HL, LO
4778, 6678; Coleman 2:351]

Grino, Daniel   To Canada. RETURNED by Halifax in 1757 [HL, LO 6678]

Hall, John, of New Salem   Was "9 miles a Bove Moriall wi ye Indians" [Coleman 2:351]

Hall, Sylvanus, of Kingston   Still missing 1758 [Coleman 2:351; PRO Adm. 1/3818]

Haniford, Benjamin, of Haverhill, in Saltonstall's co.   RETURNED Nov. 7, 1757 [MHS Saltonstall 1757; HL, LO 4778]

Hardy, Jacob, of Bradford   To Canada [MHS Saltonstall 1757; Coleman 2:351–52]

Harris, Oliver   "Carried to montriel with one arm Brok and is not Returned." Still missing 1758 [Coleman 2:352; PRO Adm. 1/3818]

Hasken, Peter   To Canada. RETURNED by Halifax in 1757 [HL, LO 6678]

Hastings, Eliphet   To Canada. RETURNED by Halifax in 1757 [HL, LO 6678; cf. *Bos. Gaz.* Oct. 9, 1758]

Heaburn, William   To Canada. RETURNED by Halifax in 1757 [HL, LO 6678]

Hewill, James   To Canada. RETURNED by Halifax in 1757 [HL, LO 4778]

Hill, George, of Taunton, in Arbuthnot's co.   Missing [Mass. Archives, 95, pp. 506–7]

Hill, Joseph   Still missing 1758 [Coleman 2:352; PRO Adm. 1/3818]

Hill, Peter   RETURNED Nov. 4, 1757 [HL, LO 4758; Mass. Archives, 95, pp. 506–7]

Hinds, Thomas, of Samuel Thaxter's co.   Missing [Maguire]

Holloway, John, of Samuel Thaxter's co.   Missing [Maguire]

Holman, Hugh   DIED in France [Coleman 2:352]

Holmes, John   To Canada. RETURNED by Halifax in 1757 [HL, LO 6678]

Howard, Nathaniel, of Tapley's co.   RETURNED by Halifax in 1757 [HL, LO 4758]

Hubbard, William, of Braintree   RETURNED Nov. 4, 1757 [HL, LO 4758; Mass. Archives, 95, pp. 506–7]

Hunter, Jabez   To Canada, still missing 1758 [Coleman 2:352; PRO Adm. 1/3818]

Hutchinson, John   Still missing 1758 [Coleman 2:352; PRO Adm. 1/3818]

Innes, Francis   To Canada. RETURNED by Halifax in 1757 [HL, LO 6678]

Jeffreys, Cato, of Braintree, in Arbuthnot's co.   Missing [Mass. Archives, 95, pp. 506–7]

Joly, Thomas   To Canada. RETURNED by Halifax in 1757 [HL, LO 6678]

Jones, John, Jr.   To Quebec. RETURNED via Halifax 1757 [HL, LO 6678; Coleman 2:352; cf. PRO Adm. 1/3818]

Jones, Thomas, of Ipswich   Taken by Indians, still missing 1758 [Coleman 2:353; PRO Adm. 1/3818]

Joseph, Joseph, of Wareham in Plymouth, "Indian man" of Samuel Nichols Nelson co.   To Montreal and an Indian town, to surrender of Montreal. RETURNED. Granted £8 [Mass. Archives, 79, p. 564]

Joseph, Nathan, Indian   Still missing 1758 [Coleman 2:353; PRO Adm. 1/3818]

Keating, Robert   To Canada. RETURNED by Halifax in 1757 [HL, LO 6678]

Keith, James (of Gloucester?), in Baily's co.   Missing [Mass. Archives, 77, p. 677; Coleman 2:353]

Keith, James, Jr., of Uxbridge   Missing [Coleman 2:353]

Kent, John, of Taunton   To Quebec. RETURNED via Halifax in 1757 [HL, LO 6678; Coleman 2:353; cf. PRO Adm. 1/3818]

Kettle, James, Jr.   Still missing 1758 [PRO Adm. 1/3818]

Kid, Michael   To Canada. RETURNED by Halifax in 1757 [HL, LO 6678]

King, Michael   To Canada. RETURNED by Halifax in 1757 [HL, LO 6678]

Knap, John, Jr.   To Canada and France. DIED aboard the *Marigold* in Dec. 1757 being carried from France to England [Curwen Family Papers, oversize, AAS]

Knight, Simeon   To Quebec, still missing 1758 [Coleman 2:354; PRO Adm. 1/3818]

Knight, Thomas, of Newbury   DIED in France [PRO Adm. 1/3818; *Bos. Gaz.* Oct. 9, 1758]

Law, Richard, Jr.   To Quebec and Halifax. RETURNED 1757 [HL, LO 4758; Mass. Archives, 79, pp. 308–9]

Lawler, John   To Canada. RETURNED by Halifax in 1757 [HL, LO 4778, 6678]

Lindse, Jacob, mulatto   Missing 1758 [Coleman 2:355; PRO Adm. 1/3818]

Linn (or Lyn), Jock, negro servant of Nathaniel Whittemore, soldier in place of master in Carver's co.   RETURNED Oct. 1760 [Mass. Archives, 79, p. 484]

Linton, Thomas, of Waldo's co.   RETURNED by Halifax in 1757 [HL, LO 4758]

Louther, David, of Taunton, in Arbuthnot's co.   To Canada. RETURNED by Halifax in 1757 [Mass. Archives, 95, pp. 506–7; HL, LO 6678; cf. PRO Adm. 1/3818]

Lowe, George   To Canada. RETURNED by Halifax in 1757 [HL, LO 4778]

McDaniel, John   To Canada. RETURNED by Halifax in 1757 [HL, LO 4778]

McDonald, John   To Canada. RETURNED by Halifax in 1757 [HL, LO 6678]

McGuire, John   Paid to August 9. KILLED [Mass. Archives, 96, p. 88]

McIntyre, John, of Tapley's co.   RETURNED by Halifax in 1757 [HL, LO 4758]

McNaire, Robert   To Canada. RETURNED by Halifax in 1757 [HL, LO 4778]

McNamara, John   To Canada. RETURNED by Halifax in 1757 [HL, LO 4778]

McWar, Robert   To Canada. RETURNED by Halifax in 1757 [HL, LO 6678]

Maley, Walter   To Canada. RETURNED by Halifax in 1757 [HL, LO 6678]

Man, James, of Palmer   To Quebec. RETURNED via Halifax in 1757 [HL, LO 4778 and 6678; cf. Coleman 2:355 and PRO Adm. 1/3818]

March, Timothy, of Methuen   To prison in Canada [Coleman 2:355]

Marshall, Joseph, of Milton, in Arbuthnot's co.   DIED in France [Mass. Archives, 95, pp. 506–7; *Bos. Gaz.* Oct. 9, 1758]

Martin, Samuel   Still missing 1758 [Coleman 2:355; PRO Adm. 1/3818]

Maylem, Ensign John   RETURNED Nov. 7, 1757, via Halifax [Mass. Archives, 95, pp. 506–7; HL, LO 4778, 6678; *Notes and Queries*, 4th ser., 4(1869): 114–15]

Merick, Timothy, of Methune, Saltonstall's co.   To Quebec [MHS Saltonstall 1757; Coleman 2:356]

Merrik, Jabez, of Ingersoll's co.   RETURNED by Halifax in 1757 [HL, LO 4758]

Miller, George   To Quebec, still missing 1758 [Coleman 2:356; PRO Adm. 1/3818]

Miller, Simon, of Roxford.   DIED in France [MHS Saltonstall 1757; *Bos. Gaz.* Oct. 9, 1758]

Morgan, Jonathan, of New Salem, in Saltonstall's co.   Missing [MHS Saltonstall 1757]

Morrison, Jonathan, servant, drummer   To Quebec. DIED in France [PRO Adm. 1/3818; *Bos. Gaz.* Oct. 9, 1758]

Morse, Gershom   To Quebec, still missing 1758 [Coleman 2:356; PRO Adm. 1/3818]

Morse, Jonathan, of Cheever's co.   Missing [Mass. Archives, 96, p. 53]

Nairl, John, of Waldo's co.   RETURNED by Halifax in 1757 [HL, LO 4758]

Oakman, John, of Salem   RETURNED by Quebec–Halifax 1757 [HL, LO 6795; Coleman 2:356]

Osborn, David, of Waldo's co.   RETURNED by Halifax in 1757 [HL, LO 4758]

Pain, Simeon, of Braintree   RETURNED Nov. 4, 1757, paid to Dec. 31 [HL, LO 4758; Mass. Archives, 96, pp. 41, 57–58]

Parker, Jesse, of Andover   To Quebec. DIED in France [MHS Saltonstall 1757; Coleman 2:356; *Bos. Gaz.* Oct. 9, 1758]

Parker, John, of New Hampshire   Still missing 1758 [PRO Adm. 1/3818; Coleman 2:357]

Peirce, John, of Charlestown   DIED in France [Coleman 2:357; *Bos. Gaz.* Oct. 9, 1758]

Peirce, Timothy, of Burk's co.   "Supposed to be with Canada Indians" [Mass. Archives, 96, pp. 41, 57–58; Coleman 2:357]

Penele, Aron   To Canada. RETURNED by Halifax in 1757 [HL, LO 6678]

Perkin, Joseph, of Bayley's co.   RETURNED by Halifax in 1757 [HL, LO 4758]

Peterson, John   To Canada. RETURNED by Halifax in 1757 [HL, LO 6678]

Petty, John, of Weymouth   Still missing 1758 [Coleman 2:357; PRO Adm. 1/3818]

Pike, Joseph, Jr., of Newport   Still missing 1758 [Coleman 2:357; PRO Adm. 1/3818]

Preston, Samuel, of Montague   RETURNED Nov. 4, died Nov. 8, 1757 [Mass. Archives, 96, pp. 41, 57–58]

Price, Corporal Jonathan, in Cheevers co.   To Canada. DIED in France [Mass. Archives, 96, p. 53; Coleman 2:338; *Bos. Gaz.* Oct. 9, 1758]

Pratt, Joseph   To Canada, still missing 1758 [Coleman 2:357; HL, LO 3893; PRO Adm. 1/3818]

Quarls, Robert   To Quebec. RETURNED via Halifax in 1757 [HL, LO 6678; Coleman 2:357; cf. PRO Adm. 1/3818]

Rand, Joshua, of Charlestown   With Ottawa beyond Michilimackinac. RETURNED 1763 [Mass. Archives, 26, p. 73; *Bos. Gaz.* Dec. 12, 1763; Coleman 2:357]

Randal, Stephen, of Thaxter's or Cheever's co. (there were 2)   To Canada. RETURNED by Halifax in 1757. [Mass. Archives, 96, p. 53; HL, LO 4778, 6678]

Richard, James, of Samuel Thaxter's co.   Missing [Maguire]

Rint, John, of Rehoboth   Still missing 1758 [Coleman 2:357–58; PRO Adm. 1/3818]

Roads, George   To Canada. RETURNED by Halifax in 1757 [HL, LO 6678]

Robens, John, of Ipswich, about 50   With "Canady Indians," still missing 1758 [Coleman 2:358; PRO Adm. 1/3818]

Robertson, Daniel, of Salem, in Saltonstall's co.   Missing [MHS Saltonstall 1757]

Rogers, Jonathan, of Newbury   To Quebec and left sick in France [Coleman 2:358; *Bos. Gaz.* Oct. 9, 1758]

Rogers, William, of Samuel Thaxter's co.   DIED in France [Maguire: *Bos. Gaz.* Oct. 9, 1758]

Root, Seth   DIED in France [PRO Adm. 1/3818; *Bos. Gaz.* Oct. 9, 1758]

Rumble, Thomas, of Marblehead, in Saltonstall's   Missing [MHS Saltonstall 1757]

Rush, James, of Milton, in Arbuthnot's co.   Sick in France, 1758 [Mass. Archives, 95, pp. 506–7; *Bos. Gaz.* Oct. 9, 1758]

Rutter, John, of Mendon   Still missing 1758 [Coleman 2:358; PRO Adm. 1/3818]

Ryford, John, of Weymouth, in Arbuthnot's   Still missing 1758 [Mass. Archives, 95, pp. 506–7; PRO Adm. 1/3818]

Salter, Joseph, of Marblehead, in Saltonstall's co.   To Quebec. RETURNED Nov. 4, 1757 [MHS Saltonstall 1757; HL, LO 4758]

Salter, William   To Quebec, still missing 1758 [Coleman 2:358; PRO Adm. 1/3818]

Sanders, Nathaniel, brother of Avery, in Bayley's N.H. co.   RETURNED by Halifax in 1757 [HL, LO 6678; Coleman 2:358; cf. PRO Adm. 1/3818]

Seers, John   To Canada. RETURNED by Halifax in 1757 [HL, LO 4778, 6678]

Severence, Joseph, of Deerfield   Escaped and RETURNED in 1757 [Coleman 2:358]

Shead, Zacheas, of Billerica, in Cheever's co.   Missing [Mass. Archives, 96, p. 53; Coleman 2:358]

Sheldon, Elisha, of Fall-Town, of Burk's co.   To Quebec. DIED in France [Mass. Archives, 96, pp. 41, 57–58; Coleman 2:358–59; *Bos. Gaz.* Oct. 9, 1758]

Shippey, Sergeant Phillip, of Waldo's co.   RETURNED by Halifax in 1757 [HL, LO 4758]

Simpson, Jeremiah   DIED in Canada [Coleman 2:352]

Sinclair, John   To goal in Canada.   RETURNED in 1758 [Coleman 2:359]

Smith, Ballard, of Newbury   To Quebec, still missing 1758 [Coleman 2:359; PRO Adm. 1/3818]

Smith, Daniel, Jr., of Ipswich   "Carried of[f] by the Indians," still missing 1758 [Coleman 2:359; PRO Adm. 1/3818]

Smith, Elisha   DIED in Canada [Coleman 2:352]

Smith, Peter, of Salem   To Canada.   RETURNED by Halifax in 1757 [HL, LO 4778; Coleman 2:359]

Spencer, Moses, of Davis's co.   RETURNED by Halifax in 1757 [HL, LO 4758]

Steel, John, of Sowhegon West, New Hampshire   To Quebec, prisoner, small-pox.   RETURNED Nov. 1758 [Mass. Archives, 78 p. 77; Coleman 2:359–60]

Stewart, Nathaniel   To Canada.   RETURNED by Halifax in 1757 [HL, LO 6678]

Stimpson, Timothy, of Reading   Wounded, and still missing 1758 [Coleman 2:360; PRO Adm. 1/3818]

Stocks, George   To Canada.   RETURNED by Halifax in 1757 [HL, LO 6678]

Stodder, Jeremiah, of Hingham   Still missing 1758 [PRO Adm. 1/3818]

Stodder, Zebulon, of Hingham, in Samuel Thaxter's co.   In Canada. [Maguire; Coleman 2:360]

Stokes, John, of Tapley's co.   RETURNED by Halifax in 1757 [HL, LO 4758]

Tansley, George   To Canada.   RETURNED by Halifax in 1757 [HL, LO 6678]

Taylor, Oliver, of Ball's co.   RETURNED by Halifax in 1757 [HL, LO 4758]

Thayer, Eleazar, Jr., of Braintree   Had "not been heard of never since," still missing in 1758 [Coleman 2:360; PRO Adm. 1/3818]

Tower, John, of Samuel Thaxter's co.   Missing [Maguire]

Travers, Daniel, of Holliston   Ran from Indians to "French."   RETURNED via Halifax 1757 [HL, LO 6678; Coleman 2:360, cf. PRO Adm. 1/3818]

Travis, John   Still missing 1758 [Coleman 2:360; PRO Adm. 1/3818]

Vandozan, Richard   To Canada.   RETURNED by Halifax in 1757 [HL, LO 6678]

Vickers, Thomas, of Samuel Thaxter's co.   To Canada.   RETURNED by Halifax in 1757 [Maguire; HL, LO 4778]

Vinal, Stephen, of Samuel Thaxter's co.   Missing [Maguire]

Wade, Lieutenant Simon   RETURNED via Halifax in 1757 [HL, LO 6795; *Notes and Queries*, 4th ser., 4(1869): 114–5]

Warden, David, in Cheever's co.   Missing [Mass. Archives, 96, p. 53]

Warner, Jesse   To Quebec, still missing 1758 [Coleman 2:360; PRO Adm. 1/3818]

Warren, William, of Amesbury, in Davis co.   To St. François. Escaped Aug. 1760 to Crown Point.   RETURNED Oct. 1760. Granted £8 [Mass. Archives, 79, p. 495; Coleman 2:360]

Weaver, Ebenezer, of Samuel Thaxter's co.   Missing [Maguire]

Webster, Peter, of Haverhill, of Saltonstall's co.   To Canada [MHS Saltonstall 1757]

Weed, Elin[?], of Newbury, of Saltonstall's co.   RETURNED from Canada
Jan. 11, 1758 [MHS Saltonstall 1757]

Weed, Joseph   To Canada. RETURNED by Halifax in 1757 [HL, LO 6678]

White, James   To Canada. RETURNED by Halifax in 1757 [HL, LO 6678]

William, John   To Canada. RETURNED by Halifax in 1757 [HL, LO 6678]

Willson, Nathaniel, of Taunton   RETURNED Nov. 4, 1757 [Mass. Archives, 95,
pp. 506–7; HL, LO 4758]

Wilson, David   To Canada. RETURNED by Halifax in 1757 [HL, LO 6678]

Wilson, Jeremiah   To Canada. RETURNED by Halifax in 1757 [HL, LO 6678]

Winter, Benjamin, of Davis's co.   RETURNED by Halifax in 1757 [HL, LO
4758]

Woodcock, Ebenezer   DIED in France [PRO Adm. 1/3818; *Bos. Gaz.* Oct. 9,
1758; Coleman 2:361]

Woods, Josiah, of Cheever's co.   Missing [Mass. Archives, 96, p. 53]

Young, Nathaniel, of Endicott's co.   RETURNED by Halifax in 1757 [HL, LO
4758]

NEW HAMPSHIRE

The muster rolls are printed in Chandler E. Potter, *The Military History of the
State of New Hampshire, 1623–1861* (Concord, N.H., 1869), pp. 179–90.
Those killed and the missing, who did not return, were paid to August 9, 1757.
Petitions preserved in the New Hampshire Records Management and Archives
are filed by date only.

Barker, Jonathan, of Bayley's co.   To Quebec, Halifax. RETURNED Nov. 8,
1757 [HL, LO 6795]

Bean, Josiah, of Brentwood, of Emery's co.   To Canada, where he had
smallpox, France, England, Newfoundland, New York. RETURNED
Nov. 30, 1758 [Coleman 2:346; petition of Dec. 26, 1758]

Belknap, Caleb, drummer, of Bayley's co.   To Quebec, Halifax. RETURNED by
Nov. 5, 1757 [HL, LO 6678; cf. *Bos. Gaz.* Oct. 9, 1758]

Bell, William, of Pelham   RETURNED via Halifax by Nov. 14, 1757 [HL, LO
4758; petition of Mar. 16, 1758]

Burns, John, of Emery's co.   Missing

Caesar, Nero, of Richard Emery's co., Major John Gilman's slave   RETURNED
Oct. 1760 [petition of Feb. 12, 1761; *New Hampshire Town Records*
11:651–52]

Campbell, William, of Mooney's co.   Missing

Carr, John, of Mooney's co.   Missing

Clement, James   To Canada, Halifax, Boston. RETURNED by Nov. 5, 1757
[petition of Mar. 22, 1758; HL, LO 4758]

Colby, Elias, of Mooney's co. Missing

Davis, John, of Emery's co. RETURNED by Nov. 5, 1757 [Coleman 2:349]

Dearborn, Stephen, of Bayley's co. Missing

Denbow, Elijah, of Mooney's co. Escaped to Montreal, sent to Quebec, had smallpox there, escaped down St. Lawrence to Louisbourg with Stobo. RETURNED in 1759. £128.2.6 granted [*N.H. Misc. Prov. Papers* 18: 508; Coleman 2:349]

Dunlap, James, of Emery's co. RETURNED by Halifax in 1757 [HL, LO 4758]

Emerson, Daniel, of Emery's co. Missing

Gale, John. RETURNED by Halifax in 1757 [HL, LO 4758]

Gile, Nathan, of Bayley's co. Missing

Glazier, Benjamin, of Mooney's co. To Canada, Halifax, Boston. RETURNED Jan. 22, 1758 [petition of Mar. 22, 1758]

Gozzal, William, of Mooney's co. Missing

Grimes, Moses, of Londonderry, in Mooney's co. To Canada, France, England, Newfoundland, New York. RETURNED Dec. 4, 1758 [petition of Jan. 5, 1759] Given £75, new tenor [Coleman 2:351]

Handcock, Jacob, of Mooney's co. To Canada, Halifax, Boston. RETURNED Jan. 1758 [HL, LO 6678; petition of Mar. 31, 1758]

Harriman, Asahel, of Bayley's co. Missing

Healey, Paul, corporal, in Bayley's co. Missing

Heath, Jonathan, of Bayley's co. Missing

Hills, Edward, of Bayley's co. To Canada. RETURNED by Halifax before Nov. 8, 1757 [HL, LO 6678]

Hilyard, Joseph, of Emery's co. DIED in France [*Bos. Gaz.* Oct. 9, 1758]

Hutchinson, Henry, of Emery's co. Missing

Hutchinson, John, of Emery's co. RETURNED by Nov. 5, 1757 [Coleman 2:352]

Johnson, Michael, of Mooney's co. To Canada, Halifax, Boston. RETURNED by Nov. 5, 1757 [HL, LO 4778, 6678; petition of Mar. 22, 1758]

Johnson, Robert, of Mooney's co. Missing

Kennedy, Robert, of Emery's co. Missing

Kidder, Benjamin, of Emery's co. To Canada. DIED in France [petition of Jan. 12, 1759; *Bos. Gaz.* Oct. 9, 1758; Coleman 2:353]

Lamson, Dr. John, of Exeter, surgeon's mate Taken by Caughnawaga, to Canada (smallpox), France, England. RETURNED Oct. 12, 1758. £100 granted [petition of Dec. 26, 1758; *New Hampshire Town Papers* 11:652; Coleman 2:355]

Little, John, of Emery's co. Missing

Little, Samuel, of Bayley's co. RETURNED by Nov. 5, 1757

Mann, Nathaniel, of Bayley's co. Missing

McColly, James, of Emery's co. Missing

McDugle, William RETURNED by Halifax in 1757 [HL, LO 4758]

McMaster, William, of Mooney's co. Missing

McQuestion, Simon, of Emery's co. Missing

Merrill, Amos, of Bayley's co. Missing

Moor, John, Jr., of Bedford, in Richard Emery's co. To Montreal, Quebec (smallpox), France, England, New York, Quebec. RETURNED Nov. 1759 [petition of Nov. 20, 1759]

Murdock, Robert, of Emery's co. Missing

Parker, Henry, Jr., of Merrimack, in Emery's co. Still missing 1758 [PRO Adm. 1/3818; Coleman 2:356]

Parker, Josiah, in Emery's co. RETURNED via Halifax and Boston in 1757 [HL, LO 4778]

Parker, Thomas, in Emery's co. RETURNED by Nov. 5, 1757

Paul, Joseph. RETURNED by Halifax in 1757 [HL, LO 4758]

Pearson, Joseph, of Emery's co. Missing

Pettingal, Benjamin, of Emery's co. "Never heard of," still missing in 1758 [PRO Adm. 1/3818; Coleman 2:357]

Prescott, Jonathan, of Emery's co. DIED in France [*Bos. Gaz.* Oct. 9, 1758]

Rackliff, William, of Mooney's co. To Canada, France, England, New York. RETURNED March 1759. Given £85 [*Bos. Gaz.* Oct. 9, 1758; petition of Apr. 10, 1759; not in muster]

Randall, Peter, of Mooney's co. RETURNED via Halifax before Nov. 5, 1757 [HL, LO 6678: cf. *Bos. Gaz.* Oct. 9, 1758]

Roberts, Benjamin, of Emery's co. Sick in France [*Bos. Gaz.* Oct. 9, 1758]

Rogers, William, of Samuel Thaxter's co. DIED in France [Maguire; *Bos. Gaz.* Oct. 9, 1758]

Russell, Pelatiah, 2nd lieutenant, in Emery's co. RETURNED via Halifax 1757 [HL, LO 6678; 4166]

Sanders, Avery, of Haverhill, in Bayley's co. Still missing 1758 [PRO Adm. 1/3818; Coleman 2:358]

Smith, Solomon. RETURNED by Halifax in 1757 [HL, LO 4758]

Stevens, Reuben, of Bayley's co. To Canada, Halifax, Boston. RETURNED by Nov. 5, 1757 [petition of Mar. 22, 1758; HL, LO 4758; Coleman 2:361]

Swain, Hezekiah, of Emery's co. Missing

Taggart, James, of Mooney's co. Missing

Thompson, William, of Mooney's co. Missing

Tobin, Patrick, of Mooney's co. To Canada, Halifax, Boston. RETURNED Nov. 14, 1757 [petition of Mar. 22, 1758]

Towle, Jonathan, of Bayley's co. Missing

Twaddel, Robert, of Mooney's co. Missing

Watson, David, of Mooney's co. Missing

Webber, Edward. RETURNED by Halifax in 1757 [HL, LO 4758]

Wheeler, William, of Bayley's co. To Canada. RETURNED via Halifax by Nov. 5, 1757 [HL, LO 6795]

Whitherweed, Joseph, servant of Benjamin Hadley, enlisted in Emery's co. To Canada. DIED in France [Hadley petition dated Jan. 12, 1759; Coleman 2:353]

Winn, Macajah, of Emery's co. Still missing in 1758 [PRO Adm. 1/3818]

Young, Jonathan, ensign, of Bayley's co. DIED in France [*Bos. Gaz.* Oct. 9, 1758]

NOTES

ABBREVIATIONS

AN   Archives Nationales, Paris

CHR   *Canadian Historical Review*

DAB   *Dictionary of American Biography*, ed. Allen Johnson and Dumas Malone, 22 vols. (New York, 1928–44)

DCB   *Dictionary of Canadian Biography*, ed. Frances Halpenny et al., 10 vols. (Toronto, 1966–)

DNB   *Dictionary of National Biography*, ed. Leslie Stephen and Sidney Lee, 63 vols. (London, 1885–1901)

HL   Huntington Library and Art Gallery, San Marino, Calif.

JP   *The Papers of Sir William Johnson*, ed. James Sullivan, 14 vols. (Albany, N.Y., 1921–65)

JR   *The Jesuit Relations and Allied Documents*, ed. Reuben G. Thwaites, 73 vols. (Cleveland, 1896–1901)

MHS   Massachusetts Historical Society, Boston

NAC   National Archives of Canada (formerly Public Archives of Canada), Ottawa

NEQ   *New England Quarterly*

NYCD   *Documents Relative to the Colonial History of the State of New York*, ed. Edmund B. O'Callaghan and Berthold Fernow, 15 vols. (Albany, N.Y., 1856–87)

PRO   Public Record Office, London

VMHB   *Virginia Magazine of History and Biography*
W&MQ   *William and Mary Quarterly*

CHAPTER 1: APPROACHES

1. *Peter Kalm's Travels in North America*, ed. Adolph B. Benson, 2 vols. (New York, 1937), 2:406–7.
2. *Kalm's Travels* sketches the Albany trade with French-allied Indians (1:345–46). For his strong aversion to Albany, see Kalm to William Johnson, September 1750, *The Papers of Sir William Johnson*, ed. James Sullivan, 14 vols. (Albany, N.Y., 1921–65), 1:304–5 (hereafter *JP*).
3. *JP* 1:228, 295–96, 304–5. On Johnson, see James Thomas Flexner, *Lord of the Mohawks*, rev. ed. (Boston, 1979) and, especially, Milton W. Hamilton, *Sir William Johnson, Colonial American, 1715–1763* (Port Washington, N.Y., 1976).
4. *Kalm's Travels* 1:350–61.
5. *Kalm's Travels* 1:361.
6. *Kalm's Travels* 1:362, 365–66. A sergeant and twelve men were posted to the site in the summer of 1757 (*General Orders of 1757 Issued by the Earl of Loudoun and Phineas Lyman* [New York, 1970], 17–18).
7. *Kalm's Travels* 1:367–73.
8. Edmund B. O'Callaghan and Berthold Fernow, eds., *Documents Relative to the Colonial History of the State of New York*, 15 vols. (Albany, N.Y., 1856–87), 6:582 (hereafter *NYCD*). P. G. Roy, *Hommes et Choses du Fort Saint-Frédéric* (Montreal, 1946). For a description of the fort in August 1746, see Arthur Latham Perry, *Origins of Williamstown*, 2nd ed. (New York, 1896), 169–70.
9. *Kalm's Travels* 2:391–92.
10. Guy Frégault, *La Civilisation de la Nouvelle-France* (Montreal, 1944), 57–58, 205–6.
11. *Kalm's Travels* 1:379–80; 2:382, 392.
12. John Norton, *The Redeemed Captive: . . . Narrative of the Capture and Burning of Fort Massachusetts . . .* (Boston, 1748).
13. Frances Halpenny et al., eds., *Dictionary of Canadian Biography*, 10 vols. (Toronto, 1966–   ), 3:168–69 (hereafter *DCB*).
14. *Kalm's Travels* 1:377–78; *NYCD*, 6:518–19.
15. *DCB* 3:168–69; Frégault, *La Civilisation*, 203–4; Marcel Trudel, *L'esclavage au Canada français* (Quebec, 1960), 92.
16. *NYCD* 6:519; Susannah (Johnson) Hastings, *A Narrative of the Captivity of Mrs. Johnson* (New York, 1841), 16 (hereafter *Johnson Narrative*).
17. *Kalm's Travels* 2:504–5; *DCB* 3:26–32; Lionel Groulx, *Roland-Michel Barrin de La Galissonière, 1693–1756* (Toronto, 1970); Max Savelle, *The Diplomatic History of the Canadian Boundary, 1749–1763* (New Haven, Conn., and Toronto, 1940), 10–11, 43.

18. *Kalm's Travels* 2:589.
19. *Kalm's Travels* 2:580–98.
20. *Kalm's Travels* 1:139; *NYCD* 6:550; U.S. Bureau of the Census, *Historical Statistics of the United States*, 2nd ed., 2 vols. (Washington, D.C., 1975), Series Z, 1–17.
21. *Kalm's Travels* 2:588.
22. *Johnson Narrative*, 3–25.
23. *Johnson Narrative*, 25–28.
24. *Johnson Narrative*, 28–36. On the number of New England women who were pregnant at the time of capture, see Laurel T. Ulrich, *Good Wives: Image and Reality in the Lives of Women in Northern New England, 1650–1750* (New York, 1982), 205.
25. *Johnson Narrative*, 36–47.
26. *Johnson Narrative*, 47–52.
27. *Johnson Narrative*, 56; *DCB* 4:293–94.
28. *Johnson Narrative*, 55–59.
29. *DCB* 3:23–25.
30. *Johnson Narrative*, 60; *DCB* 4:294.
31. *Johnson Narrative*, 63.
32. Duquesne to Spencer Phips, quoted in Emma Lewis Coleman, *New England Captives Carried to Canada between 1677 and 1760 during the French and Indian Wars*, 2 vols. (Portland, Me., 1925–26), 2:267.
33. *New York Mercury*, August 11, 1755; Coleman, *New England Captives*, 2:298–300.
34. Trudel, *L'esclavage*, 92, 117.
35. *Johnson Narrative*, 61–64.
36. Nathaniel Bouton et al., eds., *Documents and Records Relating to the Province [Towns and State] of New Hampshire from the Earliest Period of its Settlement*, 40 vols. (Concord, N.H., 1867–1943), 6:333–37.
37. Thomas Elliot Norton, *The Fur Trade in Colonial New York 1686–1776* (Madison, Wis., 1974), esp. 89–90, 124–27, 148–49, 171–72.
38. *Johnson Narrative*, 64–69.
39. *Johnson Narrative*, 70; *DCB* 3:110–11.
40. Robert C. Alberts, *The Most Extraordinary Adventures of Major Robert Stobo* (Boston, 1965), 125–38.
41. *Johnson Narrative*, 70–72.
42. *Johnson Narrative*, 72; *JP* 2:168–70.
43. *NYCD* 10:306–9.
44. *DCB* 4:425–29.
45. *Johnson Narrative*, 73–76.
46. *Johnson Narrative*, 76.
47. *Johnson Narrative*, 78–83. Susannah's smallpox is confirmed by a letter from Miriam to James printed in the Springfield, Mass., 1907 edition of the narrative, pp. 188–89.

48. *Johnson Narrative*, 75; *DCB* 4:764-66. The girls were daughters of Mrs. Howe, whose adventures as a captive are recounted in Samuel G. Drake, *Indian Captivities or Life in the Wigwam* (Buffalo, N.Y., 1854), 156-65. On the network of female captives in Canada, see Ulrich, *Good Wives*, 210.

49. *Johnson Narrative*, 85-89.

50. James Smith, a prisoner wintering with Caughnawaga, Ojibwa, and Ottawa on the Cayahoga River in 1756-1757, reported that the Caughnawaga believed that Mohawk attackers would spare them (Drake, *Indian Captivities*, 215; S. N. Katz, *Newcastle's New York* [Cambridge, Mass., 1968], chap. 7).

51. *NYCD* 6:126.

52. Philippe-Thomas Chabert de Joncaire (*DCB* 3), who was preceded among the Seneca by his father, Louis-Thomas, and succeeded by his brother, Daniel-Marie, after 1748.

53. Hamilton, *Sir William Johnson*, esp. 45ff.

54. *DCB* 3:622-24; *Daniel Claus' Narrative of his Relations with Sir William Johnson and Experiences in the Lake George Fight* (New York, 1904), 7.

55. *DCB* 3:322-23.

56. Hamilton, *Sir William Johnson*, 58-59.

57. *NYCD* 6:289-305.

58. *NYCD* 6:286-88.

59. Paul A. W. Wallace, *Conrad Weiser, 1696-1760: Friend of Colonist and Mohawk* (Philadelphia, 1945), 232-33.

60. *NYCD* 6:318-25; Hamilton, *Sir William Johnson*, 51-55; Robert Aquila, *The Iroquois Restoration: Iroquois Diplomacy on the Colonial Frontier, 1701-1754* (Detroit, 1983), 97.

61. Wallace, *Conrad Weiser*, 238-39.

62. Francis Parkman, *Half Century of Conflict*, 2 vols. (Boston, 1905), 2:230-56.

63. Hamilton, *Sir William Johnson*, 53-55; *JP* 9:15-30.

64. See Francis Jennings, "Iroquois Alliances in American History," in *The History and Culture of Iroquois Diplomacy*, ed. F. Jennings et al. (Syracuse, N.Y., 1985), 44-47.

65. C. Colden's report of August 8, 1751, in *NYCD* 6:746; Wallace, *Conrad Weiser*, 326.

66. Hamilton, *Sir William Johnson*, 55; Cadwallader Colden, *The History of the Five Nations of Canada* (London, 1747), 189-96; *DCB* 3:623; National Archives of Canada, Ottawa, MG 18, L4, vol. 8, packet 57, p. 27 (hereafter NAC).

67. John A. Schutz, *William Shirley, King's Governor of Massachusetts* (Chapel Hill, N.C., 1961), 112-18; Aquila, *Iroquois Restoration*, 98-99; George S. Snyderman, *Behind the Tree of Peace* (Philadelphia, 1948), 49-55.

68. *JP* 1:93–96; 9:15–24. Those lost included a son of Joseph Brant and "the King of the 5 Nations named Tayengaraghquere" (*JP* 9:17, 21).
69. *DCB* 3:331.
70. Hamilton, *Sir William Johnson*, 56–58.
71. Hamilton, *Sir William Johnson*, 58–59; *JP* 1:146–48; Wallace, *Conrad Weiser*, 330. Cf. Aquila, *Iroquois Restoration*, 149–55.
72. *NYCD* 6:437–52; cf. Aquila, *Iroquois Restoration*, 101.
73. *NYCD* 6:440. For negotiations in Europe on the demolition of Fort St. Frédéric, see NAC, MG5, A¹: 437, pp. 70–84; 438, p. 218; 439, p. 60.
74. *NYCD* 6:440, 448, 484–513, 520, 525–27, 544–45, 720–21; Hamilton, *Sir William Johnson*, 61–62.
75. Hamilton, *Sir William Johnson*, 64–65.
76. *NYCD* 10:186–88.
77. *NYCD* 6:738–47.
78. Lawrence H. Gipson, *The British Empire Before the American Revolution*, 15 vols. (Caldwell, Idaho, and New York, 1936–70), 5.102–6; Archives Nationales, Paris, Colonies, C11A, 90, p. 140 (hereafter AN); *NYCD* 10:263; *DCB* 4:636–38.
79. Wallace, *Conrad Weiser*, 306–7, 311–14.
80. Jennings, "Iroquois Alliances in American History," 44–52.
81. *NYCD* 6:778–79; Hamilton, *Sir William Johnson*, 94–95.
82. *NYCD* 6:782.
83. *NYCD* 6:781–88; Hamilton, *Sir William Johnson*, 95–96; Aquila, *Iroquois Restoration*, 104–5; *JP* 9:105.
84. Wallace, *Conrad Weiser*, 350.
85. *JP* 9:108–20; Hamilton, *Sir William Johnson*, 96–99.
86. *NYCD* 6:799–802, 854–56.
87. *NYCD* 6:869–70.
88. *NYCD* 6:872–73. The contest between Weiser and Theyanoguin went on behind the scenes as well. Weiser negotiated the infamous Wyoming purchase from some Iroquois sachems, prompting Theyanoguin and some fellow Mohawk to a more infamous sale of the same land to Connecticut investors (Wallace, *Conrad Weiser*, 358).
89. *NYCD* 6:860, 887, 884; Richard L. Haan, "Covenant and Consensus: Iroquois and English, 1676–1760," in *Beyond the Covenant Chain*, ed. Daniel K. Richter and James H. Merrell (Syracuse, N.Y., 1987), 44–45.
90. *NYCD* 6:908–9, 911.

CHAPTER 2: TO BATTLE FOR LAKE GEORGE

1. Reed Browning, *The Duke of Newcastle* (New Haven, Conn. 1975), 207.
2. Dominick Graham, "The Planning of the Beauséjour Operation and the Approaches to War in 1755," *New England Quarterly* 61 (1968): 551–66 (hereafter *NEQ*); *NYCD* 6:901–3; T. Roy Clayton, "The Duke of New-

castle, the Earl of Halifax, and the American Origins of the Seven Years' War," *Historical Journal* 24 (1981): 571-603; Steven Griert, "The Board of Trade and Defense of the Ohio Valley, 1748-1753," *Western Pennsylvania Historical Magazine* 64 (1981): 1-32.

3. Lee McCardell, *Ill-Starred General: Braddock of the Coldstream Guards* (Pittsburgh, 1958), 124-25; Graham, "The Planning of the Beauséjour Operation," 554-55.

4. *NYCD* 6:915-16; *Correspondence of William Shirley*, ed. Charles Henry Lincoln, 2 vols. (New York, 1912), 2:98-101.

5. Stanley M. Pargellis, ed., *Military Affairs in North America 1748-1763* (New York, 1936), 36-39; Lawrence H. Gipson, *The British Empire Before the American Revolution*, 15 vols. (Caldwell, Idaho, and New York, 1936-70), 6:60.

6. *NYCD* 6:920-22.

7. *NYCD* 6:922-24.

8. Willis E. Wright, *Colonel Ephraim Williams, a Documentary Life* (Pittsfield, Mass., 1970), 86-91.

9. *JP* 1:447-50; John A. Schutz, *William Shirley, King's Governor of Massachusetts* (Chapel Hill, N.C., 1961), 189-93; *NYCD* 6:942, 954.

10. Milton W. Hamilton, *Sir William Johnson, Colonial American, 1715-1763* (Port Washington, N.Y., 1976), 57, 116; *JP*, 1:456-59.

11. Edmund B. O'Callaghan, ed., *Documentary History of the State of New York*, 4 vols. (Albany, N.Y., 1849-51), 2:648-51; Winthrop Sargent, *The History of an Expedition Against Fort Duquesne in 1755* (Philadelphia, 1855), 300-307; Hamilton, *Sir William Johnson*, 116-20; *JP* 1:467-68.

12. *JP* 1:514.

13. *DCB* 3:214-15; *JP* 1:547, 557; 9:171; Wright, *Colonel Ephraim Williams*, 104.

14. *JP* 1:535-36.

15. *JP* 9:171-79.

16. *JP* 1:654, 659, 663; 9:189-90.

17. *NYCD* 6:964-89; *JP* 9:193-202; Hamilton, *Sir William Johnson*, 127-31.

18. *JP* 9:203-6; cf. Wilbur R. Jacobs, *Diplomacy and Indian Gifts: Anglo-French Rivalry Along the Ohio and Northwest Frontiers, 1748-1763* (Stanford, Calif., 1950), 149-57.

19. *JP* 9:203.

20. *JP* 1:491, 789-90, 795, 803-6; Huntington Library, San Marino, Calif., Loudoun Papers. no. 1106 (hereafter HL, LO); Hamilton, *Sir William Johnson*, 130-39; *Daniel Claus' Narrative of his Relations with Sir William Johnson and Experiences in the Lake George Fight* (New York, 1904), 10-12.

21. *JP* 1:468-75; Gipson, *British Empire* 6:139.

22. *JP* 1:551-56; C. Champline to Stephen Hopkins, August 14, 1755, Fort Ticonderoga Archives, no. 2028.

23. Wright, *Colonel Ephraim Williams*, 97, 100–101; James Hill, "The Diary of a Private on the First Expedition to Crown Point," *NEQ* 5 (1932): 602–5; Arthur Latham Perry, *Origins of Williamstown*, 2nd ed. (New York, 1896), 215–371 re Williams.
24. Wright, *Colonel Ephraim Williams*, 103.
25. Fred Anderson, *A People's Army: Massachusetts Soldiers and Society in the Seven Years' War* (Chapel Hill, N.C., 1984), 96–98.
26. Wright, *Colonel Ephraim Williams*, 103–6.
27. James Thomas Flexner, *Lord of the Mohawks*, 2nd ed. (Boston, 1979), 135; *JP* 1:493, 670–71; Wright, *Colonel Ephraim Williams*, 102.
28. *JP* 1:716–17, 723; Anderson, *People's Army*, 78–80.
29. Wright, *Colonel Ephraim Williams*, 106–7.
30. *JP* 1:731; 2:209–10.
31. *JP* 2:149.
32. "A Copy of a Journal Kept by James Gilbert, of Morton, Mass., in the Year 1755," *Magazine of New England History* 3 (1893): 189–90.
33. *JP* 1:730–33; Gilbert transcribed the name as "Dewoveiaygo" in his "Journal," 189.
34. Wright, *Colonel Ephraim Williams*, 109–10; *JP* 1:746–48.
35. Governor De Lancey's secretary, Goldsbrow Banyar, urged "we should deal exactly with them as they do by us, destroy and scalp as they do. They set their Indians to scalping of our poor defenceless Inhabitants, in this the necessity pleads an Excuse for following so inhuman an Example . . . (*JP* 1:772–73).
36. *JP* 1:777.
37. *JP* 1:826–27, 794–97, 823, 825.
38. *JP* 1:818; *Military Affairs*, 128–29.
39. *JP* 1:816, 818.
40. Wright, *Colonel Ephraim Williams*, 115–16, 119–20; Hill, "Diary of a Private," 604.
41. *JP* 2:163–64; Anderson, *People's Army*, chap. 4. Forces from other colonies, not just the regulars, did not share many of the New England views of military life.
42. The Fort Edward garrison erupted in violence at the beginning of September, resulting in woundings. On September 1, at least thirty of Captain John Jones's company in Ruggles's regiment marched off because they were denied "back Allowance of Rum" and others threatened to join them (*The Journals and Papers of Seth Pomeroy*, ed. L. E. de Forest [New York, 1926], 112. See also Anderson, *People's Army*, chap. 4).
43. *NYCD* 10:333–34. John E. Ferling, "The New England Soldier: A Study in Changing Perspectives," *American Quarterly* 33 (1981): 26–45.
44. Anderson, *People's Army*, 77.
45. John Shy, "The American Military Experience: History and Learning," *Journal of Interdisciplinary History* 1 (1971): 205–28; John E. Ferling, *A*

Wilderness of Miseries: War and Warriors in Early America (Westport, Conn., 1980); E. Wayne Carp, "Early American Military History: A Review of Recent Work," *Virginia Magazine of History and Biography* 94 (1986): 259–84 (hereafter *VMHB*).

46. *JP* 1:540.
47. *Pomeroy Journals*, 100–127; Hill, "Diary of a Private," 609, 610; Gilbert, "Journal," 189, 190.
48. "The Journal of Capt. Nathaniel Dwight of Belchertown, Mass., During the Crown Point Expedition, 1755," *New York Genealogical & Biographical Record* 33 (1902):7. Solomon Williams, *The Duty of Christian Soldiers when Call'd to War, to Undertake It in the Name of God* (Boston, 1755) was a striking and historical appeal.
49. Wright, *Colonel Ephraim Williams*, 120.
50. *JP* 1:783.
51. *JP* 1:861; *Pomeroy Journals*, 109.
52. *Pomeroy Journals*, 106; Gilbert, "Journal," 190.
53. *JP* 1:842; Wright, *Colonel Ephraim Williams*, 119–21; Gilbert, "Journal," 192.
54. Wright, *Colonel Ephraim Williams*, 123–25.
55. *JP* 1:825.
56. *JP* 1:855; *New York Mercury*, August 25, 1755.
57. *NYCD* 6:1000–1002; Wright, *Colonel Ephraim Williams*, 122–25; *JP* 1:879–83; Champline to Hopkins, August 14, 1755, Fort Ticonderoga Archives, no. 2028.
58. *NYCD* 6:996–97.
59. *JP* 1:880–83, 889–94.
60. *NYCD* 6:993–99; *JP* 2:6–9.
61. *JP* 2:8.
62. *JP* 2:16–17; John R. Cuneo, *Robert Rogers of the Rangers* (New York, 1959), 17–21; *Claus' Narrative*, 12.
63. *NYCD* 10:297–99.
64. *DCB* 3:185–86.
65. *DCB* 3:662–74.
66. McCardell, *Ill-Starred General*, 129; NAC, MG 5, A¹, 437, pp. 85–86, 98; *Dictionary of National Biography*, 63 vols. Leslie Stephen and Sidney Lee, eds., (London, 1885–1901), 31:44–45 (hereafter *DNB*); Schutz, *William Shirley*, 159.
67. *NYCD* 10:270.
68. Fort Halifax. AN, Marine, B 68, pp. 24–57; *NYCD* 10:275–78; L. H. Gipson, "A French Project for Victory Short of a Declaration of War, 1755," *Canadian Historical Review* 26 (1945): 361–71 (hereafter *CHR*).
69. *NYCD* 10:290–94.
70. Gipson, *British Empire* 6:106–14; *NYCD* 10:297–99; Guy Frégault, *La Guerre de la conquête*, 2nd ed. (Montreal, 1966), 128–34.

71. NAC, MG 5, A¹, 439, pp. 5–12, 76, 174–76, 180; Max Savelle, "Diplomatic Preliminaries of the Seven Years' War in America," *CHR* 20 (1939): 32.
72. Frégault, *Guerre de la conquête*, 135–36; *NYCD* 10:305–9.
73. I. K. Steele, *Guerillas and Grenadiers* (Toronto, 1969), 66.
74. *NYCD* 10:308.
75. Public Record Office, London, WO 1/4, fol. 31 (hereafter PRO). *NYCD* 10:341. Vaudreuil continued to believe that one thousand regulars were with Johnson (*NYCD* 10:321).
76. Frégault, *Guerre de la conquête*, 145–47.
77. *NYCD* 10:301; G. F. G. Stanley, *New France, the Last Phase* (Toronto, 1968), 89.
78. *NYCD* 10:311–12.
79. *NYCD* 10:329.
80. *DCB* 5:97–100.
81. *DCB* 3:374–76.
82. *NYCD* 10:327–30.
83. *DCB* 4:447–48.
84. *DCB* 4:458–61.
85. Peter E. Russell, "Redcoats in the Wilderness: British Officers and Irregular Warfare in Europe and America, 1740–1760," *William and Mary Quarterly*, 3rd ser., 35 (1978): 633–35, 641 (hereafter *W&MQ*).
86. *NYCD* 10:330–31.
87. *NYCD* 10:316, 318–19, 335, 340–41.
88. *NYCD* 10:331–34, 319–20, 316–17.
89. *NYCD* 10:317, 344; Captain Eyre was impressed with Dieskau's bold plan (PRO, CO 5/46, fols. 116–7).
90. Cuneo, *Robert Rogers*, 21.
91. *NYCD* 10:317.
92. *NYCD* 10:317, 335, 341–42.
93. See W. J. Eccles, "The Social, Economic, and Political Significance of the Military Establishment in New France," *CHR* 52 (1971): 1–22.
94. Wright, *Colonel Ephraim Williams*, chap. 7, provides the best modern account of the battle, yet it is hard to see how these two could be "stragglers who wandered off" (133).
95. Wright, *Colonel Ephraim Williams*, 133; *NYCD* 10:317.
96. *Claus' Narrative* is replete with dubious direct quotations from the last hours of his friend and teacher, Theyanoguin. Claus may well have attended to hear Theyanoguin's comments on strategy, although he does not seem to have been a witness at the "Bloody Morning Scout" (*JP* 9:229).
97. Hamilton, *Sir William Johnson*, 159; Leroy V. Eid, "'National' War among Indians of Northeastern North America," *Canadian Review of American Studies* 16 (1985): 125–54.

98. *NYCD* 10:316–18.

99. Vaudreuil, who had nothing but praise for the Indians, claimed that two Caughnawaga, suspecting that the English had been warned, opened fire (*NYCD* 10:321; *Claus' Narrative*, 13–14; Wright, *Colonel Ephraim Williams*, 135–36). Johnson later claimed that the shot was fired accidentally by someone on the French side (*NYCD* 6:1013–15).

100. *JP* 9:231; *Claus' Narrative*, 14.

101. *Pomeroy Journals*, 114, 137–39, 141–42.

102. Peter Wraxall to Henry Fox, September 27, 1755 in *Military Affairs*, 139.

103. *Pomeroy Journals*, 114, 138; *Claus' Narrative*, 14–15; *Boston Gazette*, September 22, 1755.

104. *Claus' Narrative*, 15. Captain Pierre Pouchot confirms the Canadian acceptance of Indian conventions in *Memoir Upon the Late War in North America Between the French and the English, 1755–60*, trans. and ed. F. B. Hough, 2 vols. (Roxbury, Mass., 1866), 1:37; *DCB* 3:376. Daniel Claus's re-creation of a conversation between Legardeur de Saint-Pierre and Dieskau is apocryphal, but true to the Indian perspective on battle (14–15). Wright, *Colonel Ephraim Williams*, 137; *NYCD* 10:317, 342–43.

105. *NYCD* 10:339.

106. *NYCD* 6:1005; see Shirley's view in "A Review of Military Operations in North America, 1753–1756," Massachusetts Historical Society, *Collections*, 1st ser., 7 (1800), 112 (hereafter MHS).

107. *Pomeroy Journals*, 138–39; *JP* 2:228–34; Wright, *Colonel Ephraim Williams*, 137–51; *Claus' Narrative*, 14–16; *NYCD* 10:321–23, 335–36, 343; *Military Affairs*, 139.

108. *JP* 9:231–32; Wright, *Colonel Ephraim Williams*, 144. Vaudreuil has a more elaborate, but not convincing account (*NYCD* 10:322–23). For complaints of McGinnis's men about distribution of loot, see *JP* 2:195–96.

109. *NYCD* 10:323, 336. Other accounts place the number of wounded considerably lower, at 163 or even 130 (*NYCD* 10:324, 339–40). These numbers may have been gathered later, when some of the wounded had died and others had recovered. None of the figures include all the Indian casualties.

110. *JP* 2:24–25.

111. *JP* 2:74.

112. *Pomeroy Journals*, 115–16, 142–43.

113. Hill, "Diary of a Private." 609.

114. *NYCD* 6:1005; 10:321–22.

115. One Ephraim Bennet was apparently taken to Canada as a prisoner from the battle, though other witnesses record that all of them were killed after being given to the Indians (Emma Lewis Coleman, *New England Captives Carried to Canada between 1677 and 1760 during the French and Indian Wars*, 2 vols. [Portland, Me., 1925–26], 2:362; *JP* 2:202, 400).

116. Johnson's initial estimates are in *JP* 9:231–33. Official returns are in *JP* 9:234–36 and *NYCD* 6:1006–7 but need recounting. Pomeroy's list in Forbes Library, Northampton, Massachusetts is more complete than printed versions. On September 26, Perez Marsh, now surgeon in Williams's regiment, put the figures at 216 dead and 96 wounded (Wright, *Colonel Ephraim Williams*, 148). Some of the wounded may have recovered, and others may have died in the interim; his figures did not include the 32 Iroquois dead and their 12 wounded.

117. *NYCD* 6:1015; 10:324, 336, 339–40, 354, 356; *JP* 2:44–47; AN, Guerre, A¹, 3417, pp. 81–85. Three weeks later, a scouting party returned with a Penobscot prisoner who had his thigh broken in the battle and had survived in the woods (*Pomeroy Journals*, 120). In what is probably an exaggerated account of deaths, in battle and from wounds, among Indians allied to the French, the total was given as about one hundred (*JP* 2:388).

118. *JP* 2:43, 80–81; 9:233; *NYCD* 7:55.

119. *JP* 9:300. Governor Hardy reluctantly accepted this violation of the quarter given prisoners (*JP* 2:289).

120. *JP* 2:183–85, 205, 280–81.

121. *NYCD* 6:1011–13.

122. *NYCD* 6:1005, where the Indians are referred to as "Blacks," which misled Kenneth Wiggins Porter, *The Negro on the American Frontier* (New York, 1971), 101. For Johnson's evaluation, see *NYCD* 6:1009–10.

123. Hill, "Diary of a Private," 609; *Pomeroy Journals*, 118, 124. For disputes over the distribution of plunder, see *JP* 2:195–96, 199.

124. *JP* 1:803–6; 2:80, 86, 125–28.

125. PRO, CO 5/46, fols. 113–16; *Boston Gazette*, September 22, 1755.

126. PRO, CO 5/46, fols. 116–22; Newberry Library, Chicago, Ayer Collection, no. 582; *JP* 2:146–47, 194.

127. *Pomeroy Journals*, 115; *JP* 2:38–41.

128. Frégault, *Guerre de la conquête*, 107; *Pomeroy Journals*, 120–22, 124; *JP* 2:145–48, 159–61, 174–79, 207–9, 212–15, 250–52, 257, 304–5, 319–22, 324.

129. Daniel J. Beattie, "The Adaptation of the British Army to Wilderness Warfare, 1755–1763," in *Adapting to Conditions: War and Society in the Eighteenth Century*, ed. Maartin Ultee (University, Ala., 1986), 67n.

130. *JP* 2:42–43, 53, 55, 76, 133–38; *Pomeroy Journals*, 147–48.

131. *JP* 2:78; *NYCD* 10:414.

132. *Pomeroy Journals*, 147–48; "Journal of Capt. Nathaniel Dwight," 68; *JP* 2:133–38. On October 6, Johnson reported the garrison had only 2560 effectives (*JP* 2:150).

133. *JP* 2:15–16.

134. *JP* 2:39–40, 53, 77, 82, 84–85, 99, 109, 114–18.

135. *JP* 2:150.

CHAPTER 3: FORT WILLIAM HENRY, 1755–1757

1. Late in 1757, Lord Loudoun talked of rebuilding to "protect Vessels I might build to enable me to attack Tiendroga[*sic*] in the Spring" (Stanley M. Pargellis, ed., *Military Affairs in North America 1748–1763* [New York, 1936], 400).
2. *Military Affairs*, 177–78.
3. *JP* 2:219, 262, 328–32.
4. *JP* 2:15–16.
5. *JP* 1:847.
6. John Muller, *A Treatise Containing the Elementary Part of Fortification, Regular and Irregular* (London, 1746), 198.
7. James Hill, "The Diary of a Private on the First Expedition to Crown Point," *NEQ* 5 (1932): 611; *JP* 2:117.
8. *JP* 2:117–18, 221.
9. "The Journal of Capt. Nathaniel Dwight of Belchertown, Mass., during the Crown Point Expedition, 1755," *New York Genealogical and Biographical Record* 33 (1902): 65–66; *Military Affairs*, 177–78.
10. *The Journals and Papers of Seth Pomeroy*, ed. L. E. de Forest (New York, 1926), 121; *JP* 2:221.
11. "Journal of Capt. Nathaniel Dwight," 8.
12. *Pomeroy Journals*, 123; *JP* 2:150–52, 158, 190, 277.
13. *JP* 2:164, 217, 219, 238, 261, 324.
14. *JP* 2:305–7.
15. Hill, "Diary of a Private," 613; "Journal of Capt. Nathaniel Dwight," 9.
16. *JP* 2:178, 198, 207, 217, 236, 241, 261–65, 321, 340; Johnson to Samuel Hopkins, November 1, 1755, Fort Ticonderoga Archives, no. 2031.
17. *JP* 2:241, 253–55; Hill, "Diary of a Private," 613–4.
18. *JP* 2:284, 288; "Journal of Capt. Nathaniel Dwight," 66–67.
19. "Journal of Capt. Nathaniel Dwight," 70.
20. Hill, "Diary of a Private," 616; "Journal of Capt. Nathaniel Dwight," 67; *JP* 9:304–5. The force had two 12-pounders and four 6-pounders of iron plus four 6-pounders in brass (*JP* 2:277). The 18-pounders assigned to the expedition remained in Albany.
21. "Journal of Capt. Nathaniel Dwight," 7; Hill, "Diary of a Private," 609–10, 612; *JP* 2:201, 212–16, 225, 242, 290, 295, 301.
22. Recollection of Jemima Howe, prisoner of the Abenaki on Lake Champlain (Samuel G. Drake, *Indian Captivities* [Buffalo, N.Y., 1854], 160). This quake was felt from Nova Scotia to South Carolina and toppled chimneys in Boston (*Diary and Journal of Seth Metcalf* [Boston, 1939], 17; Hill, "Diary of a Private," 617; Epaphras Hoyt, *Antiquarian Researches* [Greenfield, Mass., 1824], 282).
23. *JP* 2:140–41, 309.
24. *JP* 2:257.
25. *JP* 2:312–14, 335–36.

26. *JP* 2:354; 9:324–26.
27. *JP* 2:330–31.
28. *JP* 2:331–32.
29. *Military Affairs*, 177–78. Eyre's original plan had such an outwork, but it was to the south.
30. Report of R. Burton, James Montresor, and William MacLeod, dated August 25, 1756, printed in Stanley M. Gifford, *Fort William Henry, a History* (c. 1955), 27–31. Their instructions are in HL, LO 1424.
31. PRO, CO 5/48, fol. 4.
32. *JP* 2:691.
33. *NYCD* 10:433.
34. *Military Affairs*, 266.
35. *JP* 2:397–98.
36. PRO, WO 1/4, fols. 133–37.
37. John A. Schutz, *William Shirley, King's Governor of Massachusetts* (Chapel Hill, N.C., 1961), 227–29; ed. Allen Johnson and Dumas Malone, *Dictionary of American Biography*, 22 vols. (New York, 1928–44), 10:396–97 (hereafter *DAB*).
38. *NYCD* 10:433.
39. For Lotbinière's instructions of September 20, 1755, see Fort Ticonderoga Archives, no. 1905. By winter the walls of Carillon were reported as between five and six feet tall and fifteen feet thick (*JP* 2:201, 399). Also see Lotbinière's letter of October 31, 1756 in S. H. P. Pell, *Fort Ticonderoga, a Short History* (Ticonderoga, N.Y., 1935), 23–25.
40. *Military Affairs*, 171.
41. PRO, WO 1/4, fols. 45–46.
42. King Lawrence Parker, "Anglo–American Wilderness Campaigning 1754–1764: Logistical and Tactical Developments" (Ph.D. diss., Columbia University, 1970), chaps. 3, 4; William G. Godfrey, *Pursuit of Profit and Preferment in Colonial North America: John Bradstreet's Quest* (Waterloo, Ont., 1982), 77–81.
43. *Military Affairs*, 170, 175–76.
44. Lawrence H. Gipson, *The British Empire Before the American Revolution*, 15 vols. (Caldwell, Idaho, and New York, 1936–70), 6: chap. 7; Schutz, William *Shirley*, chap. 12; S. M. Pargellis, *Lord Loudoun in North America* (New Haven, Conn., 1933), chap. 2.
45. *Correspondence of William Shirley*, ed. C. H. Lincoln, 2 vols. (New York, 1912), 2:492–515; Pargellis, *Lord Loudoun*, 83–93; Gipson, *British Empire* 6:204–8. Loudoun, in supporting Lyman's petition for aid from the crown in 1772, said that Lyman had tried to persuade the other officers to accept the situation and had always been willing to obey orders himself (PRO CO 5/114, p. 406).
46. *Shirley Correspondence* 2:496–97.
47. Gipson, *British Empire* 6:207–8.

48. *An Enquiry into the Causes of Our Ill Success in the Present War* (London, 1757), 33. Another highly critical appraisal of Winslow's campaign, by a regular officer, is in the Chatham papers, PRO, GD 30/8/95, fols. 222–24. A Connecticut perspective is in the same source, fols. 52–53.
49. *Historical Magazine*, 2nd ser., 7 (1870): 215.
50. *Military Affairs*, 239–40; Furnis to Ordnance Board, October 3, 1756, Furnis Letterbook, Clements Library, Ann Arbor, Michigan; HL, LO 6955.
51. PRO, WO 1/4, fols. 176–81.
52. I. K. Steele, *Guerillas and Grenadiers* (Toronto, 1969), 99–101.
53. *NYCD* 10:480, 488–89, 490–92, 497.
54. Pargellis, *Lord Loudoun*, 94–95; Douglas Edward Leach, *Arms for Empire* (New York, 1973), 388–89.
55. Pargellis, *Lord Loudoun*, 179–83.
56. PRO, GD 30/8/95, fol. 223; PRO, CO 5/48, fol. 181.
57. *Adventure in the Wilderness: The American Journals of Louis Antoine de Bougainville, 1756–1760*, ed. Edward P. Hamilton (Norman, Okla., 1964), 45 (hereafter *Bougainville Journals*); Loudoun to Fox, November 22, 1756, PRO, CO 5/48, fols. 5, 10.
58. *JP* 2:398.
59. *JP* 2:167, 170, 222, 238–39, 258, 396; PRO, CO 5/48, fol. 5; HL, LO 1106, 1813.
60. *JP* 2:396.
61. *JP* 9:617.
62. *Bougainville Journals*, 31, 33, 52–53; *Journals of Major Robert Rogers* (London, 1765), 20.
63. Pargellis, *Lord Loudoun*, 98.
64. John R. Cuneo, *Robert Rogers of the Rangers* (New York, 1959), 25–26, 28.
65. *JP* 2:187, 214, 216, 225, 242; *Rogers Journals*, 1–8.
66. *Rogers Journals*, 8–10; Cuneo, *Robert Rogers*, 30–39; *JP* 2:416–17.
67. *Rogers Journals*, 11
68. *Bougainville Journals*, 47, 50–51.
69. Cuneo, *Robert Rogers*, 43; *Rogers Journals*, 18–19.
70. AN, Colonies, C11A, 101, fol. 130; *DCB* 4:513; Emma Lewis Coleman, *New England Captives Carried to Canada between 1677 and 1760 during the French and Indian Wars*, 2 vols. (Portland, Me., 1925–26), 2:355, 361–62.
71. *Bougainville Journals*, 34, 36, 40–41, 43, 45, 48; AN, Guerre, A¹, 3417, no. 205.
72. *Rogers Journals*, 27; Cuneo, *Robert Rogers*, 44–45.
73. AN, Colonies, C11A, 102, fols. 12–14; Montreuil's letter of September 20, 1756, Fort Ticonderoga Archives, no. 1906; *Bougainville Journals*, 44–61.
74. *Bougainville Journals*, 59–60.

75. *Bougainville Journals*, 40–41.
76. *Bougainville Journals*, 39; Pièrre de Kerallain, *Les Français au Canada: La jeunesse de Bougainville et la guerre de sept ans* (Paris, 1896), 50.
77. PRO, CO 5/48, fols. 48–49; HL, LO 1965B.
78. PRO, CO 5/48, fols. 29–32.
79. *Bougainville Journals*, 80–82; *DCB* 4:563–64.
80. See his report, PRO, CO 5/48, fols. 107–9 and HL, LO 2704A, and compare *Rogers Journals*, 29–33. Rogers later drew on his experience here for his "plan of discipline," pp. 43–51. Thomas Brown, *A Plain Narrative of the Uncommon Sufferings and Remarkable Deliverance of Thomas Brown of Charlestown, in New England* (Boston, 1760), indicates that at least two of those presumed killed (Thomas Brown and Robert Baker) were not.
81. *Rogers Journals*, 34.
82. Robert Baker was still a prisoner in Canada in August 1757 (HL, LO 4147).
83. *NYCD* 10:551.
84. This included 274 regulars, 72 rangers, plus 128 who were ill (PRO, CO 5/48, fol. 181).
85. PRO, CO 5/48, fols. 184–88; *Bougainville Journals*, 87–88.
86. Nearly 90 percent of the 234 craft at Fort William Henry the previous November were bateaux (HL, LO 2242). These had recently been standardized at twenty-five to thirty feet in length, eight feet in width (Daniel J. Beattie, "The Adaptation of the British Army to Wilderness Warfare, 1755–1763," in *Adapting to Conditions: War and Society in the Eighteenth Century*, ed. Maartin Ultee [University, Ala., 1986], 65).
87. PRO, CO 5/48, fols. 105–6, 173–74 and WO 34/101, fol. 89.
88. PRO, CO 5/48, fols. 184–85.
89. PRO, CO 5/48, fols. 177–88.
90. *NYCD* 10:547–55; Brown, *Plain Narrative*, 10; *Bougainville Journals*, 109.
91. AN, Colonies, C11A, 102, fols. 36–40.

CHAPTER 4: SIEGE

1. PRO, CO 5/48, fols. 29–32, 48–49, 164–65; *JP*, 2:694, 704–6.
2. AN, Colonies, C11A, 102, fols. 65–71.
3. Augustin Grignon, "Seventy-Two Years Recollections of Wisconsin," *Wisconsin Historical Society Collections* 3 (1857): 212; Paul E. Kopperman, *Braddock at the Monongahela* (Pittsburgh, 1977), 9, 24, 26; Francis Jennings, *Empire of Fortune: Crowns, Colonies & Tribes in the Seven Years War in America* (New York, 1988), 153–57.
4. *Bougainville Journals*, 5, 8–10; NAC, MG 17, A7-1, vol. 4, p. 2797.
5. *NYCD*, 10:454–56, 473–75. Jennings claims that civilians were also mas-

sacred (*Empire of Fortune*, 294–96). The prisoners taken included 138 civilian construction workers, 44 servants, 11 merchants, and at least 54 women (AN, Guerre, A¹, 3417, nos. 210, 214).

6. *Bougainville Journals*, 116.
7. *Bougainville Journals*, 66; Russell David Edmunds, *The Potawatomi, Keepers of the Fire* (Norman, Okla., 1978), 52–53.
8. *NYCD* 10: 499–518, esp. 512, and 553–63; *JP* 2:704–6. About a hundred Onondaga and Cayuga, including women and children, had come up to Sault St. Louis to visit (*Bougainville Journals*, 73). On subsequent Mohawk reluctance, see *JP* 9:665–67.
9. Pierre Pouchot, *Memoir upon the Late War in North America between the French and the English, 1755–60*, trans. and ed. F. B. Hough, 2 vols. (Roxbury, Mass., 1866), 1:81–82; *Bougainville Journals*, 127.
10. James Smith's narrative in Samuel G. Drake, *Indian Captivities* (Buffalo, N.Y., 1854), 220; John Duffy, *Epidemics in Colonial America* (Baton Rouge, La., 1953), 86–91.
11. It is possible, though unlikely, that Pontiac was at Fort William Henry (H. H. Peckham, *Pontiac and the Indian Uprising* [Princeton, N.J. 1947], 47–48). Charles Stuart found the Detroit Ottawa without a church and claimed they were particularly barbarous (see *Mississippi Valley Historical Review* 13 [1926]: 74–75; *DCB* 4:521–22). The roster of Indians has been taken from *Bougainville Journals*, 150–51, which differs slightly from that given in *Collection des manuscrits du Marechal de Lévis*, ed. H.-R. Casgrain, 12 vols. (Quebec, 1889–95), 1:89–91. Check also *NYCD* 10:607–8.
12. See Nicholas-Joseph de Noyelles de Fleurimont, *DCB*, 3:491–93. For Nissowaquet and Charles-Michel Mouet de Langlade, see *DCB* 4:563–64, 582–83.
13. *Bougainville Journals*, 114; Pouchot, *Memoir*, 1:82–83.
14. *Bougainville Journals*, 151. Little is known of these Ojibwa or the Canadians linked with them, named La Plante, Loumier, and Chesne.
15. *Bougainville Journals*, 150; Louise P. Kellogg, *The French Régime in Wisconsin and the Northwest* (Madison, Wis., 1925), 399–400; Patricia K. Ourada, *The Menominee Indians, A History* (Norman, Okla., 1979), 36–38.
16. *DCB*, 3:148–49.
17. *Bougainville Journals*, 131–32, 151. Langis' full name was Jean-Baptiste Levrault de Langis Montegron (*DCB* 3:399–400).
18. AN, Colonies, C11A, 102, fol. 84.
19. *Bougainville Journals*, 151, 152, 158, 212–13; Pierre de Charlevoix, *Journal of a Voyage to North America*, 2 vols. (London, 1761), 1:285.
20. *Bougainville Journals*, 91, 105, 120, 151. These Delaware were probably led by chief Anandomoakin (see *DCB* 4:26–27).
21. *Bougainville Journals*, 118, 120–21, 151.
22. Pouchot had about 150 women and children spend the summer with him

at Niagara while their men were on the campaign (*Memoir*, 1:85; *Bougainville Journals*, 125).

23. *Bougainville Journals*, 103, 109–10, 122–24, 150–51; *DCB* 3:328.
24. *Bougainville Journals*, 124–25, 150. Professor John Demos of Yale University had estimated the population of Caughnawaga as about twelve hundred. If the most generous estimates of militia (one in four) were applied, Caughnawaga could not be expected to contain more than three hundred warriors.
25. Paul-Joseph Le Moyne de Longueuil, *DCB* 4:463–65.
26. *Bougainville Journals*, 150; Thomas-Marie Charland, *Histoire des Abénakis d'Odanak* (Montreal, 1964); *DCB* 5:97–99; *DCB* 4:685–87.
27. Reuben G. Thwaites, ed., *The Jesuit Relations and Allied Documents, 1610–1783*, 73 vols. (Cleveland, 1896–1901), 70:100–103 (hereafter *JR*); *Bougainville Journals*, 136.
28. Vaudreuil to Moras, June 1, 1757, AN, Colonies, C11A, 102, fols. 46–51.
29. *Bougainville Journals*, 102–3, 109–10; Pouchot, *Memoir*, 1:75–76; Vaudreuil to Moras, July 12, 1757, AN, Colonies, C11A, 102, fols. 62–64.
30. *JP* 2:719.
31. Adam Williamson's journal for July 1–2, 1757 in Williamson Family Papers, NAC microfilm A 573; Webb to Loudoun, August 1, 1757, HL, LO 4020A.
32. *Bougainville Journals*, 121–22; Vaudreuil to Moras, July 12, 1757, AN, Colonies, C11A, 102, fols. 62–64; William H. Hill, *Old Fort Edward* (Fort Edward, N.Y., 1929), 123, 131.
33. Johanna E. Feest and Christian F. Feest, "Ottawa," in *Handbook of North American Indians*, vol. 15, *The Northeast*, ed. Bruce Trigger (Washington, D.C., 1978), 777; Nathaniel Knowles, "The Torture of Captives by the Indians of Eastern North America," *Proceedings of the American Antiquarian Society* 82 (1940): 151–225.
34. Quoted in Richard Waddington, *La guerre de sept ans*, 5 vols. (Paris, 1899–1914), 1:228.
35. *Bougainville Journals*, 114.
36. Pierre de Kerallain, *Les Français au Canada: La Jeunesse de Bougainville et la guerre de sept ans* (Paris, 1896), 72–73.
37. Anne-Joseph-Hippolyte de Maures, comte de Malartic, *Journal des campagnes au Canada de 1755 à 1760* (Dijon, France, 1890), 125; *DCB* 4:530–31.
38. *JR*, 70:133–37; *Bougainville Journals*, 141.
39. Malartic, *Journal*, 125–26; *Bougainville Journals*, 127.
40. *Bougainville Journals*, 140–41.
41. *Bougainville Journals*, 142.
42. Webb to Loudoun, August 1, 1757, PRO, CO 5/48, fol. 300; *Bougainville Journals*, 141–42; Williamson journal for July 24, 1757. For

the impact on the garrison, see Phineas Lyman, *General Orders of 1757* (New York, 1970), 49–56, and especially, the *Pennsylvania Gazette* of August 18, 1757. Also John Knox, *An Historical Journal of the Campaigns in North America for the Years 1757, 1758, 1759 and 1760*, 3 vols. (Toronto, 1914–16), 1:70

43. *Bougainville Journals*, 141–42; Webb to Loudoun, August 1, 1757, PRO, CO 5/48, fol. 300.

44. *Lévis MSS*, 1:85–86; *Bougainville Journals*, 141–42.

45. *DCB*, 4:347–48.

46. Webb's and Williamson's contentions, that four boats returned, seems more likely than Bougainville's claim that all but two were captured or destroyed (*Bougainville Journals*, 142–43; Webb to Loudoun, August 1, 1757, PRO CO 5/48, fol. 300; Williamson journal for July 24, 1757). See the detail offered in *Scots Magazine* (August 1757): 426 and (October 1757): 542. *New-York Historical Society Collections* 24 (1891): 510–11.

47. Lévis gave support to figures sent Loudoun by Webb and by Governor Delancey (*Lévis MSS* 1:87; HL, LO 4019, 4020A). The general figures of 100/350 (28.5%) returned are reinforced by a list of the dead and missing for two of Parker's companies. If these companies averaged seventy men, the hundred named as dead or missing would also mean 40/140 (28.5%) returned safely (*NYCD* 10:592–93).

48. *Bougainville Journals*, 142–43; *JR* 70:118–23.

49. *JR*, 70:109.

50. *Bougainville Journals*, 141–42; PRO, CO 5/48, fol. 300; Montcalm to Vaudreuil, July 27, 1757, *NYCD* 10:591, 599; Webb to Loudoun, August 1, 1757, HL, LO 4020A.

51. *JR* 70:116–17. In a later version of the incident, written about 1763, Roubaud claimed that these prisoners were saved by an order from Montcalm that he wanted to question them, which infuriated St. Luc de la Corne. By this time, Roubaud was trying to impress the British, was viciously anti-Canadian, and was particularly upset with St. Luc de la Corne (NAC, MG 23, GV5).

52. *JR* 70:124–31. *Jongleries* is here translated as "mockery." Montcalm was not receptive to the missionaries' concern (*Bougainville Journals*, 155). On the role of cannibalism among Iroquoian cultures, see Knowles, "Torture of Captives," 151–225.

53. Montcalm to Vaudreuil, July 25, 1757, Waddington, *La guerre*, 1:258; *Bougainville Journals*, 142–43.

54. *Bougainville Journals*, 144, 151; *NYCD* 10:599.

55. *Bougainville Journals*, 143, 145–46.

56. *Bougainville Journals*, 146–50; *NYCD* 10:609.

57. Bougainville counted 363 Iroquois and 337 Ottawa (*Bougainville Journals*, 150–51).

58. *Bougainville Journals*, 146–49.
59. To Holdernesse, August 16, 1757, PRO, CO 5/48, fol. 277.
60. *NYCD* 10:499, 523–26.
61. *Bougainville Journals*, 121, 152; *NYCD* 10:353–54, 441.
62. *Bougainville Journals*, 131–32, 152–53; AN, Guerre, A¹, no. 292.
63. *Bougainville Journals*, 152–53; W. J. Eccles, "The French Forces in North America During the Seven Years' War," *DCB* 3:xv–xxii.
64. *NYCD* 10:492; *Bougainville Journals*, 156.
65. PRO, GD 30/8/95, fol. 213; CO 5/48, fol. 308.
66. *Bougainville Journals*, 130–32. Parkman examined the area before the waterway was altered (*The Journals of Francis Parkman*, ed., Mason Wade, 2 vols. [London, 1947], 2:569; Francis Parkman, *Montcalm and Wolfe*, 3 vols. [Boston, 1905], 2:165–66).
67. *Bougainville Journals*, 155.
68. *Lévis MSS*, 1:88–94; cf. *Bougainville Journals*, 153–54.
69. *JR* 70:138–41; *Bougainville Journals*, 156.
70. *Bougainville Journals*, 154–57; *JR* 70:142–43; *NYCD* 10:601.
71. *Lévis MSS*, 1:94–96; *Bougainville Journals*, 157–58; *JR* 70:144–49; "A Journal Kept During the Siege of Fort William Henry, August, 1757," *Proceedings of the American Philosophical Society* 37 (1898): 146; Williamson journal for August 2, 1757.
72. Stanley M. Pargellis ed., *Military Affairs in North America 1748–1763*, (New York, 1936), 239, 255; PRO, CO 5/48, fols. 182–83; HL, LO 2065.
73. PRO, CO 5/48, fols. 223–24; Emma Lewis Coleman, *New England Captives Carried to Canada between 1677 and 1760 During the French and Indian Wars*, 2 vols. (Portland, Me., 1925–26), 2:312–13.
74. PRO, CO 5/48, fol. 228; *Military Affairs*, 370–72.
75. *Diary and Journal of Seth Metcalf* (Boston, 1939), 6, 7; Coleman, *New England Captives*, 2:368–69.
76. Williamson journal for July 2, 1757; *The Journals of Col. James Montresor* (New York, 1881), 19–20; *Metcalf Diary*, 7.
77. Williamson journal for July 4–21.
78. Williamson journal for July 24.
79. *Montresor Journals*, 23–24; *JR* 70:153; Collins' notes on gun placement (HL, LO 4923), and Webb to Loudoun, August 1, 1757 (HL, LO 4020A).
80. (Joseph Frye's journal), *The Port Folio*, 4th ser., vol. 7 (1819): 356–57; *Montresor Journals*, 23–24; Webb to Loudoun, August 1, 1757, HL, LO 4020A.
81. John A Schutz, "The Siege of Fort William Henry: Letters of George Bartman," *Huntington Library Quarterly* 12 (1948–49): 419–21.
82. *Luke Grindley's Diary for 1757* (Hartford, 1906), 47–48.
83. Transactions at Fort William Henry during its Siege in August 1757 (HL, LO 6660, p. 1).
84. HL, LO 4038, 4040A, 5275; PRO, CO 5/48, fols. 306–7.

85. Frye reported eighteen killed and "several wounded" (358); PRO, CO 5/ 48, fols. 308–9.
86. *Bougainville Journals*, 157–59; *Lévis MSS* 1:96–99; Frye journal, 357–58; "Journal Kept During the Siege," 147; HL, LO 4067.
87. HL, LO 3862, 4041A, 4281A; *NYCD* 10:626.
88. *Bougainville Journals*, 158–59; Frye journal, 357–58 "Journal Kept During the Siege," 146–47; Williamson journal for August 3; HL, LO 4048, 4040A.
89. HL, LO 4040A, 6660.
90. Williamson journal for August 4 and 5; *NYCD* 10:602; HL, LO 4061, 6660; "Journal Kept During the Siege," 147; Frye journal, 358–59; *Bougainville Journals*, 160–61; Le Blond, *A Treatise of Artillery* (London, 1746), 28.
91. HL, LO 4040A.
92. PRO, CO 5/48, fols. 308–9; HL, LO 4045A; Schutz, "Bartman Letters," 420.
93. Williamson journal for August 5; Frye journal, 359; HL, LO 6660. "Journal Kept During the Siege" entry for August 5 is a garbled collage of events of several other days, obviously reconstructed later.
94. See *Handbook of North American Indians* 15:479.
95. *Bougainville Journals*, 163–64; NAC, MG 17, A7–1, vol. 4, 2820.
96. *JR* 70:160–63.
97. NAC, MG 17, A7–1, 4, 2822.
98. *Bougainville Journals*, 164–65; *JR* 70:162–64, 168–69.
99. HL, LO 4041A, 6660; *Bougainville Journals*, 165–66; Williamson journal for August 6; "Journal Kept During the Siege," 147–48; Frye journal, 359–60.
100. M. A. Stickney, "Massacre at Fort William Henry, 1757," *Essex Institute Historical Collections* 3 (1861): 80.
101. Williamson journal for August 7; *Bougainville Journals*, 166–68; "Journal Kept During the Siege," describes August 7 under date of August 6 (148).
102. Schutz, "Bartman Letters," 422; HL, LO 4041A.
103. Williamson journal for August 7; *Bougainville Journals*, 166–67; "Journal Kept During the Siege," 148; *NYCD* 10:603; *JR* 70:166–67.
104. *Bougainville Journals*, 168; William S. Ewing, "An Eyewitness Account by James Furnis of the Surrender of Fort William Henry, August, 1757," *New York History* 42(1961): 312.
105. NAC, MG 17, A7–1, IV, 2821.
106. "Journal Kept During the Siege," 148.
107. HL, LO 4395A; PRO, WO1/51, fols. 36–38.
108. *Bougainville Journals*, 167; Frye journal, 361; *NYCD* 10:603; "Furnis Eyewitness Account," 312.
109. HL, LO 5275.

110. *Bougainville Journals*, 168–69; Frye journal, 362; "Journal Kept During the Siege," 149.
111. *Bougainville Journals*, 168–69.
112. Claims that an expedition set out and was then called back by Webb seem fictitious in the light of Lyman's detailed *General Orders of 1757*, 63–65; *Grindley's Diary*, 47–48; *Metcalf Diary*, 9; *Montresor Journals*, 26–28; *Bougainville Journals*, 333; and Rufus Putnam, *Journal of Gen. Rufus Putnam* (Albany, N.Y., 1886), 40–42. Compare David Humphreys, *An Essay on the Life of the Honourable Major General Israel Putnam* . . . (Boston, 1818), 41; James Thomas Flexner, *Lord of the Mohawks* (Boston, 1979), 181.
113. Webb to Loudoun, August 11, 1757, HL, LO 4198A; Webb to Barrington, August 17, 1757, HL, LO 4245A, and HL, LO 6660.
114. *Montresor Journals*, 27. This was the third battalion of the Royal Americans (Sixtieth) regiment, of which Lord Loudoun was colonel-in-chief (Lewis Butler, *Annals of the King's Royal Rifle Corps*, 6 vols. [London, 1913], 1:40).
115. HL, LO 4041A.
116. HL, LO 4395A.
117. HL, LO 6660, p. 6.

CHAPTER 5: "MASSACRE"

1. HL, LO 4158, 4395A; William S. Ewing, "An Eyewitness Account by James Furnis of the Surrender of Fort William Henry, August, 1757," *New York History* 42 (1961): 312–13; (Joseph Frye's journal), *The Port Folio*, 4th ser., vol. 8 (1819): 362–63.
2. James De Lancey to Thomas Pownall, August 10, 1757 (PRO, CO 5/888, fol. 54). Apparently Faesch was still being paid as a French subaltern after he began drawing pay as a British captain (PRO, WO 1/1, fol. 131).
3. "Furnis Eyewitness Account," 312–13; *Bougainville Journals*, 169–70; Frye journal, 363–65. Compare Anne-Joseph-Hippolyte de Maures, comte de Malartic, *Journal des campagnes au Canada de 1755 à 1760* (Dijon, France, 1890), 143–44. The Minorca garrison had been transferred to Gibralter.
4. The powers were not at war when Fort Necessity fell in 1754 and most of the garrison was released in exchange for French captives. The French regulars at the inglorious defense of Fort Beauséjour in June of 1755 were returned to the Louisbourg garrison under parole of six months.
5. *Bougainville Journals*, 170; *Journal du marquis de Montcalm durant ses campagnes en Canada de 1756 à 1759*, ed. H.-R. Casgrain (Quebec, 1895), 292.

6. J. W. Wright, "Sieges and Customs of War at the Opening of the Eighteenth Century," *American Historical Review* 39 (1934): 640.
7. The terms were widely printed, then and since (see *NYCD* 10:617–18).
8. Transactions at Fort William Henry during its Siege in August 1757 (HL, LO 6660, pp. 6–7).
9. L. Dussieux, *Le Canada sous la domination française*, 3rd ed. (Paris, 1883), 243; *Bougainville Journals*, 170; *NYCD* 10:650.
10. *Bougainville Journals*, 150–51.
11. *Bougainville Journals*, 170; *JR* 70:177.
12. Affidavits of William Arbuthnot and Joseph Ingersoll (HL LO 4654, LO 4660A). Arbuthnot said that he had heard of no survivors from among the sick and wounded, and Ingersoll claimed that the bodies were buried by Massachusetts soldiers who returned to the fort after the next day's turmoil.
13. *JR* 70:179. An Oneida raiding party reportedly took a human head at Montreal in October 1657, but the practice was no longer common (Raoul Naroll, "The Causes of the Fourth Iroquois War," *Ethnohistory* 16 [1969]: 52).
14. Frye journal, 367; HL, LO 6660, p. 9.
15. *Bougainville Journals*, 170.
16. *Scots Magazine* (October 1757): 543.
17. Frye journal, 365; Dussieux, *Le Canada*, 244.
18. [C.-N.] Gabriel, *Le maréchal de camp Desandrouins* (Verdun, France, 1887), 104.
19. See the petitions of Jonathan Bayley, Richard Emery, John Gilman, and Philip Johnson, in New Hampshire Archives and Records Management, Concord, N.H.
20. Malartic, *Journal*, 144–45.
21. Dussieux, *Le Canada*, 244; Malartic, *Journal*, 144–45; HL, LO 6660, p. 10; *Bougainville Journals*, 170–71.
22. Montcalm makes no mention of this event, but see Gabriel, *Le maréchal Desandrouins*, 104; *NYCD* 10:640–44; Frye journal, 365; "Furnis Eyewitness Account," 313; "A Journal Kept During the Siege of Fort William Henry, August, 1757," *Proceedings of the American Philosophical Society* 37 (1898): 149–50.
23. "Furnis Eyewitness Account," 313; HL, LO 6660, p. 10.
24. Gabriel, *Le maréchal Desandrouins*, 104–5; Dussieux, *Le Canada*, 245.
25. Frye journal, 365.
26. Frye journal, 365.
27. Dussieux, *Le Canada*, 244.
28. Miles Whitworth, surgeon to the Massachusetts regiment, later identified St. Luc de la Corne as present the next morning (Parkman MSS, XLII, 183–84, MHS).
29. *Bougainville Journals*, 150–51; *DCB* 4:512–14.

30. *Bougainville Journals*, 150–51; *DCB* 4:563–64.
31. "Remarks upon the Capitulation according to the Intelligence received from Col. Monro" sent Webb to Loudoun, August 30, 1757 (HL, LO 4332A).
32. Frye journal, 365–66.
33. Cf. Gabriel, *Le maréchal Desandrouins*, 105.
34. The line of march has not survived. With the Royal Artillery in the lead, it seems easier to account for the safe arrival at Fort Edward of Captian MacLeod and Lieutenant Thomas Collins, with the latter being among the first to arrive. Furnis nearly succeeded, and his batman did (*The Journals of Col. James Montresor* [New York, 1881], 28). See also John Maylem, *Gallic Perfidy* (Boston, 1758), lines 40–43.
35. Frye journal, 366; "Furnis Eyewitness Account," 313.
36. "Furnis Eyewitness Account," 313–14; Wright, "Sieges and Customs of War," 640–41. When the Thirty-Fifth Regiment was reassembled at Albany, it had 121 firelocks, 26 bayonets, and 54 cartouche boxes among 546 men (HL, LO 4039). Captain Cruickshank's independent company apparently lost all 49 firelocks, bayonets, and cartouche boxes (HL, LO 6664).
37. Parkman MSS, XLII, 183–84, MHS; Jonathan Carver, *Travels through the Interior Parts of North America in the Years 1766, 1767 and 1768* (London, 1778), 316–17; Frye journal, 366; "Furnis Eyewitness Account," 314; "Journal Kept During the Siege," 150.
38. *New York Mercury* and *New York Gazette* of August 22, 1757; Frye journal, 366; "Journal Kept During the Siege," 150; Emma Lewis Coleman, *New England Captives Carried to Canada between 1677 and 1760 during the French and Indian Wars*, 2 vols. (Portland, Me., 1925–26), 2:348, 350, 353.
39. Coleman, *New England Captives* 2:347–55; *Bougainville Journals*, 175; *NYCD* 10:210, 213; Kenneth Wiggins Porter, *The Negro on the American Frontier* (New York, 1971), 23–26.
40. For an Abenaki view of taking blacks, see Coleman, *New England Captives* 2:295.
41. See Paul E. Kopperman, "The British Command and Soldiers' Wives in America, 1755–1783," *Journal of the Society for Army Historical Research* 60 (1982): 14–34; Fred Anderson, *A People's Army: Massachusetts Soldiers and Society in the Seven Years' War* (Chapel Hill, N.C., 1984), 118–19.
42. On the tactical use of brutality, see Colin G. Calloway, "An Uncertain Destiny: Indian Captivities on the Upper Connecticut River," *Journal of American Studies* 17 (1983): 197.
43. Gabriel, *Le maréchal Desandrouins*, 106.
44. Frye journal, 366

45. Carver, *Travels*, 317–18.
46. Carver, *Travels*, 319. Montcalm and Bougainville blamed the Abenaki of Panaouské, but the evidence is thin. Roubaud's scalp-laden Abenaki was from St. François (Dussieux, *Le Canada*, 245; *Bougainville Journals*, 172).
47. *JR* 70:179.
48. Frye journal, 366.
49. Maylem, *Gallic Perfidy*, lines 81–82. The image appears in Cotton Mather, *Decennium Luctuosum: An History of the Remarkable Occurrences In the Long War which New-England hath had with the Indian Salvages* (Boston, 1699), 222. Esther Burr, writing in 1755, worried about the war in general, and "bring[ing] up Children to be *dashed against the Stones by our Barbarous enemies*—or which is worse, to be inslaved by them, & obliged to turn *Papist*" (quoted in James Axtell, *The European and the Indian* [New York, 1981], 310). The image may have been derived from Isaiah 13: 16.
50. "A Journal Kept During the Siege," 150. Frye's journal mentions dead women and children by the roadside (366).
51. Carver, *Travels*, 319.
52. Frye journal, 366; Frye to Thomas Hubbard, Albany, August 16, 1757, Parkman MSS, XLII, 154–56, MHS.
53. Maylem, *Gallic Perfidy*, lines 44–45; Carver, *Travels*, 318–21; "Journal Kept During the Siege," 150.
54. "Furnis Eyewitness Account," 314.
55. *JR* 70:180–81.
56. *JR* 70:178–81.
57. *JR* 70:180–81; Carver's experience supports this (*Travels*, 318–26).
58. *JR* 70:120–21.
59. *JR* 70:180–83. Monro later commented on the claim of Montcalm's personal risk: "That particular fact never came to my knowledge, though I went, after this happen'd, to his Camp, where I remain'd from the Wednesday At Noon, till Monday morning following" (HL, LO 4345).
60. Dussieux, *Le Canada*, 245; Gabriel, *Le maréchal Desandrouins*, 108–109.
61. Gabriel, *Le maréchal Desandrouins*, 112–13.
62. Gabriel, *Le maréchal Desandrouins*, 113–14. For Picquet, see *DCB* 4:636–38. For Williamson, see *DNB* 31:472–73.
63. *JR* 70:184–95.
64. *Diary and Journal of Seth Metcalf* (Boston, 1939), 10 ("above 300"); *Bougainville Journals*, 174 ("400"); Montcalm to Loudoun, August 14, in *Collection de manuscrits contenant lettres, mémoires et autre documents historique relatifs à la Nouvelle France*, 4 vols. (Quebec, 1883–85), 4:113 ("plus de 400"); "A Journal of the Expedition against Fort William Henry," *NYCD* 10:605 ("nearly 500").

65. Seth Metcalf reported that "above 300" were returned to Fort Edward on August 15 (*Diary*, 10). Bougainville claimed "four hundred English ransomed from the Indians" were returned that day (*Journals*, 174), and Montcalm claimed the same when writing to Lord Loudoun (*Collections* 4:113). Montcalm's draft letter for Vaudreuil counted fourteen hundred recovered prisoners, but that may have been a misprint (Dussieux, *Le Canada*, 245).

66. Maylem, *Gallic Perfidy*, *passim*. The trip to Montreal was not quick. A courier had left Fort William Henry early on August 8 and reached Montreal in seventy-five hours. Bougainville began the same trip the following night and reached Montreal in forty-two hours (*Bougainville Journals*, 171.

67. *JR* 70:196–97. The Nipissing were probably from Lac-des-Deux-Montagnes (Oka), led by Montcalm's supporter, Kisensik (*DCB* 3:328).

68. *Bougainville Journals*, 174–79; Gabriel, *Le maréchal Desandrouins*, 109, recalled that the Indians from the *pays d'en haut* had four hundred prisoners.

69. "Furnis Eyewitness Account," 314; for claimed losses of clothing, horses, and baggage by Furnis and White, see Furnis to Ordnance, May 30, 1758, Furnis Letterbook, William L. Clements Library, University of Michigan, Ann Arbor.

70. *Montresor Journals*, 28.

71. *Montresor Journals*, 28.

72. *New York Mercury*, August 22, 1757; PRO, CO 5/888, fols. 90–91; *Montresor Journals*, 28; John A. Schutz, "The Siege of Fort William Henry: Letters of George Bartman," *Huntington Library Quarterly* 12 (1948–49): 424.

73. "Furnis Eyewitness Account," 314; *New York Mercury*, August 22, 1757.

74. *Metcalf Diary*, 10; De Lancey to Hayman Levy, August 10, 1757, in Bartman Letters, Henry Clinton Papers, William L. Clements Library, University of Michigan, Ann Arbor.

75. Phineas Lyman, *General Orders of 1757* (New York, 1970), 79–82, 114–17; *Boston Gazette*, September 5, 1757; (Manuel Josephson?) to Hayman Levy, Fort Edward, August 10, 1757 (Henry Clinton Papers, William L. Clements Library).

76. Rufus Putnam, *Journal of Gen. Rufus Putnam* (Albany, N.Y., 1886), 37, 45; *Montresor Journals*, 28–30.

77. Putnam, *Journal*, 42; Frye to T. Hubbard, August 16, 1757, Parkman MSS, XLII, 156, MHS.

78. Carver, *Travels*, 324.

79. "The Diary of Jabez Fitch," *Mayflower Descendant* 5 (1903): 252.

80. *Montresor Journals*, 26–27; *New York Mercury*, August 22, 1757.

81. PRO, CO 5/888, fol. 54.

82. To Council, August 10, Henry Clinton Papers, William L. Clements Library.
83. PRO, CO 5/888, fols. 52, 56–58.
84. Newberry Library, Ayer Collection, no. 754.
85. Israel Williams to Pownall, Sheffield, August 11, 1757 (HL, LO 4197) and William Pepperrell to Pownall, August 13 (LO 4211). *Correspondence of William Pitt*, ed. Gertrude Selwyn Kimball, 2 vols. (New York, 1906), 1:94–98; John A. Schutz, *Thomas Pownall, British Defender of American Liberty* (Glendale, Calif., 1951), 92–97.
86. PRO, CO 5/888, fols. 18–19, 65.
87. PRO, CO 5/888, fols. 20–21.
88. Harold E. Selesky, Military Leadership in an American Colonial Society: Connecticut, 1635–1785 (Ph.D. diss., Yale University, 1984), 204–5; HL, LO 6283.
89. HL, LO 4516; Nathaniel Bouton et al., eds., *Documents and Records Relating to the Province [Towns and State] of New Hampshire from the Earliest Period of Its Settlement*, 40 vols. (Concord, N.H., 1867–1943), 6:37, 602–3, 612; De Lancey to New York Council, August 11, Henry Clinton Papers, William L. Clements Library.
90. PRO, CO 5/48, fols. 323–24; PRO, GD 30/8/95, fols. 204, 213–14; HL, LO 4271A; John Knox, *An Historical Journal of the Campaigns in North America for the Years 1757, 1758, 1759 and 1760*, 3 vols. (Toronto, 1914–16), 1:52.
91. Stanley M. Pargellis, ed., *Military Affairs in North America 1748–1763* (New York, 1936), 397; *Archives of Maryland* 9 (1890): 71; R. A. Brock, ed., *The Official Records of Robert Dinwiddie*, 2 vols. (Richmond, Va., 1883–84), 2:692.
92. August 8, 1757.
93. *JP* 2:731.
94. Webb to De Lancey, August 11, 1757 (PRO CO 5/888, fol. 90); De Lancey to New York Council and Assembly, September 2, 1757 (PRO, CO 5/1068, fols. 115–16).
95. *New York Gazette*, August 22, 1757; *New York Mercury*, August 22, 1757.
96. PRO, CO 5/888, fols. 90–91; *Montresor Journals*, 28.
97. HL, LO 4251.
98. *JP* 2:730. Seth Pomeroy raised more than six hundred men in Hampshire County, Massachusetts, to relieve Fort William Henry. They were in service less than thirteen days, marched 176 miles, and were disbanded on news of the capitulation (*The Journals and Papers of Seth Pomeroy*, ed. L. E. de Forest [New York, 1926], 151).
99. "Diary of Jacob Fitch," 75.
100. *Putnam Journal*, 46; *New York Gazette*, November 28, 1757.

CHAPTER 6: AFTERMATH

1. *The Journals of Col. James Montresor* (New York, 1881), 28–30; William Hill, *Old Fort Edward* (Ft. Edward, N.Y., 1929), 139–40; *Diary and Journal of Seth Metcalf* (Boston, 1939), 10.

2. *Metcalf Diary* 10 ("above 300"); *Bougainville Journals*, 174 ("400"); Abbé Picquet, NAC, MG 17, A7-1, 4, 2823 ("400"); Webb to Loudoun, August 17 and 20, 1757, HL, LO 4266 and 4245A ("about four hundred men"); Montcalm to Loudoun, August 14, in *Collection de manuscrits contenant lettres, mémoires et autre documents historique relatifs à la Nouvelle France*, 4 vols. (Quebec, 1883–85), 4:113 ("plus de 400"); "A Journal of the Expedition against Fort William Henry," *NYCD* 10:605 ("nearly 500").

3. Chandler E. Potter, *The Military History of the State of New Hampshire, 1623–1861* (Concord, N.H., 1869), 188n.

4. HL, LO 6660, p. 12; "The Diary of Jabez Fitch," *Mayflower Descendant* 5 (1903): 75.

5. *Montresor Journals*, 29.

6. Richard Waddington, *La Guerre de sept ans*, 5 vols. (Paris, 1899–1914), 1:268.

7. *Bougainville Journals*, 174–75; John Maylem, *Gallic Perfidy* (Boston, 1758), line 15. Other captives were taken quickly to Fort Carillon, held there for a week, and then brought to Montreal by their Indian captives in the company of the returning army (see *Boston Gazette*, September 26, 1757). Desandrouins indicated that Indians and prisoners accompanied the army ([C.-N.] Gabriel, *Le Maréchal de camp Desandrouins* [Verdun, France, 1887], 114–17). For a testimonial by Maylem and Lieutenant Simon Wade, see *Notes and Queries*, 4th ser., vol. 4 (August 7, 1869): 114–15.

8. *Bougainville Journals*, 174.

9. Abbé Picquet, "reduction du fort Georges," NAC, MG 17, A7-1, vol. 4, 2823. On Montcalm's suggestion to imprison Indians, see his draft, in Vaudreuil's name, in L.-E. Dussieux, *Le Canada sous la domination française d' apres les Archives de la Marine et de la Guerre*, 3ᵉ ed. (Paris, 1883), 246.

10. Joshua Rand was one prisoner known to be outside the settlement. Captured by Ottawa, he was taken beyond Michilimackinac, returning home six years later (see Emma Lewis Coleman, *New England Captives Carried to Canada Between 1677 and 1760 during the French and Indian Wars*, 2 vols. [Portland, Me. 1925–26], 357–58). On prices, see Abbé Picquet, "reduction du fort Georges", NAC, MG 17, A7-1, 4, 2823. Sylvanus Johnson, a young captive with the more market-conscious Abenaki, was redeemed for 500 livres that same year (Susannah [Johnson] Hastings, *A Narrative of the Captivity of Mrs. Johnson* [New York, 1841], 108).

11. *Bougainville Journals*, 178–79.

12. Only one prisoner, Joshua Rand, is known to have returned from captivity by the Ottawa (*Boston Gazette*, December 12, 1763; Coleman, *New England Captives* 2:357–58; Massachusetts Archives, vol. 26, p. 73). Pierre Pouchot, *Memoir upon the Late War in North America between the French and the English, 1755–60*, trans. and ed. F. B. Hough, 2 vols. (Roxbury, Mass., 1866), 1:85–89; *DCB* 3:534–37; *NYCD* 10:667–68, 694–95. On the smallpox epidemic, see "The Mackinac Register 1695–1821," *Wisconsin Historical Society Collections* 19 (1909): 152–58; Jonathan Carver, *Travels through the Interior Parts of North America in the Years 1766, 1767 and 1768* (London, 1778), 326.

13. Some one thousand to twelve hundred Indians defended Canada in 1759, but fewer than three hundred were from the *pays d'en haut*, and half of these were Crees, who had not come down before. The nine hundred Indians who came down to Fort Niagara with the relief expedition did not fight for the French (AN, AC, F3, XV, 272, 335v.; J.-F. Récher, *Journal du siège de Québec* [Quebec, 1959], 43; Anne-Joseph-Hippolyte de Maures, comte de Malartic, *Journal des campagnes au Canada de 1755 à 1760* [Dijon, France, 1890], 251).

14. *NYCD* 10:732–33, 803–6. Montcalm's differences with Vaudreuil had become severe by this time as well, which aggravated matters.

15. I. K. Steele, *Guerillas and Grenadiers* (Toronto, 1969), 110.

16. *Bougainville Journals*, 179.

17. NAC, MG 18 L4, vol. 8, packet 57, pp. 7–8. Schuyler smuggled his report out in October 1757. Patrick McKellar, the other prisoner thought to have prepared this report, was in London by July 1757 (see *DNB* 12:573–75; Furnis to McKellar, June 9, 1757, in Furnis Letterbook, Clements Library, University of Michigan, Ann Arbor; NAC, RG 8, II, vol. 36, pp. 1–10). Bigot confirmed the costliness in his letter of November 3, 1757 to the minister of marine (AN, Colonies, C11A, 102, fol. 193).

18. In the reports by relatives submitted to the Massachusetts government in 1758, and in the muster rolls, only three were described as definitely killed at Fort William Henry on August 10: Peter Duey, Edward Grinmon Sr., and John McQuire (see Appendix).

19. *Bougainville Journals* specified 5 killed and 18 wounded out of 2570 men (177–78).

20. HL, LO 4313A, LO 4309. Monro did not list Captains Faesch and Ormsby, who can be counted in place of the two regulars who defected during the siege. For lists of numbers in the capitulation, see *NYCD* 10:621–25; *Bougainville Journals*, 175–77. Monro listed thirty-one privates of the Royal Americans as missing, to which Captain Faesch should be added, but the November return of the battalion listed thirty-six rank and file as missing after the siege and presumed prisoners in Canada (HL, LO 5249[6]).

21. HL, LO 4313A.

22. French accounts, of forty-one English killed and seventy-one wounded,

would mean that the provincials had twenty-one killed and forty-four wounded (*NYCD* 10:625, 643, 644).

23. *Collection* 4:114–15; *Metcalf Diary*, 10; Frye to T. Hubbard, August 16, Parkman MSS, XLII, 154–56, MHS; (Joseph Frye's journal), *The Port Folio*, 4th ser., vol. 7 (1819): 366. The missing officers were lieutenants Joel Bradford, David Day, and Simon Wade, and ensigns Joseph Greenleaf and John Maylem.

24. Coleman, *New England Captives* 2:352; Massachusetts Archives, Boston, vol. 78, p. 269. Two surviving lists of men given food and lodging on their way home to Massachusetts include 189 men who had been in the capitulation. See Massachusetts Archives, vol. 77, pp. 294–95, and Ticonderoga Archives, no. 1910. The relevant muster rolls are in Massachusetts Archives, vol. 95, pp. 473–74, 506–7, and vol. 96, pp. 41, 53, 57–58.

25. Only six are known to have returned to Fort Edward after escaping from their captors on the way to Montreal (Webb to Loudoun, September 6, 1757, HL, LO 4407; *Boston Gazette*, September 26, 1757. See Rufus Putnam, *Journal of Gen. Rufus Putnam* [Albany, N.Y., 1886], 45). One thirteen-year-old boy was stolen from his Indian captors by Desandrouins, who hid the lad in the magazine at St. Jean for a week before sending him on to Quebec with the French regulars (Gabriel, *Le maréchal Desandrouins*, 114–17).

26. *JR* 70:199; PRO, WO 34/64, fols. 12, 13, 79. Peter Schuyler repaid Montcalm, and the British army reimbursed Schuyler (*NYCD*, 10:634; Loudoun's notes for December 15, 1757, Huntington Library, Huntington Manuscripts 1717, vol. IV [hereafter HL, HM]). Ormsby was back in New York by December 25, 1757 (HL, LO 6168[8], 6947, and Huntington Library, Abercromby Papers 377 [hereafter HL, AB]).

27. HL, LO 6795, 4166, 4661, 4944, 4994.

28. HL, LO 6678, 4994.

29. HL, LO 4944, 4166, 4887; *Boston Gazette*, September 5, 1757.

30. HL, LO 4716, 6795; PRO, CO 5/49, fol. 96. There were disputes about paying for the hospital (HL, LO 5134, 5574, 5611).

31. AN, Guerre, A^1 3417, no. 239; Montcalm to Belle Isle, May 8, 1759, in *NYCD* 10:970–71.

32. HL, LO 4781, 4944, 4994; AN, Colonies, C11A, 102, fols. 117–18.

33. *A Narrative of the Captivity of Mrs. Johnson* (Springfield, Mass., 1907), 188–89 (hereafter *Johnson Narrative* [*1907*]).

34. HL, LO 4730; *Johnson Narrative* [*1907*], 129–30. Susannah married again, and had seven more children and what she described as "many happy days." She saw her narrative published in 1796, and her favorite daughter, Captive, whose birthday had always been special to them both, migrated to Canada with her husband two years later. Susannah lived to be eighty. The 1907 edition of her narrative includes funeral sermons and some correspondence.

35. Coleman gathered enough evidence from petitions to determine the destination of eighty-eight parolees, and eleven (one-eighth) of these had been in the Indian villages for more than a few days. Her sources were biased against those who stayed with the Indians (*New England Captives* 2:344–61). Compare Alden Vaughan and Daniel Richter, "Crossing the Cultural Divide: Indians and New Englanders, 1605–1763," *Proceedings of the American Antiquarian Society* 90 (1908): 23–99. See also Table 2.

36. See Appendix; Robert C. Alberts, *The Most Extraordinary Adventures of Major Robert Stobo* (Boston, 1965), 202–36. Denbow may have posed as a servant to an officer in the New Jersey Blues, but he was in Hercules Mooney's New Hampshire company (Nathaniel Bouton et al., eds., *Documents and Records Relating to the Province [Towns and State] of New Hampshire from the Earliest Period of its Settlement*, 40 vols. [Concord, N.H., 1867–1943], 18:508–9).

37. See Appendix concerning the missing Indians, Jonathan George and Nathan Joseph, as well as Elijah Denbow, Francis Finney, Benjamin Goodnow, Joseph Joseph, Joshua Rand, and William Warren.

38. La Corne had twenty-four Indian and Negro slaves in 1760; the governor had sixteen, most of whom may have been inherited; and his brother owned two (Marcel Trudel, *L'esclavage au Canada français* [Quebec, 1960], 137, 139, 141).

39. Article 47 in *NYCD* 10:1107–19.

40. See Appendix concerning Caesar, Caesar Nero, Canada Cuggo, Jacob Lindse, and Jock Linn.

41. *NYCD* 10:825–26, 878–84.

42. *NYCD* 10:883, where John Steel is listed as Stillé; *Johnson Narrative*, 99–102; Appendix.

43. Massachusetts Archives, vol. 78, pp. 77, 751.

44. AN, Guerre, A^1 3417, no. 239; Montcalm to Belle Isle, May 8, 1759, in *NYCD* 10:970–71.

45. See Appendix concerning Josiah Bean, John Lamson, Wells Coverly, John Moor, and William Rackliff.

46. Thomas L. Purvis, "The Aftermath of Fort William Henry's Fall: New Jersey Captives Among the French and Indian," *New Jersey History* 103 (1985–86): 75–77. Contrary to his claims, he was granted some help in Plymouth, England (New Jersey Archives, Trenton, Colonial Wars, Box 3, no. 214).

47. Petition of Selectmen of Tewksbury, Massachusetts, September 22, 1758 (New Hampshire Records Management & Archives, Concord, N.H.).

48. See Massachusetts petitions of Jonathan Bailey, William Furbish, Zachariah Gilson, and John Steel; New Hampshire petitions of Josiah Bean, Elijah Denbow, Dr. John Lamson, and John Moor; HL, LO 4716; John Duffy, *Epidemics in Colonial America* (Baton Rouge, La., 1953), 86–91.

49. To the 175 soldiers listed as of unknown fate, it seems reasonable to add 10

noncombatants. Non-military camp followers are difficult to estimate, but certainly could not have added 10 percent to the casualties. Eighty women (3.2%) were said to have been with the 2400 man garrison. Eleven women and 4 children (6.4%) accompanied 218 men in the two Halifax-bound flag-of-truce vessels with adequate passenger lists (HL, LO 6678, 6795; Paul E. Kopperman, "The British Command and Soldiers' Wives in America, 1755–1783," *Journal of the Society for Army Historical Research* 60 [1982]: 14–34). In 1757, the Fourth Battalion of the Royal American regiment had 60 women and 34 children (10.3%) with 823 men, and the Twenty-second Regiment had 60 women with 996 men (5.7%) (HL, LO 3794, 3647). It is also worth remembering that women and children were more likely to be adopted by Indian tribes than were men. All the teamsters caught in the siege were soldiers because of Loudoun's reforms.

50. HL, LO 4654, 4660A; *JR* 70:176.

51. *JR* 70:180–81; Parkman MSS, XLII, 183–84, MHS.

52. HL, LO 6660.

53. PRO, CO 5/1068, fols. 52–61; *NYCD* 7:276–79; *JP* 9:900–905; *New York Gazette*, October 3, 1757; Francis Jennings, *Empire of Fortune* (New York, 1988), 414–17.

54. October 1757 issue, p. 542.

55. *Scots Magazine*, November 1757, 601–2.

56. See *Daily Advertiser* and Public Advertiser, October 12, *London Evening-Post* and *London Chronicle*, October 13 and 15.

57. HL, LO 4786A, 4788. Forty-five French and Canadian prisoners were returned from Boston to Louisbourg by the Massachusetts government (HL, LO 6970). Vaudreuil sent a party to Fort Edward in February 1758, ostensibly to see if there were others to be returned (HL, LO 5561).

58. His admission that these people were in a separate category was dated before the end of October (AN, Guerre, A¹ 3417, no. 239).

59. NAC, MG 23 K34 (3); John Knox, *An Historical Journal of the Campaigns in North America for the Years 1757, 1758, 1759 and 1760*, 3 vols. (Toronto, 1914–16), 1:181–82, 238; HL, AB 79, 99, 117, 142, 144, 215, 394, 397, 398, 408.

60. Thomas Mante, *The History of the Late War in North America* (London, 1772), 207. On Amherst's later policy, see Bernhard Knollenberg, "General Amherst and Germ Warfare," *Mississippi Valley Historical Review* 41 (1954): 489–94, and, especially, Donald H. Kent's reply in ibid., 762–63.

61. NAC, MG 23 K 34 (3) and MG 18, M 15; Knox, *Historical Journal*, 1:181–82, 238, 267.

62. *DCB* 4:20–26.

63. *NYCD* 10:1054–57; Lawrence H. Gipson, *The British Empire Before the American Revolution*, 15 vols. (Caldwell, Idaho, and New York, 1936–70), 7:360–65.

64. John R. Cuneo, *Robert Rogers of the Rangers* (New York, 1959), 101; *Correspondence of William Pitt*, ed. Gertrude Selwyn Kimball, 2 vols. (New York, 1906), 2:220-22.

65. *Johnson Narrative* [*1907*], 132-33; Coleman, *New England Captives*, 1:29; Henry Trumbull, *History of the Indian Wars* (Boston, 1846), 144-47; J. H. Temple and G. Sheldon, *History of the Town of Northfield, Massachusetts* (Albany, N.Y., 1855), 306; Francis Parkman, *Montcalm and Wolfe*, 3 vols. (Boston, 1905), 3:93-101; Thomas-Marie Charland, *Histoire des Abénakis d'Odanak* (Montreal, 1964), 107-18; Gordon M. Day, "Rogers' Raid in Indian Tradition," *Historical New Hampshire* 17 (1962): 3-17.

66. Charland, *Abénakis*, 118; Coleman, *New England Captives* 2:329; *Johnson Narrative* [*1907*], 133-35.

67. *DCB* 4:481.

CHAPTER 7: PERCEPTIONS

1. *Boston Gazette*, August 22, 1757, and August 8 and 15, 1757.

2. Apparently by order of Lieutenant Governor James De Lancey, who was at Albany on August 11. On that day, Colonel Webb wrote to De Lancey from Fort Edward about the arrival of part of the army "in the most distressing Situation" and their reporting that Indians "had fallen upon them with Spears and Hatchets" murdering women, children, and some men. He also claimed "all accounts seem to agree the French connived at this most inhumane Treatment." This letter, which also complained about the New York militia (who "continue to go back as fast if not faster than they came up") was obviously intended to urge more effort from New Yorkers Webb's report on the same day to General Loudoun was much more tempered. De Lancey needed little beyond what Webb told him in order to believe what was printed on the nineteenth (Webb to De Lancey, August 11, 1757, PRO, CO 5/888, fols. 90-91; Webb to Loudoun, August 11, 1757, CO 5/48, fols. 312-13). For De Lancey's own fears on August 10 and 11, see his letter to Governor Pownall (PRO, CO 5/888, fols. 54, 58). These initial reactions do not support L. H. Gipson's claim that authorities in the northern colonies minimized the disaster to encourage recruitment (*The British Empire before the American Revolution*, 15 vols. [Caldwell, Idaho, and New York, 1936-70], 7:87n). For Governor Pownall's proclamation of August 13 concerning the Acadians, see PRO, CO 5/888, fol. 65.

3. *New York Mercury*, August 22, 1757.

4. The *New York Mercury* of April 24, 1758, warming up for the new campaign, argued that the "poor Indians" had been duped into becoming butchers for the French. The article also denounced the claims of cowardice that Montcalm had made against the victims. The explanation

given was fear of immediate reprisals by the French if they violated parole, not lack of ammunition.

5. L.-É Dussieux, *Le Canada sous la domination française d'apres les archives de la marine et de la guerre*, 3rd ed. (Paris, 1883), 220; *Collection de manuscrits contenant lettres, mémoires et autre documents historique relatifs à la Nouvelle France*, 4 vols. (Quebec, 1883–85), 4:115–17; *NYCD* 10:598.

6. *Collection de manuscrits* 4:112–15. Monro's remark is reported in HL, LO 4226A.

7. *Collection de manuscrits du Marechal de Lévis*, ed. H.-R. Casgrain, 12 vols. (Quebec, 1889–95), 1:101–2. Monro denied the claim "which is really not fact, As I my self saw every drop of liquor distroy'd immediately After the Capitulation was sign'd" (HL, LO 4345).

8. *JR* 70:195–99; Dussieux, *Le Canada*, 149.

9. Montcalm to Webb and to Loudoun, August 14, 1757, *Collection de manuscrits* 4:112–15.

10. Bougainville to M. de Paulmy, August 19, 1757, *NYCD* 10:605–16.

11. *Bougainville Journals*, 170; *Journal du marquis de Montcalm durant ses campagnes en Canada de 1756 à 1759*, ed. H.-R. Casgrain (Quebec, 1895), 292.

12. Montcalm to M. de Palmy, September 8, 1757, see *NYCD* 10:630–31 concerning Montcalm's preparation of the Vaudreuil letter. A copy arrived, although Vaudreuil did not agree to it, and was eventually printed in Dussieux, *Le Canada*, 242–48. Vaudreuil's letter of August 18 is quoted in Richard Waddington, *La Guerre de septs ans*, 5 vols. (Paris, 1899–1914), 1:269. For a translation of the official French version of the incident, see *NYCD* 10:645–51.

13. See *Daily Advertiser* and *The Public Advertiser*, October 12; *London Evening Post* and *London Chronicle*, October 13, and another account in the *London Chronicle*, October 15, including the New York news of August 22 that only ten or twelve were thought to have been killed in the massacre.

14. *Gentlemen's Magazine*, October 1757, 474 and ff.

15. *Scots Magazine*, November 1757, 598–600.

16. *An Enquiry into the Causes of our Ill Success in the Present War* (London, 1757), anonymous but attributed to political writer, Ralph Griffiths.

17. *The Yale Edition of Horace Walpole's Correspondence*, ed. W. S. Lewis, 48 vols. (New Haven, Conn., 1937–83), 21:144.

18. *The Political Journal of George Bubb Dodington*, ed. John Carswell and Lewis A. Dralle (Oxford, 1965), mentions that the fort was taken (366); *Memoirs from 1754 to 1758 by James Earl Waldegrave one of his Majesty's Privy Council* . . . (London, 1821) makes no mention of the siege, surrender, or massacre.

19. A draft is in the Saltonstall Papers, Massachusetts Historical Society, Boston. See Richard Slotkin, *Regeneration through Violence* (Middletown, Conn., 1973), 248–50.

20. John Entick, *The General History of the Late War: Containing its Rise, Progress and Event in Europe, Asia, Africa, and America*, 5 vols. (London, 1763), 2:394–401; *DNB* 17:378. Compare with Entick, *The Complete History of the Late War* (Dublin, 1763), 40–41

21. Thomas Mante, *The History of the Late War in North America* (London, 1772), 97. Mante translated works by Joly de Maizeray, published in 1771 and 1781 (see *DNB*).

22. Some details are not traceable. Mante mentioned that the Abenaki chief Gvisensick was active in an earlier chase on Lac St. Sacrement (*History of the Late War*, 90). He followed Entick in claiming that Webb withdrew "a strong train of artillery" from Fort William Henry just before the attack, and he identified the bearer of Montcalm's initial call to surrender as "Sieur Fonvive" rather than Fontbrune (91).

23. Mante, *History of the Late War*, 95.

24. Mante, *History of the Late War*, 95–98; William G. Godfrey, *Pursuit of Profit and Preferment in Colonial North America: John Bradstreet's Quest* (Waterloo, Ont., 1982), 259–60.

25. Tobias Smollett, *The History of England from the Revolution to the Death of George II*, 5 vols. (London, 1790), 5:37–41.

26. Smollett, *History of England*, 42.

27. Thomas Hutchinson also was writing the third volume of his *History of Massachusetts Bay* (Cambridge, Mass., 1936), in England in the mid-1770s. His paragraph on the incident began with "reports were spread among the people, that, after the surrender of the fort, the garrison had been massacred by the Indians, by the countenance and connivance of the French general." Hutchinson recorded that many were stripped: "Some few were killed, or never heard of; the rest came in, one after another, many having lost their way in the woods, and suffered extreme hardships." Hutchinson concluded by commenting that the prisoners admitted that the French attempted, in vain, to restrain the Indians (44).

28. Jonathan Carver, *Travels through the Interior Parts of North America in the Years 1766, 1767 and 1768* (London, 1778), 313. There were London and Dublin editions in 1779 and a third in London in 1781, the year of the first French edition.

29. See *DAB*, E. G. Bourne, "The Travels of Jonathan Carver," *American Historical Review*, 11 (1905–6): 287–302. Carver was a private in Captain John Burk's company (Ticonderoga Archives, no. 1910).

30. Carver gives the besiegers eleven thousand regulars and Canadians, plus two thousand Indians (314). This version of the Montcalm–Monro negotiation gained even wider currency once James Fenimore Cooper adopted it.

31. Carver, *Travels*, 318–19.
32. Carver, *Travels*, 324–25.
33. At least as early as 1792 Oliver Wolcott wrote to Jedidiah Morse that Carver could not be relied on and may not have written his book at all (see Bourne, "Travels of Jonathan Carver," 292).
34. Carver, *Travels*, 319–20.
35. Carver, *Travels*, 325–27. E. P. Hamilton echoes this in *The French and Indian Wars* (Garden City, N.Y., 1962), 210.
36. Carver's book went through three London editions and one Dublin issue by 1781, when the accounts of Père Roubaud and Pierre Pouchot were printed. The first French translation of Carver was published in Paris in 1784, and this may have been what provoked Jean-Nicholas Desandrouins to write "Notes sur le voyage de M. Jonathan Carver dans l'Amerique septentrionale, au sujet du massacre des Anglois, par les Sauvages, après la capitulation du fort William-Henry, en 1757."
37. Roubaud's account reprinted in *JR* 70:90–203. See also Joseph P. Donnelly, *Thwaites' Jesuit Relations: Errata and Addenda* (Chicago, 1967).
38. On Roubaud see *DCB* 4:685–86; Gustave Lanctôt, "La vie scandaleuse d'un faussaire," *Royal Society of Canada Transactions*, 3rd ser., vol. 50 (1956), section 1, 25–48, and "Le Prince des faussaires en la Nouvelle-France," *Royal Society of Canada Proceedings*, 3rd ser., vol. 40 (1946), section 1, 61–78.
39. Lanctôt cast no doubt on the authenticity of the letter, but cited it as "Lettre du P. Bouchard Octobre, 1757" in his account of the massacre (*A History of Canada*, 3 vols. [Toronto, 1963–65], 3:146–48). Parkman said, rather jauntily, of Roubaud: "He was an intelligent person, who may be trusted where he has no motive for lying" (*Montcalm and Wolfe*, 3 vols. [Boston, 1905], 2:202–3). Roubaud's reconstruction of the exchange between Montcalm and Monro on August 3, indicated an excellent grasp of the point and the ploys of the letters, though the Jesuit was apparently recalling without the documents (*JR* 70:156–57). Roubaud was expelled from the Jesuit order in 1760, before his career of forgery really began (*JR* 70:173).
40. Fr. Jean-Baptiste de Saint-Pé, who had been in Canada from 1720, was then the superior at Quebec (*DCB* 3:579–80).
41. *JR* 70:95 ff.
42. *JR* 70:114.
43. *JR* 70:125.
44. Roubaud displayed much curiosity, but little enthusiasm for the untouched natives or their lives. The need to civilize and Christianize was his assumption. See the earlier Jesuit position as explained by George R. Healy, "The French Jesuits and the Idea of the Noble Savage," *W&MQ*, 3rd ser., vol. 15 (1958): 143–62.

45. "Sans doute que tous les coins de l'Europe ont retenti de cette triste scène, comme d'un attentat dont l'odieux rejaillit peut-être sur la Nation, et la flétrit" (*JR* 70:175).
46. *JR* 70:180, 199.
47. David Humphreys, *An Essay on the Life of Israel Putnam* (Hartford, Conn., 1788), 42–43.
48. *DCB* 3:534–37. Originally published in Yverdon, a translation of Pouchot's account by F. B. Hough appeared as *Memoir upon the Late War in North America, between the French and the English, 1756–60* . . . , 2 vols. (Roxbury, Mass., 1866). See also *NYCD* 10:667–68, 694–95.
49. *Memoir upon the Late War* 1:85. Bougainville's list of Indians with Montcalm's army includes ninety-four "Kiscacous" and ten "Magnonjans" among the Ottawa (*Bougainville Journals*, 151).
50. *Memoir upon the Late War* 1:89.
51. The only source for this lost document is Abbé Charles Nicolas Gabriel, *Le Maréchal de camp Desandrouins, 1729–1792* (Verdun, 1887), which quotes extensively from "Notes sur le voyage de M. Jonathan Carver . . . ," which appears to have been lost in World War I.
52. Gabriel, *Le Maréchal Desandrouins*, 104–5.
53. In his "Memoire de Canada," written between 1758 and 1770, Desandrouins offers a few telling comments on the massacre. Particularly significant is his comment that "les sauvages, voyant qu'ils emportaient tous leur effets, se jetèrent dessus, en massacrèrent quelques-uns et leur pillèrent tout" (*Rapport des Archives du Québec, 1924–25*, 131, 96; *DCB* 4:211–12).
54. This defense of Vaudreuil displays some breadth of understanding that was not shared by Montcalm.
55. This confirms the remarks of Bougainville and Maylem.
56. Desandrouins' earlier "Memoire de Canada" had claimed that "some" had been massacred.
57. Gabriel, *Le Maréchal Desandrouins*, 103–12.
58. It remains possible, though unlikely, that Gabriel chose not to include some discussion of this matter in his biography.
59. Humphreys, *Israel Putnam*, 40–41. The account makes no mention of meeting Montcalm when Putnam was a prisoner of the French.
60. Humphreys, *Israel Putnam*, 42–43.
61. Putnam's kinsman, a private in the Massachusetts regiment, recorded in his journal that Israel set out from Fort Edward on August 21 to scout (*Journal of Gen. Rufus Putnam 1757–60* [Albany, N.Y., 1886], 43). The *New York Mercury*, September 5, stated that Putnam and a lieutenant from Otway's regiment had been out scouting and reported the complete demolition of the fort.
62. None of the specifics of Putnam's description, except the "half-con-

sumed" bodies, are recognized consequences of the burning of human bodies. (I am grateful to Owen Wills, veteran London fireman, for this observation.)

63. Humphreys, *Israel Putnam*, 43; John Fellows, *The Veil Removed, or, Reflections on David Humphreys'. . . Life of Israel Putnam* (New York, 1843).

64. (Joseph Frye's journal), *The Port Folio*, 4th ser., vol. 7 (1819): 355–68; *DAB*; Rufus Putnam reported the safe arrival of Colonel Frye at Fort Edward on the night of August 11–12 (*Putnam Journal*, 42); Hutchinson says that Frye had wandered in the woods for "some days" (*History of Massachusetts Bay* 3:44).

65. Frye journal, 365.

66. Frye journal, 366.

67. Epaphras Hoyt, *Antiquarian Researches* (Greenfield, Mass., 1824), 293, 288–95.

68. *DAB* 5:577–78; Timothy Dwight, *Travels in New England and New York*, ed. Barbara Miller Solomon, 4 vols. (Cambridge, Mass., 1969), 1:ix–xlvii.

69. Dwight, *Travels in New England* 3:243, 263.

70. Dwight was misleading his readers when he claimed "by a letter in my possession, written from Albany, August 15th, by a gentleman who was at Fort Edward on the 9th." The famous letter appeared in both New York papers on August 22, 1757.

71. Dwight, *Travels in New England* 3:265, Jeremy Belknap, *History of New Hampshire* [1784–92], 2 vols. (Dover, N.H., 1831), 1:317, citing *New Hampshire Gazette*, no. 49. The muster rolls indicate that fifty-seven were killed or initially captured (see Table 1).

72. Dwight, *Travels in New England* 3:265–66.

73. Dwight, *Travels in New England* 3:267.

74. See Marcel Clave, *Fenimore Cooper: Sa vie et son oeuvre: La jeunesse (1789–1826)* (Aix-en-Provence, France, 1938); David P. French, "James Fenimore Cooper and Fort William Henry," *American Literature* 32 (1960): 28–38; and Thomas Philbrick, "The Sources of Cooper's Knowledge of Fort William Henry," *American Literature* 36 (1964): 209–14.

75. Paul A. N. Wallace clarifies how Cooper was misled by John Heckewelder in "John Heckewelder's Indians and the Fenimore Cooper Tradition," *Proceedings of the American Philosophical Society* 96 (1952): 496–504, and "Cooper's Indians," *New York History* 35 (1954):423–46.

76. James Fenimore Cooper, *The Last of the Mohicans: A Narrative of 1757* (Philadelphia, 1826; Albany, N.Y., 1983), 138.

77. Cooper, *Last of the Mohicans*, 169.

78. Cooper, *Last of the Mohicans*, 174–75.

79. Cooper, *Last of the Mohicans*, 154.

80. Cooper, *Last of the Mohicans*, 170.

81. Cooper, *Last of the Mohicans*, 179.
82. Cooper, *Last of the Mohicans*, 180.
83. Cooper, *Last of the Mohicans*, 179.
84. Cooper, *Last of the Mohicans*, 179n.
85. Compare the 1846 edition of Henry Trumbull, *History of the Indian Wars* (Boston, 1846), 140-44, with Hoyt, *Antiquarian Researches*, 288-93. Also see Slotkin, *Regeneration through Violence*, 432-37.
86. In addition to reprinting sources on the Pequot war and King Philip's war, Drake wrote *Biography and History of the Indians of North America*, which went through at least twelve printings between 1820 and 1857. The related *The Book of Indians* had nine printings between 1833 and 1845, and his *Indian Captivities* was printed thirteen times between 1839 and 1873. He also published *Tragedies of the Wilderness* (Boston, 1845) and *A Particular History of the Five Years French and Indian War* (Boston, 1870) concerning 1744 to 1749.
87. John Frost [William V. Moore], *Indian Wars of the United States from the Discovery to the Present Time* (Philadelphia, 1856), 194-97.
88. George Minot, *Continuation of the History of the Province of Massachusetts Bay from the year 1748*, 2 vols. (Boston, 1798-1803); Benjamin Trumbull, *A Complete History of Connecticut*, 2 vols. (New Haven, Conn., 1818), 2:382-83. William Smith, *The History of the Late Province of New-York . . .* , 2 vols. (New York, 1829-30), 2:245-49, was both brief and preoccupied with politics.
89. James Grahame, *History of the United States of North America, from the Plantation of the British Colonies till their Assumption of National Independence*, 4 vols. (London, 1827-36), vol. 3, and second edition, 2 vols. (Philadelphia, 1850), 2:264-65; Michael Kraus, *A History of American History* (New York, 1937), 194-98.
90. George Bancroft, *History of the United States*, 10 vols. (Boston, 1852), 4:270. See Russel Blaine Nye, *George Bancroft, Brahmin Rebel* (New York, 1944).
91. Bancroft, *History of the United States* 4:265, 259-71.
92. See Kraus, *History of American History*, 181-83, 215-39.
93. M. A. Stickney, "Massacre at Fort William Henry, 1757," *Essex Institute Historical Collections* 3 (1861): 79-84.
94. In their *History of the Town of Northfield, Massachusetts* (Albany, N.Y., 1855), J. H. Temple and G. Sheldon end a graphic account of the incident with: "The numbers massacred could never be known; but it fell little short of 300" (301).
95. Samuel Niles, "A Summary Historical Narrative of the Wars in New England with the French and Indians in the Several Parts of the Country," *Massachusetts Historical Society Collections*, 4th ser., vol. 5: 311-600.
96. Niles, "Summary Narrative," 442, 444.
97. Francis Parkman, *Montcalm and Wolfe* (Boston, 1884). Citations are

from the three-volume Frontenac edition of 1905. On Parkman, see Mason Wade, *Francis Parkman, Heroic Historian* (New York, 1942); Howard Doughty, *Francis Parkman* (New York, 1962): Richard C. Vitzthum, *The American Compromise: Theme and Method in the Histories of Bancroft, Parkman, and Adams* (Norman, Okla., 1974); W. J. Eccles, "The History of New France According to Francis Parkman," *W&MQ*, 3rd ser., vol. 18 (1961): 163-75; and Francis Jennings, "Francis Parkman: A Brahmin Among Untouchables," *W&MQ*, 3rd ser., vol. 42 (1985): 305-28.

98. [Francis Parkman], "The Works of James Fenimore Cooper," *North American Review* 74 (1852): 155.

99. Margry edited the six-volume *Découvertes et établissements des français dans l'Ouest et dans le Sud de l'Amérique septentrionale 1614-1754* (Paris, 1876-1886).

100. Most French accounts appeared in Casgrain, *Collection des manuscrits du Maréchal de Lévis*. Anne-Joseph-Hippolyte de Maurès, Comte de Malartic, *Journal des campagnes au Canada de 1755 à 1760* . . . , was published in Dijon, France, in 1890. On the Bougainville journal, see Edward P. Hamilton, "Parkman, Abbé Casgrain, and Bougainville's Journal," *Proceedings of the American Antiquarian Society* 71 (1961): 261-70.

101. R. C. Vitzthum, "The Historian as Editor: Francis Parkman's Reconstruction of Sources in *Montcalm and Wolfe*," *Journal of American History* 53 (1966-67): 471-86, esp. 476-77; *The Journals of Francis Parkman*, 2 vols. (London, 1947) 2:567-73.

102. Parkman, *Montcalm and Wolfe* 2:185, 193; See *NYCD* 10:625, 643, 644, where casualties are listed as 108 or 112. Parkman followed a more propagandist French publication that converted the total casualties into dead and added 250 wounded (*NYCD* 10:651.

103. Parkman, *Montcalm and Wolfe* 2:198.

104. Parkman, *Montcalm and Wolfe* 2:197.

105. Parkman, *Montcalm and Wolfe* 2:198.

106. Parkman, *Montcalm and Wolfe* 2:167.

107. Parkman, *Montcalm and Wolfe* 2:194.

108. Parkman, *Montcalm and Wolfe* 2:195.

109. Belknap, *History of New Hampshire* 2:317; Parkman, *Montcalm and Wolfe* 2:199.

110. Parkman, *Montcalm and Wolfe* 2:201-2.

111. Parkman, *Montcalm and Wolfe* 2:202.

112. *Journals of Francis Parkman* 2:567-81; H.-R. Casgrain, *Francis Parkman* (Quebec, 1872).

113. Serge Gagnon, *Le Québec et ses historiens de 1840 à 1920* (Quebec, 1978), 288-324; Gustave Lanctôt, *Garneau, historien national* (Montreal, 1946); James S. Pritchard, "Some Aspects of the Thought of F. X. Garneau," *Canadian Historical Review* 51 (1970): 276-91.

114. François-Xavier Garneau, *Histoire du Canada*, 2nd ed., 4 vols. (Quebec, 1852), 2:258–64.
115. Dussieux, *Le Canada*, 242–45.
116. Dussieux, *Le Canada*, 140–45. In addition to Paris editions of 1855 and 1862, there had been a Quebec edition in 1863.
117. J.-B.-A. Ferland, *Cours d'histoire du Canada*, 2 vols. (Quebec, 1861–65), 552–55.
118. James MacPherson Le Moine, *La Mémoire de Montcalm vengée ou le massacre au Fort George. documents historiques* (Quebec, 1864). On McClellan, see *DAB* 6:581–85.
119. Gagnon, *Le Québec et ses historiens*, 173.
120. H.-R. Casgrain, *Guerre du Canada 1756–1760. Montcalm et Lévis*, 2 vols. (Quebec, 1891), 1:195–207.
121. Casgrain, *Guerre du Canada* 1:233–37.
122. Gabriel, *Le Maréchal Desandrouins*.
123. Casgrain, *Guerre du Canada* 1:281–85. Casgrain provoked René de Kerallain to publish a well-documented defense of his ancestor, *La Jeunesse de Bougainville* (Paris, 1896).
124. Casgrain, *Guerre du Canada* 1:287.
125. William Kingsford, *The History of Canada*, 10 vols. (London, 1887–98), 4:58.
126. Kingsford, *History of Canada* 4:48–69.
127. Richard Waddington, *La Guerre de sept ans*, 5 vols. (Paris, 1899–1910), 1:256–71.
128. Felix Martin, *Le Marquis de Montcalm et les dernières années de la colonie française au Canada*, 4th ed. (Paris, 1888), 126–28. The first edition was published in 1867. More generally, see Georges Robitaille, *Montcalm et ses historiens, étude critique* (Montreal, 1936).
129. See also Charles de Bonnechose, *Montcalm et le Canada français*, 5th ed. (Paris, 1882), 53–63. This popular history went through twelve editions between 1877 and 1908.
130. A. Doughty and G. W. Parmelee, *The Siege of Quebec*, 6 vols. (Quebec, 1901), 1:190. On Chapais's authorship of *Le Marquis de Montcalm (1712–1759)*, see Gagnon, *Le Québec et ses historiens*, 175–78.
131. Chapais, *Marquis de Montcalm*, 144, 280.
132. Chapais, *Marquis de Montcalm*, 286–88. See also Thomas Chapais, "Montcalm et la capitulation de William Henry," *La Nouvelle-France* 9 (1911): 529–41; Robitaille, *Montcalm et ses historiens*, 107–16; and Aegidius Fauteux, "Montcalm," *CHA Annual Report* (Ottawa, 1924), 25–44. For a modern scholarly appraisal of Montcalm, see W. J. Eccles, "Montcalm, Louis-Joseph de, Marquis de Montcalm," in *DCB* 3:458–69.
133. Lionel Groulx, *Histoire du Canada Français*, 4th ed., 2 vols. (Montreal, 1960), 1:350. On Abbé Groulx, see Ramsay Cook, *Canada and the French Canadian Question* (Toronto, 1967), 119–42; Jean-Pierre Ga-

boury, *Le Nationalisme de Lionel Groulx: Aspects idéologiques* (Ottawa, 1970); and Susan Mann Trofimenkoff, ed., *Abbé Groulx: Variations on a Nationalist Theme* (Toronto, 1973).

134. Kingsford, *History of Canada* 4:64.
135. See John W. Fortescue's dismissive treatment of the "episode" in *A History of the British Army*, 13 vols. (London, 1899–1930), 2:305–6. Arthur Granville Bradley's vigorously written, moralistic, professedly English, and undocumented *The Fight with France for North America*, 3rd ed. (London, 1908), denounced Indians, Canadians, and Montcalm for the "massacre" of an estimated one hundred prisoners (186–99).
136. Fortescue, *History of the British Army* 2:306.
137. Stanley M. Pargellis, *Lord Loudoun in North America* (New Haven, Conn., 1933), chap. 9, esp. 243–50. Also see Stanley M. Pargellis and Norma B. Cuthbert, "Loudoun Papers," *Huntington Library Bulletin*, no. 3 (1933): 97–107. The Loudoun Papers include Monro's casualty list for the regulars (LO 4313A), reports of captains Faesch (LO 6795, 4944) and Shaw (LO 4898), and Governor Pownall (LO 4778) on the return of prisoners, as well as the "Transactions" journal (LO 6660).
138. Gipson, *British Empire* 7:62–89, esp. 87. The casualty estimate is not derived from his numerous sources.
139. For example, "about twenty" for Douglas Edward Leach, *Arms for Empire* (New York, 1973), 181; "little more than a hundred" for J. R. Rutledge, *Century of Conflict* (Garden City, N.Y., 1956), 444; at least 120 to 150 victims for Hamilton, *French and Indian Wars*, 205; "about two hundred" for H. H. Peckham, *The Colonial Wars 1689–1762* (Chicago, 1962), 163.
140. Guy Frégault, *La Guerre de la conquête* (Montreal, 1955), 215.
141. Lanctôt, *History of Canada* 3:146–48; G. F. G. Stanley, *New France, the Last Phase* (Toronto, 1968), 161; W. J. Eccles, *France in America* (New York, 1972), 190–92.
142. This is true of Francis Jennings' intriguing, but unconvincing, use of some of the sources in *Empire of Fortune: Crowns, Colonies & Tribes in the Seven Years' War in America* (New York, 1988), 312–22. Wilbur R. Jacobs, whose work has also expanded our understanding of Indian values, did not seek such an opportunity in "A Message to Fort William Henry: An Incident in the French and Indian War," *Huntington Library Quarterly* 16 (1953): 371–80, and "A Message to Fort William Henry: Drama of Siege and Indian Savagery," in *Dispossessing the American Indian: Indians and Whites on the Colonial Frontier* (New York, 1972), 68–74.

INDEX

241